JEWISH LIFE IN AMERICA

Historical Perspectives

JEWISH LIFE IN AMERICA

Historical Perspectives

edited by GLADYS ROSEN

Institute of Human Relations Press
of The American Jewish Committee

KTAV Publishing House, Inc.

Library of Congress Cataloging in Publication Data
Main entry under title:

Jewish Life in America.

Includes bibliographical references.
1. Jews in the United States—History Addresses, essays, lectures. 2. United States—History—Addresses, essays, lectures. I. Rosen Gladys Levine.
E184.J5J57 973'.04'924 78–16560
ISBN 0–87068–346–2

MANUFACTURED IN THE UNITED STATES OF AMERICA

TABLE OF CONTENTS

PREFACE

By Richard Maass

President, The American Jewish Committee

Every culture develops characteristic ways of recalling and interpreting the past. Pre-literate civilizations accumulate great oral traditions; literate societies continually record their events, concerns and customs—whether on clay tablets or parchment, marble or magnetic tape—so that future generations may know.

Among the Jewish people, the tradition of preserving the past and looking to it as a guide to the future has always been strong. For a millennium and a half, the Talmud has enjoined us: "Know whence you have come and whither you are going." The sense of connectedness, of having a place in the universe, which emerges from understanding the past has helped sustain us in good and bad times; it still sustains us today.

In 1972, as the nation was drawing up plans for celebrating its 200th anniversary, the American Jewish Committee convened a Bicentennial Planning Council to consider how a Jewish intergroup relations organization could most appropriately join in marking the occasion. The Council unanimously recommended that AJC illuminate the Jewish experience in the United States through a series of lectures by outstanding writers and scholars, which would eventually be published to reach a wider audience.

The lectures were delivered in a number of American cities. They are now assembled in this volume, which highlights the distinctive ways in which Jews have helped build American society, illustrates how they have in turn been affected by it, and offers what we think are important insights into the interaction between Jewish values and American freedoms.

The lectures and the present publication were made possible, either directly or indirectly, by generous members and friends of the American Jewish Committee. Thus, the Edward M. Chase Estate funded lectures by Richard B. Morris in Boston and Eli Ginzberg in Dallas, and helped subsidize the present volume. AJC's Jacob Blaustein Institute for the Advancement of Human Rights supported lectures by Milton R. Konvitz in Baltimore, and Marshall Sklare in Los Angeles. The Neal S. Breskin and Louis A. and Hazel Breskin Foundation underwrote the lecture by I. I. Rabi in Chicago, and the family of Edward Elson did the same for that by Norman Podhoretz in Andover, Massachusetts. Joyce and Avern Cohn honored the memory of their four grandparents by supporting Irving Howe's lecture in Detroit, and AJC's Institute for Pluralism and Group Identity sponsored Moses Rischin's lecture in New York as a memorial to a deceased staff member, Judith M. Herman.

The hospitality of the Central Synagogue in New York helped make Naomi W. Cohen's lecture a success. Equally valuable help and hospitality were offered by the Adas Israel Synagogue in Washington, Baltimore Hebrew College, Boston University, Hebrew Union College in Los Angeles, Midrasha College of Jewish Studies in Detroit, Phillips Academy in Andover, Massachusetts, Spertus College of Judaica in Chicago, Temple Beth El in Birmingham, Michigan, the University of Judaism in Los Angeles, and the Wilshire Boulevard Temple also in Los Angeles. To them, as well as to all others who helped and encouraged this project, the American Jewish Committee tenders warmest thanks.

FOREWORD

This is a book of essays about Jewish life in America from the late eighteenth century, when fewer than 3,000 Jews were scattered throughout the colonies, to the late twentieth, when the Jewish community of the United States—successful, acculturated and integrated—numbered close to six million. In these pages, outstanding scholars examine the roles this community has played in American history, and the values and beliefs by which it has lived in this land.

In the beginning, "America was promises" (Archibald MacLeish). It offered freedom and a safe haven to those who had been oppressed in the old country because of their religion or social class. Steeped in Old Testament tradition, committed at the same time to the individualistic ideals of John Locke and Thomas Jefferson, and unhampered by Europe's deep-rooted anti-Semitism, the United States was, and remained, singularly attractive to Jews. Through massive immigration, almost unrestricted for the first century and a half, this originally Anglo-Saxon nation gradually became an amalgam of the most varied religious and ethnic groups; and among these, the Jews were unique in possessing a multi-faceted identity—as a people, a religious community and a cultural group.

The ways in which Jews perceived America and adjusted to it were determined to a large extent by their long history of alternating toleration and persecution, of suffering and survival in other lands. Whether they arrived as individuals ahead of their families, in family groups, or as part of towns that emigrated in a body, Jews came here with the firm intention to stay—to make this country their permanent home. Even in the worst of times, they re-emigrated in far smaller numbers than any other ethnic or religious group.

From the earliest days, the lives of Jews in America have been closely intertwined with the nation's expansion and growth. They helped win independence, joined in the westward trek, fought on both sides in the Civil War; they pioneered in industrial growth, business, science, the arts. Yet most of them, while joining the American mainstream, kept their Jewishness, easy though it would have been to discard. Even more than most other American subcultures, Jews have clung to their special identity, their sense of mutual responsibility and their historic roots.

This persisting "mystery of Jewish distinctiveness," as Irving Howe calls it, has engaged the attention of all contributors to this volume. The essays illustrate how, from the Revolutionary War to Vietnam and beyond, Jews have existed "as a recognizable and—despite their small numbers—a highly significant segment of American society" (Marshall Sklare), influencing American life styles, values and viewpoints in distinctive ways, and in turn being reshaped by America's social, economic and intellectual challenges. The perspectives outlined here should be instructive as a case history in how ethnic and religious minorities in America have come to be what they are.

The publication of this work has benefited from the help and advice of many friends and colleagues. The members of the American Jewish Committee's Bicentennial Planning Council gave generously of their time and energy, as did AJC's staff and its members in the cities where these essays were first presented as Bicentennial lectures. Sonya F. Kaufer, AJC's Director of Publications, and her staff contributed invaluable editorial counsel and encouragement. Selma Hirsh, Associate Director of AJC, and Yehuda Rosenman, Director of the Jewish Communal Affairs Department, were unstinting in their cooperation.

We trust this volume will serve both as a stimulus and as a resource for further exploration of the Jewish experience in America.

Gladys Rosen

ABOUT THE AUTHORS

Ronald S. Berman

Ronald S. Berman headed the National Endowment for the Humanities from 1971–1977 and is now visiting Scholar at the American Enterprise Institute in Washington and Professor of Renaissance Literature at the University of California at San Diego.

Dr. Berman also taught English at Columbia University, and Kenyon College. He has written for many national magazines and literary reviews, including the *Kenyon Review* with which he served as Editorial Associate, 1963–1970.

Among Professor Berman's published volumes are *America in the Sixties: An Intellectual History* and a *A Reader's Guide to Shakespeare's Plays.*

Gerson D. Cohen

Gerson D. Cohen is Chancellor and Jacob H. Schiff Professor of History at the Jewish Theological Seminary of America, where in earlier years he was the Librarian and later Visiting Professor of Jewish Literature and Institutions. From 1950–1960, Dr. Cohen was the Gustav Gottheil Lecturer in Semitic languages at Columbia University, and from 1963–1970, he was Professor of History and Director of the Center of Israel and Jewish Studies. He is a Fellow of the American Academy for Jewish Research and the former editor of its proceedings.

Among Rabbi Cohen's major publications is a critical edition and commentary for Abraham Ibn Daud's *Book of Tradition.*

Naomi Weiner Cohen

Naomi Weiner Cohen is Professor of History at Hunter College, where she teaches courses in both American History and

American Jewish History. Dr. Cohen has written numerous articles for scholarly journals and is the author of *A Dual Heritage: The Public Career of Oscar Straus* and *Not Free to Desist: The American Jewish Committee, 1906–1966.* Her most recent book is *American Jews and the Zionist Idea.*

Eli Ginzberg

Eli Ginzberg, economist, educator and author is the A. Barton Hepburn Professor of Economics at Columbia University, and Director of the Conservation of Human Resources Project since its establishment in 1950. He also heads the National Commission for Manpower Policy and serves as a consultant to the Departments of State, Defense, Labor and HEW as well as numerous private agencies and businesses. Dr. Ginzberg is the author and editor of many important volumes on the American economy and its human resources. His most recent book is *American Jews: The Building of a Voluntary Community.*

Irving Howe

Irving Howe, author of the best selling *World of Our Fathers,* is Distinguished Professor of English at City University of New York Graduate School and Hunter College and has taught at Brandeis and Stanford Universities. Together with Eliezer Greenberg, Dr. Howe has translated and edited *A Treasury of Yiddish Stories, A Treasury of Yiddish Poetry,* and *Voices from the Yiddish,* and is co-editor of *Dissent* magazine.

Milton Konvitz

Milton Konvitz, author, editor and a leading authority on constitutional law, is Professor Emeritus of Industrial and Labor Relations Law at Cornell University. Dr. Konvitz holds a doctorate in philosophy as well as a law degree, and is one of the few Americans to be awarded honorary degrees from all four American institutions of Jewish learning. He has written extensively in the spheres of philosophy, intellectual history and religious thought. In 1973–1976, Dr. Konvitz was the recipient of a fellowship from the National Endowment for the Humanities for a book contributing to the celebration of the Declaration of Independence and the United States Constitution. The volume, *Judaism and the American Idea* will soon be published by Cornell University Press.

Richard B. Morris

Richard B. Morris, Special Lecturer and Gouverneur Morris Professor Emeritus at Columbia University, and one of the country's foremost authorities on the American Revolution, has also taught at the City University of New York, Princeton University, University of Hawaii, and the Hebrew University in Jerusalem. In 1976, Professor Morris was Chairperson of the New York State Bicentennial Coordinating Council, and President of the American Historical Association. Among his principal works are *The Peacemakers: The Great Powers and American Independence* for which he received the Bancroft Prize in History and *Seven Who Shaped Our Destiny: The Founding Fathers as Revolutionaries.* He also served as editor of the *Encyclopedia of American History* from 1953 through the Bicentennial edition.

Norman Podhoretz

Norman Podhoretz, Fullbright Scholar, writer, lecturer and literary critic, has been editor-in-chief of *Commentary* magazine since 1960. He has contributed articles and reviews to major American magazines, and has lectured extensively on American culture, literary trends and Jewish concerns. Mr. Podhoretz is the author of *Making It, Doing and Undoings: The Fifties and After in American Writing* and editor of *The Commentary Reader: Two Decades of Articles and Stories.*

Isidor Isaac Rabi

I. I. Rabi, University Professor Emeritus at Columbia University, is one of America's most distinguished scientists. He received the Nobel Prize in Physics in 1944 for recording the magnetic properties of atomic nuclei. In 1955, Dr. Rabi was vice-President of the International Conference on Peaceful Uses of Atomic Energy, and in 1958 he served as United States Delegate to the Atoms for Peace Conference in Geneva. Recipient of numerous awards and honorary degrees, he has held several of the most responsible scientific advisory posts to the United States Government, among them Chairperson of the General Advisory Committee to the Atomic Energy Commission.

In addition to his scholarly scientific publications, Dr. Rabi is the author of *Science: The Center of Culture,* published in 1970.

Moses Rischin

Moses Rischin is Professor of History at San Francisco State University, President of the Immigrant History Society, and Director of the Western Jewish History Center in Berkeley. He serves as editor of *Minorities in American History* and *The Modern Jewish Experience* series for the Arno Press. Dr. Rischin is the author of *The Promised City: New York's Jews 1870–1914, The American Gospel of Success: Individualism and Beyond* and, most recently, *Immigration and the American Tradition.*

Gladys Rosen

Gladys Rosen, a Program Specialist in the American Jewish Committee's Jewish Communal Affairs Department, has taught Hebrew and Judaic studies at Brooklyn College, Rutgers, and the Jewish Theological Seminary of America, and was Executive Associate of the American Jewish History Center of the Jewish Theological Seminary of America from 1960 to 1970.

She has written articles and book reviews and frequently appears on radio and television as guest or interviewer for programs featuring such subjects as Jewish education, history, Jewish women and the Jewish family.

Dr. Rosen's most recent publication is "Jews in American Life: A Guide to Local Programming for the Bicentennial."

Marshall Sklare

Marshall Sklare, the leading sociologist of American Jewry, is the Appleman Professor of American Jewish Studies and Sociology at Brandeis University. Formerly Professor of Sociology at Yeshiva University, he has served as President of the Association for the Sociological Study of Jewry, and taught at Hebrew University in Jerusalem and other institutions of higher learning. Dr. Sklare was Director of Scientific Research for the American Jewish Committee for a number of years. A frequent contributor to magazines and scholarly journals, Dr. Sklare's many books include *Jewish Identity on the Suburban Frontier: A Study of Group Survival in the Open Society, Conservative Judaism, America's Jews, The Jews in American Society* and its companion volume *The Jewish Community in America.*

GERSON D. COHEN

The Meaning of Liberty in Jewish Tradition

Although doubtless a coincidence, this Sabbath marks the conjunction of three points that are of special significance to all Jews and particularly to us who are assembled here. We meet when our nation is celebrating the bicentennial of its independence. Secondly, we celebrate the seventieth anniversary of the American Jewish Committee, which has had a profound impact on the life of Jews everywhere and of freedom-loving people everywhere, especially in our own country. Finally, it is on this Sabbath that in synagogues the world over—and I venture to hope even in those corners where Jews are still forbidden to, or prevented from, congregating to worship—the words of the Torah will be chanted aloud: "You shall hallow the fiftieth year, and you shall proclaim liberty throughout the land for all its inhabitants." Such a conjunction of events, however fortuitous, augments the meaningfulness of this occasion and bids us halt and assess afresh the meaning of liberty in the Jewish tradition, the impact of this legacy on our immediate past, and its potential significance for the present and proximate future.

I believe this is important on several counts. In the first place, the task of recapturing the original vitality of what has often been reduced to the cliche or the platitudinous is one that faces every sensitive person. That the vision of liberty underlies much of our

An Address to the Seventieth Anniversary Meeting of the American Jewish Committee (May 14, 1976)

tradition, from the moment of the birth of the children of Israel as a people and at many major turning points of our history, may perhaps be well known but that does not absolve us of the duty of actively recalling that past. Our biblical and rabbinic ancestors rightly understood how easily and quickly the fundamental principles underlying our identity can become hackneyed phrases that are, for all intents and purposes, sapped of meaning and, therefore, of the stimulus they were intended to provide.

For the fathers of this organization, the American Jewish Committee, the record will show that the ideal of liberty meant not only freedom *from*, but also the right and duty *to*. Among the values they held most dear was the translation of their Jewish heritage into contemporary terms and the rediscovery of its genuine spiritual moorings in ways that would be apposite to their lives. They appreciated the role of synagogue, school, and seminary as an indispensable component of their enterprise, if the battle for liberty was not to be reduced to philanthropy for others, to an expiatory quittance, that would not commit them and their children and their communities to the continuity and expansion of their ideals. I believe that many of us have rediscovered the acuteness of their perception of the realities of a healthy Jewish life. I would hope that all Jews deeply committed to the safety of the State of Israel, to the loosening of the fetters that bind our brothers in the Soviet Union, to the propagation of freedom in every corner, would see that for Jews to be committed to those values requires a strong sense of Jewish identity, and that that identity is sapped of its vitality and cut from its moorings if it is not rooted in transcendent principles that alone make any sense of Jewish brotherhood. I know that many of us do feel and live this way. I think that the future of this Jewish enterprise, indeed of any collective Jewish enterprise, depends on the transmission of the sense of dignity and duty that are reflected in the ancient concepts of the covenant and of freedom under God that it implies.

Accordingly, I believe that the verse I have just cited from this week's portion in the Book of Leviticus reminds us that freedom does not come automatically. It must be proclaimed afresh, and only through such proclamation and release of the enslaved and the oppressed can the years of our lives be hallowed. Sanctity is not something automatically achieved but a state gained through affirmation and action. Moreover, it is never gained once and for all. It must be reaffirmed and reproclaimed.

Above all, its original components must be isolated and examined afresh so that the reasons for the ascendancy of different notions of freedom in varying periods of our history will be understood. An examination of our classical sources will reveal that the Jewish notion of freedom was woven of two threads that became inseverably intertwined in the course of our history. However, originally two discrete notions of freedom circulated in ancient Israel. The first, a priestly one in origin, emphasized personal liberty, equality before the law, and religious freedom. A second thread, derived from the prophetic sources of the Bible, emphasized political restoration to independence and the ingathering of the exiles. It was from the prophets that our ancestors learned to see in the very fact of dispersion and exile a form of subjection. Hence, freedom could not be considered complete unless the Temple was rebuilt and the Jews restored to their historic homeland. In consequence of the Maccabean wars, the Hadrianic persecution, the rise of Christianity as the established religion of the Roman Empire, and finally the spread of Islam, these originally discrete notions of freedom were blended so that the two separate threads became one.

While in rabbinic and medieval Judaism, freedom could not be considered total until both elements were realized, our ancestors thought this would come to pass only in the messianic era. This was to be a divine intervention in history. For the interim, the Jew had to content himself with as much personal freedom as he could gain. Much of the Jewish theology of the Talmud and the Middle Ages centers on rationalizing theories of freedom and subjection. In modern times the intellectual leadership of European Jewry determined to gain total freedom for the Jew as a Jew. But here again the notion of liberty and the course to be followed was a subject of an acrimonious debate that in general terms may be classified as the approaches of West European and East European Jewry. Curiously, the debate consisted in selecting certain strands of the Jewish legacy on the ideal of freedom and emphasizing one component at the expense of the other. It was German Jewry that adopted the priestly ideal, while it was Russian and Polish Jewish spokesmen who identified with the prophetic dream of restoration.

West European Jews took as their point of inspiration and departure the achievement of the Jews of France in 1791, and proclaimed that Jewishness was a matter of private conviction. They demanded and ultimately gained citizenship on the clear understanding that liberty meant political equality and nothing more. Judaism was now one confession among many, the Jewish people a memory of the dark ages of the past. The dream of corporate liberation and national regeneration was renounced, or relegated, even in Orthodox circles, to immutable liturgical formulae that were said to have no pragmatic implications. In a word, this group proclaimed *Judaism* to be very much alive but the Jewish people at an end or in its last stages of existence. Not all West European Jews agreed with this ideology, but it was clearly the dominant one. Liberty to Jew and to non-Jew alike in Western Europe meant the acceptance of the nation-state as the only legitimate framework of political interest, let alone of political loyalty.

The concern with dual loyalty, or hyphenated Jewishness, is a memory of a past that is not too distant to be recalled even in this country. To many Jews it was the source of a genuine dilemma, which in all fairness was not of their making but the consequence of the axiomatic role of modern nationalism. Judaism, accordingly, was defined merely as a religion, and a man had a right to his own religion. That many a Gentile refused to believe the Jewish protestations that Judaism was only a religion was, of course, only too obvious, and explained as a reflection of the abiding virulence of a medieval hatred whose days were hopefully numbered.

Indeed, the persistence of bigotry only added fuel to the Jewish claim that Judaism had a genuine mission in the world, and that was to bring what was inaccurately called the prophetic ideal of the brotherhood of man to all corners of the earth.

We do classical Reform and German neo-Orthodoxy an injustice if we accuse them of naivete or ostrichlike behavior in the face of the realities that stared them in the face. They had consciously translated the ancient Jewish ideal of messianic deliverance from exile and alienation into a theological doctrine and political program that they believed to be apposite to their days. Jews became liberals because they hoped for, and believed in, the reasonableness of their fellow human beings. That they were grievously disappointed is an indictment not of them but of the general society. Parenthetically, it should be noted that when the futility of these liberal hopes became apparent, many of these Western Jews either migrated to America or became militant Zionists of the more extreme wing, even in the nineteenth century.

East European Jewish intellectuals were no less seized by the vision of liberty, but they saw the stumbling block not in Jewishness but in Judaism. To the East European Jew of modern orientation, religion was a relic of the past, and Jewish religion was responsible for Jewish passivity and immobility. Liberation, in short, consisted not only in the removal of civil disabilities that were imposed by a bigoted and tyrannical regime, but equally in the breaking of the shackles and restrictions of rabbinism and its complex of life. Liberty could come to the Jew only by internal regeneration and by the mobilization of collective Jewishness to a new and revitalized form of collective life. Jewish freedom could be attained only by collective *national* regeneration. Only as a member of a free Jewish people could the individual Jew attain freedom. The great historic consequence of this view were, of course, the rebirth of the Land of Israel, the ancient language of Israel, and finally, the State of Israel. However, not all East European Jews of this orientation were Zionists. Indeed, some were bitterly anti-Zionist and yet Jewish nationalists in their orientation and program. Thanks to the Holocaust and the suppression of any vestige of collective Jewish expression by some of the great "people's democracies," Zionism and the State of Israel remain the only living testimonies to that great dream. To be more accurate, the State of Israel and our own American Jewish community are the living links of continuity with that great mass drive for liberation, for one of the most salient manifestations of the new aspiration for liberty was the massive movement of migration westward.

Apart from the State of Israel, the single greatest by-product of that migratory wave was the growth in America of the largest body of Jews within one state in all of history.

In our country the notion of freedom has taken on new vitality. American Jewry has displayed not only great communal achievement, but the ability to fashion a Jewish and American identity that can transcend and overcome the extreme polarities of the nineteenth century European Jewish debate. American Jewry has cultivated Jewish religious movements that are unanimous in affirming Jewish peoplehood and a commonality of Jewish destiny and aspirations irrespective of political allegiance. The concern with dual loyalty has all but gone with yesteryear's frost. Conversely, there appears to be emerging a growing interest on the part of so-called secularists and the religiously unaffiliated in the roots of Jewish identity that transcends the latest political crisis for the State of Israel or the annual needs of Jewish social services. Jewry and Judaism are increasingly being acknowledged as inseparable and indivisible, and neither Jews nor Gentiles feel that this requires any apology. In a word, we have ceased to measure our legitimacy by yardsticks appropriated exclusively from the outside world, especially the hostile portion of it.

Outside the State of Israel, in America alone the Jewish expression and the Jewish experience have attained a recognition and respect in the forum of cultural expression that have opened new channels of Jewish creativity and unprecedented forms of dialogue between Jew and Gentile. Both Judaism and Christianity have been enriched by the new encounter with each other, and a sympathetic exchange of ideas that was unthinkable in Europe has here become a phenomenon so common as no longer to generate any special notice. And this has been achieved without the cloying apologetic so common in Western Europe and the hopeless chasm of separation between Jew and non-Jew underlying East European discussion. We are in America not only a religious group but an ethnic group and bearers of a civilization that, for all its faults and flaws, is growing in quality as well as quantity. No, I am not suggesting that the messianic age has arrived, but I do contend that liberty has not only attained new dimensions in America but has compelled the two great religious traditions of the Western world to face each other not only with tolerance but with respect.

If there is cause for concern, it is that the setbacks in our social fabric of recent years will undermine our sense of determination to capture new frontiers of freedom. To us, liberty has meant responsibility and the right to be ourselves on all levels and in all dimensions—religiously, culturally, institutionally, and corporately. However embarrassing the proposition may sound, I submit that all Jews have a mission—to be a light unto the nations by being ourselves. By being true to our heritage we will, perforce, be concerned with, and have a share of responsibility for, the liberty and the welfare of the world as a whole. But as an American Jewish Committee our road to that goal is to rediscover our roots in the memory of our past as a stimulus to our future. Only thus will we hallow our years and help shake America and the free world of the fatigue of morale that has overcome large portions of it. We can best do so, I believe we can *only* do so, by taking seriously the two roots of our drive for liberty and by strengthening those institutions that inculcate the Jewish spirit of sanctifying space and time.Thus, our political and social aspirations cannot help but achieve the renewed faith that is necessary if we are to continue to proclaim liberty throughout the land for all its inhabitants.

RICHARD B. MORRIS

The Role of the Jews In the American Revolution in Historical Perspective

The story of the American Revolution is not complete without some acknowledgment of the role the Jews played in that conflict, and, in a broader sense, of the contribution of Jews and other minorities to the recognition of rights and values which are now considered an integral part of the American tradition.

Some fifty years ago an American President of New England origin, taking a phrase he attributed inaccurately to Lecky, paid tribute to the "Hebraic mortar which cemented the foundations of American democracy." Calvin Coolidge was acknowledging that strong sense of literary identification with the ancient people of Israel shared by Puritans and Pilgrims alike. The American Puritan tradition was immersed in Hebraism. A crucial and distinctive principle of its system—the covenant theology—is rooted in the Old Testament. The covenant theology was the keystone to the democratic control of church government under the Puritan Congregational system, and explains what looks like a revolutionary principle of government embodied in the Mayflower Compact, and in the settlements in Connecticut, New Hampshire, and Rhode Island. It is government based upon the consent of the people. This relationship between the Hebrew concept of the covenant and the Puritan concept is summed up in a remark of the Puritan thinker Joshua Moody: "We are all the children of Abraham; and therefore we are under Abraham's covenant."

Not only the Puritans but a later generation of Revolutionary Founding Fathers took almost daily inspiration from the Old Testament. John Jay, in his famous Address to the Convention of the State of New York in late 1776, argued that the persecution suffered by the American colonists at the hands of the British was worse than that suffered by the Jews from the tyrants of Egypt. Washington urged that the "most atrocious" war profiteers "be hung on gallows five times as high as Haman's," and innumerable like quotations from the Revolutionary years can be readily culled.

What these worthies are speaking about are the people of the book, not the Jews of flesh and blood of their own times, for many Americans, by the time of the Revolution, had probably never met a Jew. For the first hundred years or so of their existence in the colonies, the Jews constituted a minuscule minority. By the time of the Revolution there could not have been more than 2,000 Jews out of a total population of 2,500,000. At the start, then, the question might well be asked whether so tiny a minority could exercise a meaningful role in the great events that were about to transpire. In answering that question one should bear in mind that, though small in numbers, the Jews in America were literate, propertied, and often well connected, that they lived chiefly in the principal towns that were tinderboxes of revolt, and that the network of imperial blood relationships of which they formed a part gave them a special advantage in overseas transactions. One could say that they had a stake in the establishment without being a part thereof.

First of all, though, we should not allow filiopietism to blind us to a realization that the American Revolution, as a civil war, found Jews divided among themselves over support or resistance to revolt. Like other inhabitants of the colonies, Jews obeyed the dictates of conscience and exercised the right of dissent from whichever party might be the prevailing one in their particular communities. The coming of the Revolution found Jewish families, like those of other faiths, torn asunder and Jewish congregations split wide open. Perhaps most conspicuous on the Loyalist side was the Franks family of Philadelphia, one that lacked a strong sense of Jewish identity. Historians still narrate the role of Rebecca Franks, a society belle in her time, who acted as one of the two "Queens of Beauty" and graced an Italian medley which was performed in the Quaker City in the late spring of 1778 in honor of a departing and less-than-triumphant British general, Sir William Howe. Her father, David Franks, an outstanding merchant, played an ambivalent role during the Revolutionary crisis, his actions seemingly motivated by opportunism rather than conviction.

Appointed by the Continental Congress to serve as agent to supply American prisoners in British hands with provisions and other necessaries, he was permitted to go into British-held territory on condition that he not "give any intelligence to the enemy" and return to Philadelphia. What he wrote and what he did aroused increasing suspicions. He was jailed several times for suspect behavior, and finally permitted to leave for the enemy lines. Even though he was reimbursed by the British government in recognition of his loyalty and zeal for the cause, at war's end he returned to Philadelphia, along with other prominent Loyalists. Despite rumors to the contrary, he had not, unlike his daughter, forsworn his faith. In the records of the Federal District Court in Philadelphia, we have a deposition of his attested to "on the five Books of Moses."

In the tight Jewish communities of New York and Philadelphia, this divided allegiance was most apparent, whereas it was least demonstrable in communities of the deep South. Overall, the evidence suggests that the Jews of Spanish and Portuguese extraction, the long-term residents in the colonies, seem to have been enthusiastic Patriots, while the Ashkenazim were more evenly distributed between Tory and Whig. Most of the Sephardim—merchants like Aaron Lopez, for example—left Newport with the colonial forces, while the Hart and Pollock families of that town remained to work for the British cause, and perhaps suffered more for their decision than any other Jewish families in the colonies. In 1780 the properties of Isaac and Samuel Hart and the latter's son, Samuel, Jr., were confiscated by the Rhode Island Assembly. Moving to long Island, Issac Hart fell in defense of an improvised fort which the Loyalists had manned. Rivington's *Gazette* reports that he was "inhumanly fired upon and bayonetted," but the fact is that Hart had forfeited such immunity as might have been due him as a civilian. Jacob and Moses Hart received modest compensation from the British Commissioners of Forfeited Estates.

Closely allied to the Harts and sharing their political views were the Pollocks of Newport. Edmund Burke took up the cause of the Pollocks in an eloquent speech in the Commons, wherein he related that one of the Pollocks had been driven from Rhode Island for importing tea contrary to the nonimportation agreement, and after being forced to flee Long Island, where the British army had turned some lands over to him, he settled in St. Eustatius, there once more suffering substantial losses after the British capture of that Island, on which occasion the whole Jewish community of a hundred persons was rounded up, and each one searched and stripped of his possessions. Ezra Stiles lists seven other Jews who remained behind at Newport after the British occupation, suggesting that their Patriot sympathies were at best lukewarm, and an official list of Newport Tories includes another five known to be Jews.

In New York City the Jewish community was also split. The Congregation Shearith Israel was torn by dissension. The majority of the membership, following the lead of Gershom Mendes Seixas, decided to disband the congregation, and on the arrival of the British forces in the summer of '76 sought refuge in Connecticut or Philadelphia, while the Jewish Tories remained in the city. Others remained not out of choice, but were given little peace. I refer to those resting in the old Jewish cemetery set atop an elevation near Chatham Square on the outskirts of the Patriot fortifications overlooking the East River. While skirmishes were fought on and around the site, the British soldiery removed the lead plates bearing inscriptions and melted them down for ammunition. Very much alive, however, were Jewish supporters of George III like the Hessian soldier Alexander Zuntz, who doubled as commissary for the Hessian general staff and served as president of the rump Jewish congregation. The signatures of some fifteen Jews, some of them relatives of Patriot families like the Myers, Nathans, and Hayses, signed the ardent Loyalist address presented to Admiral

Lord Richard Howe and his brother Sir William on October 16, 1776.

If I have dwelt at some length on the role of Jews as Tories or neutrals, it is merely to put in perspective the assertions of that early proto-Zionist, Mordecai Noah, that his co-religionists had been one hundred percent pro-Revolution. That was a pardonable exaggeration, considering the patriotic antecedents of Noah himself, but the roster of American Jewish participants on the side of the Revolution is so impressive that it is clear that Whiggish Jews constituted an overwhelming majority of the scattered Jewish communities in the thirteen colonies. With the Catholics they stand as an exception to the generalization that the Tories were an aggregation of conscious minorities whose status was threatened by the Revolution. Perhaps because of their involvement with commerce, Jewish protesters against the new British revenue program were proportionately more numerous than those of any other ethnic or religious group.

Even before the formal start of the war, Jewish merchants were prominent in signing the nonimportation agreements, and their role in active military support and in financing, provisioning, and supplying the Continental and state military forces is a conspicuous one. Let us take two examples out of at least a hundred that could be selected. Immediately there comes to mind Francis Salvador.

Elected a member of the South Carolina Assembly, preceded only by Joseph Ottolengui of Georgia as a Jew in a colonial legislature, Salvador also served in his state's first and second Revolutionary Provincial Congresses. He accompanied the Presbyterian evangelist William Tennent into the heart of Tory country in North Carolina to persuade the Loyalists to join the Association. On July 24, 1776, Chief Justice Drayton wrote Salvador: "No news yet from Philadelphia; every ear is turned that way anxiously waiting for the word 'Independence.' I say, 'God speed the passage of it.' 'Amen,' say you." On August 1 Salvador was shot and scalped in an Indian and Tory ambush. Probably he never learned that the American Congress had declared that independence for which he had given his life. As evidence of divisions over the war even in Jewish families, it is worth mentioning that back in England Salvador's brother-in-law, Samuel Prado, was fearful, because of his loyalty to the Crown, that estates which he had never visited in South Carolina had been confiscated, and he filed a claim of loss just to be on the safe side.

Of David Solebury Franks, history tells us a great deal. Because he defended the right of a demonstrator to protest against George III—in this case the bust of the king at Montreal was daubed over with the words, "This is the pope of Canada and the fool of England"—Franks was jailed. Once he got out, he sought a more liberal climate, and although he is known to have been president of the Spanish-Portuguese Congregation of Montreal, he removed from that city to Philadelphia in 1775 and enlisted in the Continental army. He became a major and aide-de-camp to Benedict Arnold. Arnold's treason cast a shadow over the patriotism of Richard Varick and David Franks, Arnold's principal aides. Varick was acquitted in a court-martial, and all charges were dropped against Franks. Indeed, he was sent abroad with diplomatic dispatches as a mark of Congress's esteem, delivering to John Jay in Madrid Congress's commission to negotiate the peace. Promoted to the rank of lieutenant-colonel, he was sent abroad once more with a copy of the ratification of the Definitive Treaty of Peace. He served in 1784 as Vice-Consul at Marseilles, and the following year accompanied the American agent to Morocco to negotiate with that piratical nation a treaty, which he brought back to the United States early in 1787. Thus, the Jews and the Arabs got involved with each other very early.

Salvador and Franks are the best known among the Jewish military figures; but the list of those distinguishing themselves in military action is impressive. The Southern contingent of Jews in the rebel military forces seems all out of scale with their slender numbers. Almost the entire adult Jewish male population of Charleston, augmented by Jews who fled from Georgia, served in Captain Lushington's Company, which became known as the "Jew Company," a distinction attesting to the fact that the Jews and non-Jews in the company were about equally divided. One of those who was to give a good account of himself under fire was

Jacob I. Cohen. Some years later, as a member of the Richmond firm of Cohen and Isaacs, he hired a frontiersman named Daniel Boone to survey his land on the Licking River in far-off Kentucky. Enraged at the Patriot activities of the Sheftalls and Philip Minis, Governor James Wright of Georgia wrote the authorities, in the course of the war, that the Jewish Whig refugees should not be permitted to return to Georgia and that other Jews should be prevented from emigrating to the colony. "For these people, my lord, were found to a man to have been violent rebels and persecutors of the king's loyal subjects. And however this law may appear at first sight," Wright insisted, "be assured, my lord, that the times require these exertions and without which the loyal subjects have no peace or security in the province." Elsewhere I have likened this advice to the blind panic that led to the wholesale arrest and incarceration of the Nisei immediately after Pearl Harbor, a deed which has stained America's record for civil rights.

Apart from the battlefield, Jews from their connections and expertise in shipping, trade, and finance, made substantial contributions to the successful operation of the war. The Jewish share of privateering, to cite one example, is estimated at six percent of the total, a figure far out of proportion to its slender population, and including the activities of such prominent figures as Moses Michael Hays of Boston, Isaac Moses, a partner of Robert Morris in the Black Prince, and the firm of Moses Levy and Company. A chief victim of privateering depredations was the great merchant shipper of Newport, Aaron Lopez. At the outbreak of the Revolution he was the owner of thirty vessels engaged in European and West Indian trade and the whale fisheries. Lopez's espousal of the American cause virtually wrecked his business; nearly all his vessels were lost before the war was over; some of them, according to his memorial to the Continental Congress, had been captured by American privateers, and the Congressional Court of Admiralty and Appeals sustained him in at least one suit.

In the Southern theater of military operations, no Jew played a larger civilian role than Mordecai Sheftall, leader of the Savannah Jewish community, and chairman of the insurgent Committee of Christ Church Parish. He was nominated in 1778 for the post of

Deputy Commissary General of Issues to the Continental troops in South Carolina and Georgia and Deputy Commissary General of Purchase and Issues to the militia, but fell into enemy hands before the formal commission could be confirmed by Congress. When the British occupied Savannah in December 1778, Sheftall was captured by a body of Highlanders, transferred to a prison ship, listed as "Chairman Rebel Committee," and regarded as barred thereby from holding a public office in royal Georgia. His claim to reimbursement of advances made as Deputy Commissary General of Issues was rejected by Congress, although persistently pressed. Sheftall's fortune was apparently depleted, if not entirely liquidated, as a result of his war involvements, despite his efforts to recoup his losses by privateering operations after his release from imprisonment. In the Western theater of operations, Simon Nathan advanced large sums for George Rogers Clark's campaign, only to be repaid in worthless Continental paper.

Perhaps no Patriot in the American Revolution boasted a more romantic and seemingly improbable career than Haym Salomon, a Polish immigrant who arrived in New York in 1772 and set himself up as a commission merchant, dealer in securities, and ship broker. He soon struck up a friendship with Alexander McDougall, a leader of the Sons of Liberty, with whom he cast his lot. When, in September 1776, New York City was burned ("whether by Providence or some stout fellow," as George Washington put it), the irate British occupation forces sought scapegoats. Salomon was picked up as a suspect and thrust into jail, probably the Old Sugar House located on what is now Liberty Street. Owing to his fluency in German as well as in five other languages, the British found him useful in communicating with the Hessians, who numbered about half the occupation troops. Because of these services, he was released from jail and permitted to resume his business activities. Whether or not he continued to use his military contacts to have access to prisons or prison ships, it seems clear that Salomon was soon involved in underground activities to help American prisoners of war escape. With the evacuation of Philadelphia and the rebuff at Monmouth, the British in New York became panicky. Salomon was arrested in early August

1778, and jailed this time on suspicion of espionage and sabotage. Sentenced to death in a drumhead court-martial, Salomon effected a miraculous escape with the aid of his friend McDougall, now a Patriot general. On August 25, 1778, we find him in Philadelphia, petitioning Congress that his war activities had cost him all his effects and credit to the amount of five or six thousand pounds sterling.

In Philadelphia, Salomon was picked by the Chevalier de La Luzerne, the French minister to Congress, to serve as paymaster-general of the French forces in America. At his brokerage office in Front Street, feverish financial activities were carried on. It was only natural that when, in February 1781, Congress named Robert Morris to be Superintendent of Finance, virtually endowing him with the powers of a financial dictator, Morris should lean on Salomon. The latter had already advanced the government considerable sums of money on the dubious security it offered because, as we know, the federal government had gone bankrupt in its efforts to finance the war. Now, with his own personal endorsement, Salomon sold Morris's bills of exchange, providing much of the funds that kept the government in motion, and charging only one-fourth of one percent commission, perhaps a third of the going rate. In the three-year period of Morris's Superintendency of Finance, Salomon had no less than seventy-five transactions with Morris, advancing in hard currency over $200,000.

The later career of Salomon proved tragic. With the war's end, Salomon planned to move his operations back to New York, but the transfer was never effected. His health seriously impaired as a result of his wartime imprisonment by the British, he died at the age of forty-five. The Revolution had not enriched him. His total assets amounted to $44,732; his debts to $45,292. His estate was insolvent by $560. Had the liquidation of his estate not been forced, the loan office, treasury, and state certificates that Salomon's estate held, to the extent of over $150,000, would have been redeemed at par when Alexander Hamilton became Secretary of the Treasury—a fact nobody knew in 1785, and all the Salomon family would have suffered would have been a loss on the worthless Continental currency. Thus Salomon, who had lost two fortunes in the course of the Revolutionary War, had risked his property and pledged his credit on behalf of the Revolutionary Congress when a crisis of confidence existed.

In short, from Aaron Lopez to Mordecai Sheftall to Haym Salomon, every single conspicuous Jewish figure who was involved in financing or supplying the Continental forces ended up broke.

If the American Revolution proved to be a liberating movement for various minorities, including the Jews, there were moments when Jews in America felt that they were being singled out for discrimination. Both sides in the Revolution required the inhabitants to take loyalty oaths. One of the earliest oaths of loyalty to the Revolutionary cause was that exacted by the Rhode Island Assembly in June 1775, of male inhabitants over sixteen years of age "suspected of being inimical to the United American Colonies." The officers of the Rhode Island brigade soon listed seventy-seven inhabitants of Newport suspected of "inimical" views, among them three known Jewish Tories and Moses M. Hays. When four members of the General Assembly tendered the test to the Newport suspects, Isaac Hart refused to sign the test until it was required from all alike; Myer Pollock declined on the ground that it was "contrary to the custom of Jews," but Moses Michael Hays, who in fact was no Tory, refused on more elaborate grounds. He demanded that his accusers come forward and asked that the accusation be read, which was done. Although avowing "the strongest principles and attachments to the just rights and privileges of this my native land" and his support for the war as a "just" one, he declined to subscribe, first, because the burden of proof of his inimical status rested on his accusers; secondly, because as a Jew he was not allowed to vote, contrary to the state's constitution; thirdly, because the test was "not general," and finally because neither the Continental Congress nor the state assembly had ever singled out "in this contest . . . the society of Israelites to which I belong." He followed up this refusal with a petition to the General Assembly avowing his attachment to the Patriot cause and insisting upon "the rights and privileges due other free citizens." So far as the records disclose, this ended the controversy.

If there is an overtone of anti-Semitism in this incident, or a forecast of the McCarthyism of the 1950s, it in no wise reflects the climate of opinion prevailing in the American colonies on the verge of rebellion. When one considers that the American Revolution was a civil war, that leading Patriots held a deep and abiding prejudice against Roman Catholics, that the rhetoric of abuse in which both sides indulged has seldon been surpassed except in our own time, and, further, that the Jews seemed especially vulnerable since they provided scapegoats on both sides of the conflict, it is astonishing how little anti-Semitism was stirred up in America as a result of the Revolutionary crisis. Contrariwise, prejudice and animosity toward Jews was widespread in contemporary England. Jews were humiliated and physically attacked on the streets, which resounded to the tunes of anti-Jewish ballads, anti-Semitism was a part of the religious indoctrination of the High Church, and the prominence of Jews in finance was reflected in the frequent caricatures of the Jew as a moneylender. One of the most celebrated of Gillray's caricatures depicts the Earl of Shelburne, with a booted and spurred French courier on his left just arrived from Paris, bearing news that the Preliminaries had been signed with America on November 30, 1782, and on his right a group of Jewish moneylenders waiting to receive payment of sums allegedly advanced on the security of the Shelburne House and about to be paid off with the fruits of stock manipulation. The conversion of the eccentric Lord George Gordon to Judaism hardly cooled latent English anti-Semitism. Nor did Lord George's proposal, dated barely a month before the signing of the Definitive Peace with America and addressed to Elias Lindo and Nathan Salomons on behalf of the Portuguese and German Jews respectively. On the verge of conversion, the irrepressible peer proposed that Jews could stop the war by withholding credits. It was the playwright-diplomat Richard Cumberland who, single-handedly, stepped into the breach, and through his periodical, *The Observer* and his play *The Jew* sought to correct the current image in England of the Jew as rogue, usurer, or buffoon.

Unlike England, the tie-in of Jews with usury and sharp financial dealings was rarely made in America of Revolutionary times, although isolated instances may be found. One Loyalist who sought to exploit the traditional view of the Jewish usurer was Miers Fisher, a Quaker lawyer and former Tory exile, who, on his return to Philadelphia at the end of the war, sought to obtain a charter for the Bank of Pennsylvania, a potential competitor of Robert Morris's Bank of North America. He contended that the chartering of his bank would reduce the rate of interest, thus protecting the people against the exactions of the Jewish brokers. Not only was this a diversionary maneuver by which Tories attempted to exonerate themselves by inciting prejudice against Jews, but it was an implied attack on Robert Morris and his bank, which had received strong support from Jews. A "Jew Broker," the pseudonym believed to have been used in this case by Haym Salomon, sent a scorching reply to the press. Denouncing the aspersions "cast so indiscriminately on the Jews of this city at large," the writer not only accused Fisher of libeling the Jews but of injuring that liberty of conscience which the Jews enjoyed. Defending the Jews as having been "early uniform, decisive Whigs," and "second to none" in their "patriotism and attachment" to their country, he insisted on the injustice of denigrating an entire group "for the faults of a few."

This exchange must be put down as exceptional. Anti-Semitism was definitely out of fashion in the America of the Revolutionary era. When Ezra Stiles reported that in May 1773 Governor Wanton of Rhode Island, together with Judges Oliver and Auchmuty, sat with the president of the congregation at a Jewish religious service held at the Newport synagogue, he was very casually reporting an event which would have been impossible to parallel in Europe at that time. When, in 1809, John Adams, taking exception to the anti-Semitism of Bolingbroke and Voltaire, insisted that "the Hebrews have done more to civilize men than any other nation," he was merely voicing sentiments that President Washington, perhaps less effusively had placed on the records a good deal earlier. I need hardly add that John Adams was expressing his affection for the people of the book, not for contemporary Jewry. Behind the effusive acknowledgment of affirmative Jewish qualities lurked a hope on the part of Hebraists like Ezra Stiles of

Yale that someday the Jews would see the light and unite with Christians in accepting the religion of the majority.

Having reviewed the individual experience of the more conspicuous Jewish figures in the American Revolution, it is now fitting that we should consider the role played by the scattered Jewish communities and community leaders in acting, along with other minority groups, as a catalyst to quicken demands for equal rights and civil liberties. Just as the Catholics played a decisive role in the passage of the Maryland Toleration Act of 1649 to reassure Protestant settlers, and the Baptists sparked the passage of Virginia's revolutionary legislation for religious liberty, so, too, the Jews had, from the beginning of their settlement in America, fought Director-General Stuyvesant in New Netherland to win the basic right of settlement, economic privileges, the right of public worship, and various political rights. The fact that the Jews back in the seventeenth century had waged the battle of other minority groups as well as their own is clear from Stuyvesant's warning to the Dutch West India Company. "Giving them liberty," he declared, "we cannot refuse the Lutherans and the Papists."

Was the Jew in America an alien? The issue was raised not many years after the passage of the Navigation Act of 1660, which barred aliens from the colonial trade, and a draft of the Act of 1696, which by its phrasing seemed to bar Jews who had succeeded in obtaining naturalization in the colonies. The Jewish traders petitioned the government, asserting that "those of the Hebrew Nation do look upon what ever Countrey they retire" to "as their native country." The Jews were supported by a similar representation from a group of French Huguenots acting in behalf of their co-religionists in Carolina and New York. As finally enacted, the statute of 1696 omitted the objectionable provision, an omission which was a resounding victory for minority groups both in England and the colonies.

By the time of the American Revolution Jews had achieved civil rights and rights of worship, but their political position was by no means clarified. In 1737 New York disqualified the winner of an election to the legislature because Jews had voted for him. The legislature was persuaded by the contention of a New York attorney of prominence, William Smith, who pointed out that Jews were disqualified from voting in English Law, and to clinch his case he reminded his hearers of the guilt the Jews allegedly bore for the Crucifixion. In Rhode Island the Superior Court held that no Jews could hold any office or vote in choosing others—this in the plantation found by Roger Williams!

Considering the fact that the Jews in America enjoyed civil rights long before they were accorded them in England, and that the great campaign for the admission of Jews to the British Parliament was not secured until 1858, it is not surprising that some American states proved dilatory about letting down political barriers to such minorities as Catholics, Jews, Deists, or nonbelievers. Even states like Virginia, which acted boldly in providing for religious freedom, did not at once remove political discrimination against various minorities. The great exception was the New York State Constitution, whose two-hundredth anniversary was appropriately commemorated on April 20, 1977. That constitution, which imposed on the Jews no disabilities whatsoever, justified the encomiums of contemporary New York leaders of being "wisely framed to preserve the inestimable blessings of civil and religious liberty," and may well be, as one American Jewish historian claims, "the first emancipatory law in modern history."

New York's example heartened religious minorities and the friends of religious liberty in other states, notably in Pennsylvania, where an unusually democratic constitution guaranteed freedom of worship, but at the same time fixed a religious test for office-holding, one which effectively barred Jews. Early in 1784 a group of Jewish leaders of the Philadelphia synagogue, including their "rabbi," Gershom Seixas, their president, Simon Nathan, and the associates of their council—Asher Myers, Bernard Gratz, and Haym Salomon—petitioned the Pennsylvania Council of Censors "in behalf of themselves and their brethren Jews, residing in Pennsylvania." They protested the tenth section of the state constitution, requiring members of the assembly to subscribe to a declaration which ended in these words: "I do acknowledge the Scriptures of the old and new Testament to be given by divine inspiration." Very properly the memorialists pointed out that this clause violated the second paragraph of the state's declaration of rights, asserting "that no man who acknowledges the being of a God can be justly deprived or abridged of any civil rights as a citizen on account of his religious sentiments." The point was made that the disability of Jews to serve in the assembly might impel Jewish immigrants to go to New York or to such other places in the United States where no such discrimination prevailed. While disavowing strong political ambitions, the memorialists denounced the exclusion test as "a stigma upon their nation and their religion," particularly undeserved in view of the Patriot contribution of the Jews to the cause of the Revolution and their losses suffered as a result of their participation. While the memorial was tabled at that time, Pennsylvania in its new constitution of 1790 removed the New Testament reference, which had in effect excluded Jews from public office.

In addition to Pennsylvania, various other states, following New York's example and Virginia's Notable Act for Religious Freedom of 1785, removed political restrictions against the Jews. Georgia acted in 1789; South Carolina did so simultaneously with Pennsylvania; Delaware removed the bars in 1792; and Vermont a year later. Still other states were slower to respond to Enlightenment currents. For example, the disqualification in the Maryland Constitution of 1776 barring Jews from public office was not removed until 1825. Rhode Island did not secure equal rights for the Jews until the adoption of its state constitution in 1842, and North Carolina not until 1868.

If Jews contributed to making the Revolution both a war for independence and a broad movement for change and reform, still they and other religious minorities were beneficiaries of the movement in the original thirteen states to guarantee religious liberty, separate church and state, and drop the religious bars to public office-holding. But it was the federal government rather than the states which provided the most vigorous impetus to the movement. On July 13, 1787, the Congress of the Confederation, meeting in New York City, enacted the Northwest Territory Ordinance, whose first article ordained that "no person, demeaning himself in a peaceable and orderly manner, shall ever be molested on account of his mode of worship, or religious sentiments, in the said territory."

Would the Federal Convention meeting simultaneously in Philadelphia adopt so liberal a stance? Since its sessions were secret, nothing was known to the public of what had been decided prior to the adjournment of the Convention. On August 20, Charles Cotesworth Pinckney had submitted to the Convention, for reference to the Committee on Detail, a number of propositions, among them: "No religious test or qualification shall ever be annexed to any oath of office under authority of the United States." This proposition was referred to the Committee on Detail without debate or further consideration. When the Committee reported back on August 30, Pinckney then moved to amend the article with the addition of these words: "but no religious test shall ever be required as a qualification to any office or public trust under the authority of the United States." Roger Sherman thought the clause unnecessary, "the prevailing liberality being a sufficient security against such tests," But Gouverneur Morris and General Pinckney approved the motion, which was agreed to unanimously. The entire article was adopted, with only North Carolina voting no and Maryland divided.

Not knowing what had transpired, Jonas Phillips, a long-time patriot of New York, who had removed to Philadelphia before the start of hostilities and served in the Philadelphia militia, memorialized the convention on September 7, which he carefully described as "24th Ellul 5547." Using arguments similar to those the synagogue leaders of his city advanced to the Pennsylvania Council of Censors in 1784 in arguing against the test oath, Phillips urged that, should the Convention omit the phrase regarding the divine inspiration of the New Testament, "then the Israelites will think themselves happy to live under a government where all religious societies are on an equal footing." Jonas Phillips appears to have been unduly concerned. In its final form, Article VI of the Federal Constitution requires all federal and state officials to take an oath or affirmation to support the Constitution, with the proviso "but no religious Test shall ever be required as a qualification to any office or public trust under the United States." Finally, of course, one should mention the first article of the Bill of Rights, forbidding Congress to make any law respecting an establishment of religion or prohibiting the free exercise thereof.

It was only fitting that Jews should publicly express their rejoicing when the Constitution was ratified, and Jews joined in public celebrations with their fellow Americans. In Philadelphia their sensibilities were observed by providing for them a special kosher table. Quite properly could Washington applaud the "enlarged and liberal policy" of the new nation, in which "all possess alike liberty of conscience and immunities of citizenship." Significantly, the new President extolled the example of the new nation "which gives to bigotry no sanction, to persecution, no assistance," as "a policy worthy of imitation," lifting the eloquent phrasing from a memorial to him from Yeshuat Israel Congregation of Newport. Or, as he phrased it in a communication to the members of the New Church in Baltimore: "In the enlightened Age and in this land of equal liberty it is our boast, that a man's religious tenets will not forfeit the protection of the Laws, nor deprive him of the right of attaining and holding the highest Offices that are known in the United States."

On this point Washington proved an optimist, because while a Catholic has attained the Presidency, to date the very highest office in the land still eludes non-Christians.

In sum, there is abundant evidence not only from the Revolutionary era but from the whole century of a Jewish presence in America preceding it, to demonstrate that where the Jews gained the equal protection of the laws other minorities were likely to profit thereby, and, further, that the struggles of Presbyterian minorities or French Huguenot minorities or German Pietist minorities or Baptist minorities or Catholic minorities were inseparably tied to the security of the Jewish community. After all, had there been no minority groups in this country, colonial and early national America would have been quite differently structured and doubtless less vital and democratic than the emerging nation proved to be in fact. At least forty percent of the population of the American colonies was of non-English stock, and the followers of the Church of England, though that church was established in a number of colonies, were in fact a numerical minority themselves. Accordingly, toleration and equal rights were the keys to effective functioning of government. Without them discord and civil strife would have stifled opportunity, discouraged immigration, and even have caused a breakdown of law enforcement.

America's toleration toward Jews and other religious minorities, and the steps taken to guarantee their civil and political rights, served as a spur to the movement on the European continent for the emancipation of the Jews, so long victims of discriminatory laws. In their petition to the French National Assembly of January 1790, the Jews of France pointed to America, citing that Revolutionary land for having "rejected the word toleration from its code," for, they cogently reasoned, "to tolerate is, in fact, to suffer that which you could, if you wished, prevent and prohibit." In Western Europe the emancipation of the Jews was finally achieved by the French Revolution and the Code Napoléon. Moses Mendelssohn, that foremost spokesman for Jewish emancipation, and a grand product of the *Aufklärung,* was so stirred by the secular spirit evoked by America's War of Independence that he wrote a new foreword to an older work, using the American Revolution as a pretext to set forth his ideas on the separation of church and state.

Thus, a great world leader in the movement of Jewish emancipation took heart from the grand events on this side of the Atlantic, events in which the voice of the Jews had been raised on numberless occasions on behalf of religious liberty, in opposition to political discrimination, and in support of civil rights for all, and would continue to be raised in the years ahead down to our own time.

A final point. The people of the "Hebrew nation," or "Israelites," as they chose to style themselves, made every effort to join the mainstream of American life. Some assimilated so completely that even the most skilled genealogist cannot trace their descendants. Others, probably a majority of that Revolutionary generation, saw no difficulty in maintaining their identification with Judaism while regarding themselves as Americans on an equality with their non-Jewish associates. With Washington, they recognized the need to develop a "national character," with Hamilton, the vision to "think continentally." Without renouncing their faith, they were quite prepared to be "Americanized," to use a term first coined by John Jay in 1797.

Indeed, the early role of the Jew in America should be borne in mind at a time when notions of cultural pluralism have portrayed society as a collection of minorities and given priority to minority concerns over collective interests. Pushed to extremes, pluralism has spawned separatist Quebec, a tragic bomb-wracked Northern Ireland, Scottish, and Welsh separatism, not to speak of rising bilingualism in some regions of the United States, with its disunifying implications, and the reality of ethnic politics to which every American politician pays obeisance.

The belief that all the varied groups in America could co-exist in a kind of natural harmony was a theory advanced a half-century ago by Horace Kallen,* an early and active Zionist. Since then ethnicity in America, from university curricula to popular culture, has assumed directions that might well have given even a Kallen pause. Where pluralism denotes a theory of culture, I would embrace it, especially for its appropriateness to minorities like the Jews, who wish to preserve their religious identity and their blood ties to Israel, and are not likely to forget the rise of Nazism, the Holocaust, and the coercion under which Jews now live in totalitarian states. Where pluralism denotes a theory of power, I confess to grave misgivings. Ethnic pluralism as a basis of power immobilizes government and erodes the national purpose. Most plural societies are either tyrannized by one of the constituent groups or operate under constant instability, thereby posing a threat to the continued functioning of democratic institutions.

In the third century of our national existence, as I see it, our tasks as American Jews steadfast to the traditions of the American Jewish past are, first, to cherish our distinctive cultural values. Irving Howe's brilliant analysis of the process of Americanizing the

*See below "Jews and Pluralism" by Moses Rischin.

Jewish immigrant has shown how greatly Jewish ethical and cultural values, traditions, and even personality traits have spurred that growing awareness in the larger community of intellectual values and the need for social reform, while at the same time contributing so much to Jewish self-discovery. To maintain our own cultural values constitutes by itself an enormous challenge in a society where family ties are disintegrating and swift technological change is homogenizing our life and culture without rendering either more homogeneous or more enriching.

We Jews have another task before us, as I see it. While maintaining our respect for diversity, we should take the lead in marking out those political and cultural values and bases of creativity which served to bind together all Americans in achieving a common purpose, consistent with our democratic traditions and the image of America as an "asylum for liberty," a common purpose that will lift our sights and unite us, one that will inspire us with the kind of dedication that impelled Jews and other minorities of Revolutionary days to sacrifice life and treasure for a noble cause.

MILTON R. KONVITZ

The Quest for Equality and the Jewish Experience

America is the great exception in Jewish history. As recently as 1975, when the *New York Times* reported the death of the celebrated cellist Gregor Piatigorsky, the obituary mentioned the fact that before he was fourteen years of age, Piatigorsky had lived through a pogrom in Russia. Indeed, I myself recall my parents discussing a pogrom that they had lived through. For almost two thousand years, persecution and discrimination were part of the common life of the Jewish people almost everywhere in the world. The Talmud records that early in the second century, when a non-Jew asked to be converted, the rabbis said to him: "What reason have you for seeking conversion? Do you not know that Israelites today are in travail, that they are persecuted, that they are driven from place to place, that they are harassed and full of suffering?"[1] It is precisely in these terms—in terms of ceaseless persecution, trouble, expulsion, harassment, and suffering—that the history of the Jews of almost every country in the world, not excepting even England or France, can be written.

When we survey the history of Jews in America, we cannot help but see and cry out how different, how radically different, has been the American Jewish experience.

I

In the late 1960s, when militant blacks staged demonstrations in various churches demanding a half-billion dollars in "reparations" for three hundred years of subjugation and discrimination, a writer in an Anglo-Jewish journal[2] formulated a demand for "reparations" from various nations on behalf of the Jewish people, including a demand on the Vatican for the harm done by teaching that the Jewish people were guilty of deicide, and for promotion of the blood libel; a demand on Spain for the Inquisition and the expulsion of Jews in 1492; on Germany, France, Austria, and Italy, as successors of the Holy Roman Empire, for imprisoning Jews in ghettos; on Arab governments for oppression of the Jews for hundreds of years; on Russia for forcing Jews to live in the Pale of Settlement, for prohibiting them from owning land, for imposing on Jews the quota system which severely restricted their admission to high school or the universities, and for the forgery of the notorious *Protocols of the Elders of Zion.* These are only some of the claims that could be made against governments and nations. But no Jewish writer would for a moment think that America owes the Jews anything, that American Jewry would be warranted in demanding "reparations" from the United States government for any wrongs or outrages against the Jewish people.

Indeed, historians, in searching and sifting the facts of American history, claim that they have found only a single instance of a governmental action against the Jewish people. This refers to General Order No. 11, issued in December 1862 by order of Maj. Gen. Ulysses S. Grant, which provided for the expulsion of "the Jews, as a class," from the Department of the Tennessee, "within twenty-four hours" of receipt of the order. Post commanders were instructed by the order to see that "all of this class of people" be furnished passes and be required to leave.[3] The General Order was issued in the midst of a scandal of widespread illegal cotton speculation and illegal trading in which thousands of people were implicated, including federal agents, army officers, and even General Grant's father.

But the Jews who were directly affected by the expulsion order did not accept the affront and injustice supinely. Three Jewish citizens of Paducah, Kentucky, at once sent a telegram to President Lincoln protesting

> this inhuman order, the carrying out of which would be the grossest violation of the Constitution and our rights as citizens under it, [and] which will place us . . . as outlaws before the whole world.

Receiving no reply (it is not known whether Lincoln was ever shown the telegram), one of the Paducah expellees alerted the press and especially Jewish community leaders, and hastened to Washington, where he induced a friendly member of Congress to arrange for an immediate appointment with the President, to which he was accompanied by the Congressman. The report of the meeting in the White House shows that Lincoln had known nothing about the order. As soon as he heard the facts, Lincoln instructed the General-in-Chief to send a telegram canceling General Grant's order. Three days later Rabbi Isaac Mayer Wise, Rabbi Max Lilienthal, and delegations of Jews from Cincinnati and Louisville arrived in Washington and were taken at once by two Ohio Congressmen to the White House, where they expressed to Lincoln their gratitude for his prompt and firm cancellation of the odious General Order No. 11.

In fairness to Grant it should be noted that apart from this incident, there is no proof that he ever revealed any antipathy toward Jews. During his two terms as President, Grant appointed many Jews to major and minor offices; he appointed a Jew as Governor of the Washington Territory, and he offered the position of Secretary of the Treasury to Joseph Seligman, who declined the post; and when pogroms broke out in Rumania in 1870, he appointed the Grand Master of B'nai B'rith as American Consul at Bucharest, as part of the government's effort to exert pressure on the Rumanian government to desist from its anti-Semitic actions.

The case of General Order No. 11 is deserving of our attention for three reasons. *First,* as we have noted, historians point to it as "the only instance of collective punishment of Jews in American history,"[4] or as the "first instance of something approaching explicit ideological anti-Semitism."[5] I think that one can accept the judgment that "American antisemitism has almost never been official or governmental";[6] but the exceptions to the rule must include, I think, besides General Grant's order, the restrictive immigration laws that were in effect until 1965.[7] *Second,* the case of General Grant's order is significant for the Jewish reaction it caused. Jews of Kentucky who were personally affected, and Jewish community leaders, rabbis and laymen, reacted to the order with vigor, expedition, self-regard, and dignity. After all, this was not the Old World, this was America, and no one, not even Major General Grant, and not even in a time of civil war, could be allowed to unjustly abuse them and use Jews as scapegoats. *Third,* the telegram sent by Jewish citizens of Kentucky protested the violation of their constitutional rights. There was nothing cringing in their words, no plea for mere toleration or compassion; the Jews took their stand on their legal, civil rights, on their rights as American citizens.

Although it is admittedly hazardous, if not worse, to formulate laws of history, I submit that the course of American Jewish history over the past two centuries demonstrates the following two generalizations; namely, that whenever American Jews felt themselves to be unjustly treated, they did not suffer the injustice or wrongdoing passively, insensibly, or obsequiously, but reacted with forthright courage, with head erect, and with proud-minded steps; and furthermore, when they felt themselves discriminated against, their resistance was placed on the high ground of constitutional principle and legal rights. In these important respects American Jews have always acted as a civil rights movement.

Indeed, one can go back to the earliest days of our Colonial history for the original precedent of this principled Jewish response to a threatened deprivation. Soon after the first Jews—twenty-three of them—settled in New Amsterdam in 1654, Peter Stuyvesant, the Governor, prohibited them from trading with Indians on the Delaware and the Hudson. On November 29, 1655, three of the Jewish settlers wrote a petition to the Governor and his Council in which they respectfully but firmly protested against his action and called attention to the fact that the Lords Directors of the West India Company had given them permission and consent, "like the other inhabitants, to travel, reside, and trade here, and enjoy the same liberties . . ."[8] Also in 1655 Stuyvesant denied Jews the right to keep "watch and ward" and imposed on them a special tax in lieu of the military service from which he had barred them. Two of the settlers, Asser Levy and Jacob Barsimson, petitioned the Governor and Council for either the right to bear arms or exemption from the onerous Jews' tax. Although the petition was not granted, the records show that by the spring of 1657 Asser Levy was in fact serving in the guard.

When they were denied recognition as burghers, they brought a court action, and when they lost in the court, they appealed to the Governor and Council, and in their petition the Jews of New Amsterdam said:

> Further, that our nation enjoys in the city of Amsterdam in Holland the burgher right . . . as appears by the burgher certificate hereto annexed; also that our nation, as long as they have been here, have, with others, borne and paid and still bear, all burgher burdens.[9]

In reply, on April 20, 1657, the authorities acted to admit the Jews of their town to the rights of burghership.

As the Jewish refugees from Brazil won the rights to trade with Indians and to stand guard, and their status as burghers, their successes in their struggles for civil and political rights

> obtained benefits not only for themselves but also opened the door for other disenfranchised groups. The intolerant Stuyvesant, writing to the Directors in Amsterdam in October, 1655, had thought of this too: "Giving them liberty, we cannot refuse the Lutherans and Papists."[10]

II

According to Maimonides, a proselyte, as he is received into the people of Israel, is forewarned and comforted in these words:

> and though you see Israel in distress in this world, good is in store for them [in the world to come], for they cannot receive overmuch good in this world like the other nations, lest their heart become proud and go astray and lose the reward of the world to come, as it

> is said, "But Jeshurun waxed fat, and kicked"; and the Holy One, blessed is He, does not inflict too much punishment upon them in order that they should not perish.[11]

Maimonides, having witnessed, at the age of thirteen, religious persecution in his native Cordoba, and wandering with his parents for eight or nine years from place to place, settling in Morocco, where he found life for a Jew intolerable, fleeing to the Holy Land, and then to Egypt, yet could he thank God for not inflicting "too much punishment" on the people of Israel, for they had not altogether perished; and certainly he could thank God for not having bestowed on Israel "overmuch good in this world," such as other nations enjoyed; and being an Aristotelian, Maimonides was reconciled to the idea that happiness is attained through following the mean, through avoidance of extremes, which he probably thought the history of the Jews providentially manifested: persecution falling short of extinction, prosperity falling short of absolute security.

At long last, however, after several thousand years, Jewish history can now cite an instance of a Jewish community which, Maimonides might say, has in fact received "overmuch good in this world like the other nations," and perhaps even surpassing "other nations."

For according to the best available evidence and the judgment of the most knowledgeable scholars, American Jewry constitutes "a relatively prosperous" people, "which in its income and occupational profile compares favorably with the nation's high-status Protestant founding groups."[12] This is a relatively conservative or moderate judgment. Another reputable scholar puts the matter as follows: "the Jews have become in every measure one could care to choose the most successful group in American society," and he adds that this is "a fact which no one at this point would presume to deny."[13] What do the facts show?

A survey taken in 1972 by the Census Bureau showed that of the eight ethnic groups surveyed, comprising 102 million Americans, the Jews had the highest median family income.[14] The Jews had the highest percentage of high school and college graduates: 26 percent of the Jewish population, 25 years of age and over, were college graduates; the next ethnic group were the English with 18 percent, and after them the Germans with 12 percent. With respect to occupational distribution, 77.8 percent of the Jews were white-collar workers, only 17.2 percent were blue-collar workers. The next ethnic group were the English, with 49.2 percent white-collar and 39.4 percent blue-collar workers.

Using a religious rather than an ethnic identification approach, Andrew M. Greeley, of the National Opinion Research Center in Chicago, finds that the Jews are the best educated Americans, with fourteen as the average years of education. Next come Episcopalians with 13.5, Presbyterians with 12.7, Methodists with 11.9, and Catholics with 11.5. While the spread between Jews and Episcopalians may not be substantial, that between Jews and Catholics is certainly notable.[15] Looking at educational mobility, that is, given where they started educationally, the Greeley study concludes that while Catholics are catching up with Episcopalians, "Jews are leaving the rest of the American population far behind."[16]

Looking at the occupational pattern,

> Jews and Episcopalians and Presbyterians represent the elite of non-Spanish white Americans, Methodists and Catholics and Lutherans, the middle class, and Baptists the less successful.[17]

With respect to income, the Greeley study says that "Jewish income success seems to have kept pace with and benefited by Jewish educational success." The average Jewish family income was $13,340. Next followed Catholics with $11,374, and Episcopalians with $11,032, and Baptists in seventh place with $8,693. With a national average of $9,953 in 1974, the Jewish family's income was above by $3,387, around $2,300 more than the family income of Episcopalians, and around $4,600 more than that of Baptists.[18]

During the years of the Vietnam War, 88 percent of young Jews attended college; the next groups, with 65 percent each, were Episcopalians and Presbyterians; then came Methodists and Catholics, with 45 percent each, Lutherans with 43 percent, and lowest of all, Baptists with 28 percent. Today, "the odds of a young Jew attending college are better than seven to one." At the turn of the century, the order of rank among denominations attending college was quite different; Presbyterians were first with 48 percent, Jews were fourth with 17percent, which was then the national average. The rise of the percentage of Jews attending college has been steady and substantial since then: from 17 to 88.[19] If the trend should continue, the time will come when every American Jew will be a college graduate.

Based on seven surveys by the National Opinion Research Center, Jews rate first with respect to years of education, prestige of occupation, percentage of white-collar jobs, and family income.[20] This holds true among ethnic as well as religious groups. The Jews, says Father Greeley, who directed these studies and surveys, "are America's most impressive success story."[21]

These surveys and studies are substantiated by others made since World War II, although some scholars tend to put their conclusions in more guarded terms than those of Father Greeley. Thus, e.g., Professor Nathan Glazer puts the matter this way: American Jews have become "an extremely prosperous group, probably as prosperous as some of the oldest and longest-established elements of the population of the United States."[22] But Professor Glazer has noted that the relative prosperity and success of Jews could be seen even at the turn of the century. Reviewing the data for that time, Glazer concluded that "there is no question that the Jews earned more than did non-Jews," although the average Jewish immigrant at that time landed with only $9 in his pocket.[23] Although the immigrant Jews tended to settle in ghetto areas in large urban centers, they also tended to leave these ghettos as quickly as possible, and, indeed, more rapidly than did other immigrant groups.[24] Writing in 1954, in connection with the American Jewish Tercentenary Celebration, Glazer concluded that the statistics

> demonstrate that the rise in the social and economic position of the Jews has been extremely rapid, far surpassing that which can be shown for any other immigrant group, and indeed surpassing, for

the period, changes in the socio-economic position of long-settled groups.[25]

In a study prepared for the American Jewish Committee in 1970, in which he surveyed and summarized the extensive literature, Professor Sidney Goldstein concluded that the "fact remains that, on the whole, both the average income of Jews and the proportion of Jews in high income groups are well above those of most of the population."[26]

The success of Jewish academicians has deservedly received special attention, for the facts are impressive. A study conducted by the Carnegie Commission on Higher Education in 1969 showed that 9 percent of those teaching in colleges and universities identified themselves as Jews. In the elite colleges and universities, the percentage of Jewish professors was 19. In the Ivy League schools, of the professors under fifty years of age—which would mean those who were hired since the end of World War II—a quarter were Jews. When the schools in the Carnegie study are rank-ordered according to academic quality, 32 percent of the Jewish professors are at schools which are in the highest quality category, while only 9 percent of Christian professors are teaching at such schools; and conversely, over 40 percent of the Christian professors are at the lowest quality category schools as compared to 13.5 percent of the Jews.[27] Jews have been named presidents of leading universities and deans of leading colleges and professional schools. These developments have been especially dramatic and impressive since they have taken place in the lifetime of many who remember when it was possible to name only a total of five or six Jews who had the honor to hold professorships.[28]

III

Just as Americans in general tended to forget that there were millions of poor among them until Michael Harrington's *The Other America* (1962) forcefully propelled the facts to front-page space, so, too, American Jews have only belatedly recognized the fact that success and affluence have bypassed hundreds of thousands of their people. It was not until 1971 that the existence of "the other Jews" came to be talked about. At about the same time the so-called Black Panthers of Israel attracted international attention by their demonstrations against the existence of poverty especially among the Jews who had emigrated from North Africa and Yemen.[29]

Just how many Jewish poor there are in the United States is uncertain; the estimates run from 350,000 to 700,000. A report of the Federation of Jewish Philanthropies of New York, made in 1972, showed 272,000, or 15.1 percent of the Jewish population of New York, as poor or near-poor. In addition, there were 423,000 persons, or 25 percent of the Jewish population, who were between near-poverty level and the moderate level of living as fixed by the Bureau of Labor Statistics standards.[30]

Who are these poor among American Jews? They can be divided into two classes. (a) As many as two-thirds are old Jews, sixty years of age or older. The proportion of aged among Jews is far larger than among America's poor generally—the proportion of persons sixty-five or over within the Jewish population was 14 percent, and is expected to reach 18 percent by 1979. Writing about this class of Jewish poor, Bertram H. Gold, Executive Vice President of the American Jewish Committee, noted that

> Many of the aged poor are in ill health. For the most part, they do not live close to hospital care. . . . They live in wretchedly neglected houses, in neighborhoods no longer Jewish. Many are so afraid of crime in the street—with good reason—that they rarely venture out even to shop or see the doctor and do not visit with friends at all.[31]

(b) The other one-third are young and middle-aged, and who are poor because they are Jews:

> The Hasidic and other strictly Orthodox Jews, whose beliefs obligate them to raise large families, use only *glat* kosher foods and send their children to cheder and yeshiva rather than public school [i.e., in schools where they are required to pay tuition and fees]. The Hasidim are additionally held down in their earning capacity by

> their deep-rooted tradition of limited secular education, of excluding certain aspects of the modern world from their society and their children's schooling.[32]

These people, both the old and the young among the Jewish poor, were neglected by the Jewish community and overlooked by the federal and local anti-poverty programs. These programs were directed toward neighborhoods occupied by blacks or Puerto Ricans—of the twenty-six community operations in New York, only five had Jewish representatives; furthermore, the poverty programs made no provision for the special cultural and economic needs of the Jewish poor.[33] It perhaps was not because of purposeful discrimination that the poverty programs simply overlooked the Jewish poor; the fact is that American society no longer sees the Jews as a "minority." In his speech accepting the Democratic Party nomination for President of the United States, Jimmy Carter said: "It is time to guarantee an end to discrimination because of race or sex." He made no reference to discrimination because of religion or creed or national origin. This was not an oversight, nor was it intended as an expression of indifference or animosity toward Jews—not at all. It was simply that the Jews are no longer thought of as belonging to the class of Americans who need special attention, special laws, and special massive appropriations of funds to help them in their various needs.

IV

But this poverty that afflicts from 5 to 10 percent of American Jews is hardly more than an aberration—like the 12 percent of the American people who are classified as poor.[34] It is the wart on the face. Jewish poverty only tarnishes but does not belie the fact that American Jews constitute the most successful or affluent ethnic group or religious denomination in the country that is the most affluent or wealthiest country in the world.[35] What accounts for this Jewish success, for this dramatic movement from rags to riches? A variety of theories have been offered, but generally only timidly, mostly by way of suggestion.

Father Greeley, reviewing the findings of the various studies, especially those of the National Opinion Research Center, notes that while the most wealthy American group is the Jews, the ethnic Catholic groups—the Irish Catholics, the Italian Catholics, the German and Polish Catholics—follow right after the Jews, in a rank order of family income, ranging from $13,340 for Jews to $11,298 for Poles, and the latter are followed by Episcopalians and Presbyterians. At the bottom of the ladder are other Protestant groups.[36] Can it be, Father Greeley asks, that the so-called Protestant ethic has been not merely refuted but reversed? The question, he says, is a good one, but there is no obvious answer to it. Greeley has, however, less trouble explaining the specifically Jewish success. He says:

> The Jewish immigrants were the product of two millennia of ancestors who had to live by their wits. Many of them were craftsmen, tradesmen, inhabitants of small towns or even cities. They were people of the Book, believing firmly in education and practical learning. It is not difficult to see why they would be successful in the United States.[37]

At the end of his report to the Ford Foundation, facing the success of the Jews and of other ethnic groups, Father Greeley ventures to suggest a psychological theory:

> Might we be seeing a phenomenon for which I can find no other name but "overthrust" (though you might also want to try overcompensation)? Could it be that the first stage cohort of a population group that "makes it" in American society does so with such tremendous energy and such tremendous "need for achievement," that they not only do as well as everyone else, but better, because of the sheer, raw power of their elemental drive for respectability and success? May it be that in another generation or two, the effect may wear off, and the Catholic and Protestant and Jewish ethnic groups will have relatively similar levels of achievement—while the blacks and the Spanish-speaking profit from the "overthrust" phenomenon?[38]

This point is similar to one that has frequently been made about the nations of the world; that is, that the Western industrial nations are bound to lose their nerve and vigor, and that their primacy will be lost to nations of the Third World. But "overthrust" is hardly an explanation; it is a pejorative label placed on a phenomenon; it leaves unanswered why, in the first place, there was a "thrust" by one group and not by another, why one group had such an "elemental drive for respectability and success" while other groups lacked it.

Father Greeley projects also the theory that achievement can be explained by a group's culture. "There are, it turns out," he says, "strong relationships between culture and achievement."[39] But what precise aspects of Jewish culture, that are different from the components of other groups' cultures, can explain the attainments of American Jews? As we have seen, Greeley mentions some well-known facts: that for some two thousand years Jews have had to live by their wits, that Jewish immigrants brought with them to American shores certain skills or aptitudes that prepared them to become craftsmen and traders; that they came ready for urban life; and that they had been prepared to seek education and practical knowledge.[40]

Now it is these and related cultural factors that other scholars have also pointed to as being somehow causally related to Jewish achievement. Professor Glazer, in his Jewish Tercentenary article,[41] explains Jewish success in America by pointing to the following facts:

> The Jews for generations were engaged in middle-class occupations, in the professions, in buying and selling.
>
> The middle-class occupations are associated with certain characteristic habits—habits of care and foresight. The Jew was trained to save money so that with the capital, and with intelligence and ability, he may be able to advance himself. He was taught generally to postpone his pleasures—to save himself and his money for enjoyment later.
>
> Judaism, for at least fifteen hundred years before Calvinism, has emphasized the traits that businessmen and intellectuals require; and so it is no wonder that it is in a modern society like America that the Jews, who have been stamped with the values that make for

good businessmen and intellectuals, should flourish. Long before Calvinism, Judaism placed emphasis on study and learning, on habits of foresight, care, and moderation. The bent given to them by religion and culture was strengthened by their economic experience.

While Jews were traders, businessmen, and scholars, a large group of them were artisans; but unlike Christian artisans, they were not members of guilds and corporations [from which they were excluded], consequently Jewish artisans were actually or potentially tradesmen, with middle-class habits, psychology, and ambitions. The Jewish artisans carried with them the values conducive to middle-class success, and so, under proper circumstances, they easily turn to trade and study. The Jewish artisans were the sons and grandsons of traders and scholars, and could readily turn their minds to ways and means of improving themselves that were quite beyond the imagination of their fellow workers. Business and education were therefore not remote but familiar and attainable possibilities. With the prospect of success beckoning, it became worthwhile for the Jewish immigrants to work harder and save more than other immigrant groups.

Unlike other scholars, Glazer does not consider the urban experience of Jewish immigrants important, for large numbers who came from Germany and Eastern European countries were from small towns and villages that were scarcely "urban." I think that Glazer is right about this, for the experience of the *shtetl* could hardly be thought a preparation for what the immigrant faced in New York, Chicago, Kansas City, or Rochester. If not the experience of the *shtetl,* the experience of the Jew did, in subtle and complex ways, prepare the Jewish immigrant for the challenges and opportunities that America offered people with intelligence, imagination, enterprise, courage, and habits of prudence and moderation. In any case, as Glazer says,

the pattern of foresight and sobriety so essential for middle-class success was so well established in Jewish life that it was maintained even when there was no prospect of going into business. The Jews did not drink; the Jewish students were docile, accepting—as lower-class children rarely do today—today's restraints for tomorrow's rewards; the Jewish workers stayed out of jail. When we look at the working-class Jewish neighborhoods of the great American cities of the 1920s and 1930s, it is clear we are not dealing with ordinary workers. It was not dangerous to walk through the New York slums at night when they were inhabited by Jews.[42]

Significantly, Jewish workers tended to join more organizations than Christian workers, and even more than Jewish white-collar workers, and they wrote more frequently to their Congressmen than even high-income Catholics or Protestants.[43] As Glazer wrote a few years later in his book *American Judaism:*

> The Jewish working class had a broader horizon than the working class of other groups. They tended to form powerful unions, which helped improve their conditions. And they made sure their children would not also be workers. As early as 1900, so authoritative a historian of the American working classes as John R. Commons observed that "Jewish women are employed [in factories] to a much less extent than the women of other nationalities, and their children are kept in school until 15 or 16 years of age. It is quite unusual for Jewish tailors to teach their children their own trade." With the Jewish mother at home, the Jewish child received a better education and better care, as shown in lower delinquency and death rates. . . . Never were teachers in slum schools happier than when they had Jewish pupils; never were settlement-house workers more delighted with the results of their work than when the Jews filled the slums of the large cities.[44]

Professor Joseph L. Blau, in his recent book *Judaism in America,* published in 1976, lists substantially the same characteristics that account for or have contributed to the success of the Jewish immigrant; that is, the ethos of hard work, thrift, the readiness to defer satisfaction for the sake of goals to be achieved later, an intense desire for respectability, and the secular application of the traditional conception of study and scholastic achievement; but he adds another characteristic that is significant: "a strong sense of family that produced innumerable instances of mutual assistance." In part, Blau explains, this characteristic

> may derive from the age-old Jewish tradition that it would be a scandal if any one of their number was forced to ask and accept assistance from the non-Jewish public. It was a matter of pride to the Jewish community that it took care of its own. . . . The family was a source of mutual aid for its members not only in times of adversity, but even in times of prosperity. Any Jew who moved ahead saw to it that he carried others with him, as far as it was possible for him to do so.[45]
>
> . . . Every family of whatever background envisions a brighter future for the new generation. What is outstanding is the sacrifice that all members of the Jewish immigrant family were willing to make to advance those who showed potential for fulfilling the vision. Noteworthy is the extent to which those who did scale the heights—having benefitted from their family's sacrifice—used their achievements and prominence to ease the living of those who supported and encouraged them.[46]

V

There is no doubt that the Jewish immigrants from Germany, Russia, Rumania, the Austro-Hungarian Empire, and other parts of Europe brought with them energies, talents, and gifts that greatly contributed to their usefulness, enterprise, and success. There are scholars who would reduce all the Jewish aptitudes to the simple fact that the Jewish immigrants came with an urban background and that they were equipped thereby to engage in types of activities that went with urban status and life;[47] but I believe that this oversimplifies a complex cultural, historical event.

In any case, the great talents and gifts which the Jews possessed cannot alone explain their success, for they had the *same gifts* before they emigrated from the Old Country, and there they had been only paupers, failures—the poor, the "huddled masses," the "wretched refuse" of whom Emma Lazarus wrote. It is obvious that America provided certain ingredients without which the Jewish adventure in the United States would have turned out quite differently. The American Jewish success story is the story of a partnership. To this partnership, America—to use terms made familiar by Toynbee—provided the Challenge, and the immigrant

Jews provided the Response. America provided challenges that fortunately were of a "salutary severity" that stimulated these immigrants and their children to an ordeal that was, as the results have shown, "a creative response."[48] To see only what the Jews brought with them is to see only a part, which is not fully understandable in isolation from the whole. A complex social, historical phenomenon can be studied only by the holistic approach, which sees causes as part of a complex web rather than in a simple chain-link relationship.

First of all there was the great bounty that nature and a rapidly developing industrial society provided. As Father Greeley graphically put it:

> How has a society of such diverse components as the United States survived? The country's richness of natural resources and its resultant economic prosperity have had something to do with the success of pluralism. People seem less inclined to go after their neighbors with a rock, club, or knife when they have just consumed a succulent steak from the backyard barbecue.[49]

Secondly, the social order put relatively few obstacles in the way of economic and social progress. There were no kings and royal retinue; there was no aristocracy by birth. The original church establishments in the colonies were feeble institutions and were not even memories when mass Jewish immigration took place. There were no guilds to dominate the crafts and the lives of artisans and workers. The economic and social structure was such as to encourage fluidity. The movement from peddling to storekeeping encountered no artificial obstacles. It was often relatively easy for a man who had himself worked at tailoring to open a small shop and set other tailors to work for him. Thus Jewish jobs became transformed into middle-class businesses in a social order that needed to value a man for his function and the quality of his performance. As Macaulay noted in 1831, when the civil disabilities of the Jews of Britain were under consideration: it was certainly better to have one's shoes mended by a heretical cobbler who knew his work well than by a person who had subscribed to the Thirty-Nine Articles but had never handled an awl.[50] This proposition needed to be debated in Great Britain, where religious and class lines were still prominent and effective, but Americans did not need to have the obvious demonstrated to them.

The late Chief Rabbi Herzog once wrote that "We are apt to speak of Jews and Gentiles as if the human race consisted of one half Jews and the other half non-Jews."[51] We are apt to forget that of the forty-six million immigrants who have settled America, only perhaps two million were Jews. The non-Jews who came here also brought with them various energies, talents, gifts, attitudes, and prejudices, some of which they sooner or later discarded and replaced with others; and it was the new and old elements in their mental and spiritual baggage that made the secure settlement of the Jews possible and that became the basis for the ultimate achievement of equality by the Jewish settlers and their children and grand-children.[52] The host nation brought as much to the success of the Jews as the immigrant Jews themselves did.

What the Jewish immigrants found when they came here by the tens of thousands[53] was not only a country superlatively rich in natural endowment, but also one in which the social environment was receptive and hospitable to the immigrants' qualities of character. America's institutional conditions welcomed individual initiative; it offered strong incentives for risk-taking, for industrial and commercial pioneering, for self-reliant action, for newness, for creativity, for ingenuity, for productivity, for enterprise—for, indeed, every form and aspect of human endeavor.

Thirdly, it is important to see the ineluctable connection that existed between America's opulence and the ideal of equality, both of which features of American life and promise loomed large in the dreams, hopes, and lives of the Jewish immigrants. The late David M. Potter has cogently described that connection:

> Abundance has influenced American life in many ways, but there is perhaps no respect in which this influence has been more profound than in the forming and strengthening of the American

> ideal and practice of equality, with all that the ideal has implied for the individual in the ways of opportunity to make his own place in society and emancipation from a system of status.
>
> The very meaning of the term "equality" reflects this influence, for the connotations to an American are quite unlike what they might be to a European. A European, advocating equality, might very well mean that all men should occupy positions that are on roughly the same level in wealth, power, or enviability. But the American, with his emphasis upon equality of opportunity, has never conceived of it in this sense. He has traditionally expected to find a gamut ranging from rags to riches, from tramps to millionaires. To call this "equality" may seem a contradiction in terms, but the paradox has been resolved in two ways: first by declaring that all men are equal in the eyes of the law . . . ; and, second, by assuming that no man is restricted or confined by his status to any one station, or even to any maximum station. . . . At one end of the scale might stand a log cabin [or shall we say, a peddler's pack], at the other the White House [or shall we say, a department store]; but equality meant that anyone might run the entire scale. This emphasis upon unrestricted latitude as the essence of equality in turn involved a heavy emphasis upon liberty as an essential means for keeping the scale open and hence making equality a reality.[54]

Equality, for the American, carried the connotation of upward mobility, without the need to overcome legal impediments or deeply rooted vested and institutionalized interests. But—and this is of crucial importance—unless objectively there was a large measure of abundance, created by nature intermixed with the energy and ingenuity of man, equality of opportunity would have been a mere fantasy. Given abundance in fact, equality of opportunity meant the fulfillment of the promise of success. The result has been that "America has had a greater measure of social equality and social mobility than any [other] highly developed society in human history."[55]

And while questions have been raised about the degree of actual mobility or advancement from status to status shown by Americans generally (quite apart from the problem of blacks, American Indians, and Spanish-Americans), no such questions have been raised about American Jews. Indeed, the facts show that while other immigrant groups have also left their ghettos or first places of settlement, the Jews left them more rapidly and in greater numbers, and in general their rate of social-economic mobility was greater than that of other groups.[56]

VI

The Jewish masses came to America from countries where they had been hated and persecuted because of their religion. Although there were, without doubt, other factors which contributed to the drive to hate and destroy Jews—economic competition and envy, hatred of the stranger—religious difference was felt to be an intolerable affliction on the body politic; for a people's religion was conceived of as the single spiritual tie that held them together and kept them from devouring one another. Religion had, therefore, to be homogeneous, single; religious difference was heresy or treason or both; religious persecution was, therefore, altogether legitimate, necessary, and even honorable and meritorious.

The Jews who came to the United States found this country to be indeed a New World. For the first time in their lives they did not need to apologize for their religious difference. The United States Constitution guaranteed religious liberty and banned any religious establishment. The Constitution prohibited oaths which tested a person's religious beliefs. No official stigma could attach to a man because he was a Jew.

More than that, in the Old World, even within the Jewish community itself, a Jew was not as free as he may have wanted to be. The Jewish communities in Germany and Russia were organized on the principle that Jews were defined by their religion—they were not a nation, or a nationality, or an ethnic group, but a religious society, and the Jewish religion was Judaism—a single religion, without inner divisions into denominations or sects. When, e.g., Rabbi Samson Raphael Hirsch wanted to organize an Orthodox Jewish community in Frankfurt-on-the-Main, separate from the Reform community, which alone had official recognition, it took him years until he was able to induce the Prussian Parliament to enact a law that permitted him and his followers to withdraw from the official Jewish community and establish their own religious association. The "Law of Secession," the *Austrittsgesetz,* passed in July 1876, permitted a Jew to leave his local congregation, without leaving Judaism, and this law, whose centenary has been noted in 1976, was considered in its day a significant victory for religious conscience and Judaism.[57] The Jewish immigrants to the United States had no need to petition the government for permission to perform any religious function, or for permission to be free from any religious prohibitions or restrictions. Synagogues and temples were organized on the congregational model and were wholly voluntary associations, in which membership was altogether voluntary.[58] Professor Blau is quite right in stressing the fact that this principle of voluntaryism, "or the idea that a man's religious affiliations are his own concern and not the business of the community," was "a novelty of the American scene." It was no part of the Jewish or European experience, and was part of the American environment that was "a novelty to practically all Jews at the time of their arrival in America."[59]

Jews were not only freed from disabilities and restrictions because of their religion, but in time even won recognition precisely because of their religion. Instead of speaking of Christian civilization or Christian ideals, Americans learned to speak of the Judaeo-Christian tradition, thus making Judaism an equal partner with Christianity when pointing to America's living ideas. Although Jews constitute less than 3 percent of the population, Judaism is looked upon as the Third Faith and given equal status with Protestantism and Catholicism. Thus, even nonreligious Jews have become identified as Jews-by-religion—not, however, for the imposition of disabilities, but rather for the recognition of their equality with Christians.[60] Whatever may be the case with regard to other ethnic groups, Jewish ethnic concerns are filtered through Jewish religious institutions, symbols, communities, and ideals.

But once again we want to stress that these developments serve as sources of strength for American Jews, who can look to their status as a religious community for a guarantee of freedom from discrimination and a guarantee of equality of treatment and dignity with Protestants and Catholics. American Jews thus have the best of both worlds; they can be as religious or as secular as they please and in either case enjoy the benefit of the Religion Clauses of the First Amendment. And this is consistent with the halakhic principle that one remains a Jew even if he strays: "Even if he has sinned, he remains an Israelite."[61]

Possibly one factor contributing to this result—admittedly impossible to measure—is that Christianity shares with Judaism passionate devotion to the Hebrew Scriptures. Whatever vilification the Jewish people suffer from some writers of the New Testament, the impact of the Hebrew Scriptures—of Genesis, Deuteronomy, the Psalms, Job, Ecclesiastes, the Song of Songs, Micah, Amos, Jeremiah, the various Isaiahs—could not be totally lost. Because of the pervasive Protestant, especially Puritan, influence, American culture perhaps has been more strongly influenced by the Hebrew Scriptures than has the English—and the influence has, at least until recent years, assimilated itself into the very substance and basic fabric of the American mind. What Shakespeare has been to English literature and thought, the Bible, and especially the Hebrew Scriptures—and the large elements of them that are absorbed into the New Testament—has been to American language and thought. This thought and language link Christians and Jews with a common past, a common set of ideals, a common set of sentiments, which together make up the essence of a common tradition.[62]

Jews are differentiated, even sharply, among themselves. They are attached to different Judaisms—Orthodox, Conservative, Reform, and each broken down into various shadings; Hasidim, rationalists, and just nondescript Jews; Hebraists and Yiddishists; pious Jews and secularists; Zionists and enemies of Israel. But just as in the dark, as Hegel noted, all cows are black, so to the Christian all Jews are defined by their religion, which is, to the outsider, a single, undifferentiated Judaism. They are identified, not ethnically but denominationally, and they thus, providentially, find themselves—even against the wishes of some of them—under the beneficent shelter of the First Amendment. This has been, and continues to be, a boon, the extent of which is beyond our capacity to measure.

And when we think of American Jews as defined by their religion, which differentiates them from Catholics and Protestants, and compares them with British or Israeli Jews, one of the great differences that strikes us is the fact that it is largely only American Jews who are differentiated *among themselves* denominationally as Reform, Conservative and Orthodox, and that each of these groupings is made up of a variety of subgroups. This is a distinctively American, not Jewish, phenomenon, for the Israeli Jews, e.g., have no such divisions. In Israel the Jews are either Orthodox or nonreligious. The Reform (or Progressive) and Conservative congregations in Israel are very few, and their congregations are made up largely of American and other English-speaking Jews (often those who attend their services are mainly American tourists). While Reform Judaism had its origin and early development in Germany, it made relatively little headway there; it became largely an American development; and Conservative Judaism is almost exclusively an American phenomenon. While Reform had an early start (1840) in England, it developed along conservative lines and made so little headway that in 1901 a new movement appeared under the name of Liberal Judaism with a more radical position respecting beliefs and practices, and in 1910 established in London the Liberal Jewish Synagogue; but neither of these movements has ever attracted more than small numbers of Jews. The masses of British Jews are either members of Orthodox congregations that are affiliated with the United Synagogue or the Federation of Synagogues, or belong to no religious group.

This phenomenon—the pluralistic character of American Judaism and Jewry—is, as we have said, an American contribution to Jewish historical development. It is rooted in the voluntaryism that is characteristic of American civilization, and especially of the history of religion in America. Once it became clear that the state had no power in any matter affecting religious belief or worship, ecclesiastical organization, or religious association, it followed that no other agency could assert such power, and that every man was absolutely free to choose, change, or deny his religion; that there can be no official compulsion in any matter relating to religion, and that no government official has the power to declare what is orthodox or heretical. The result is a great proliferation of religions, denominations, and sects, such as is not to be seen anywhere else in the world, and among them is the variety of Judaisms that one finds in the United States today—variations of a common core of tradition that compete with each other and yet feel themselves united by a common history and a common destiny. There are those who bemoan this as fragmentation, and there are those who see in the phenomenon a flowering of the Jewish religious spirit that is an enrichment and a blessing. In any case, what we witness is the fact that for the first time in history, Jews are wholly free to make of Judaism whatever they choose it to be, from Habad Hasidism to Jewish humanism, with an infinite variety of stations between. In a unique way American Jews can say, in the words of Moses: "Not with our fathers did the Lord make this covenant, but with us, who are all of us here alive this day."[63]

VII

The liberties and rights of Americans have their roots partly in English history. The Bill of Rights of the United States Constitution can hardly be understood when totally separated from its background in Magna Carta, the Petition of Right (1627), and the Bill of Rights of 1688.[64] But this is not true of the rights of American Jews. With respect to them, the reverse situation is true: the rights and liberties of American Jews became a model for England. Although English Jews enjoyed a large measure of social and economic freedom, they were under severe civic and political disabilities. It was not until 1835 that they were admitted to the office of sheriff, and ten years later to other minor offices; and in 1846 the Religious Opinions Relief Bill removed minor disabilities. But they could not take their place as Members of Parliament because they could not take the Christian oath of office which the law required. Lionel de Rothschild, though elected by the City of

London as its parliamentary representative time after time from 1847, could not take his seat. It is notable that Macaulay, in his great speech in Parliament in 1829, in support of a bill to remove the civil disabilities of Jews, observed that in the United States "the Jews are already admitted to all the rights of citizens"; and in his second speech on the subject in 1833 Macaulay stated that it is "an undoubted fact that, in the United States of America, Jewish citizens do possess all the privileges possessed by Christian citizens."[65] Although Dissenters and Roman Catholics had been admitted to full civil and political rights in 1828 and 1829, it was not until 1858 that Baron Rothschild was permitted to take his seat in Parliament upon passage of the Jews' Disabilities Bill.

In America, although Jews were subject to some civil and political disabilities in the colonies, and even at times in some of the states,[66] as citizens of the United States they enjoyed full equality with all other citizens. This was the guarantee of the First Amendment, which all branches of the federal government have observed in full measure. But James Madison's insight is still relevant. "Is a bill of rights a security for religion?" he asked in 1788. If all the people of the United States belonged to one sect, he said, "a bill of rights would be a poor protection for liberty." If the states enjoy freedom of religion, Madison went on to say, this is due to the "multiplicity of sects . . . which is the best and only security for religious liberty in any society."[67] Since at least 40 percent of the population of the American colonies was of non-English stock, and followers of the Church of England were in fact a minority,[68] religious liberty and equality were indispensable conditions for the effective operation of government, for the development of the country and its resources, for the encouragement of immigration, and for the enjoyment of civil life in peace and prosperity.

Despite, however, these fortunate conditions, Jews often found themselves the victims of prejudice and discrimination. The Constitution of the United States and the constitutions of the various states shielded them from unfriendly or discriminatory official acts, but most constitutional guarantees were not restrictions on the actions of private persons. Special legislative enactments were therefore required to prohibit private discrimination. The movement for such enactments, which came to be known as civil rights laws, began in 1865, when Massachusetts enacted the first such law, banning discrimination based on race or color in places of public accommodation. By 1966 there were civil rights acts in thirty-six states. These laws generally prohibit discrimination on account of race, color, creed, or national origin, in hotels, restaurants, theaters, and other places of public accommodation. Thirty-nine states had fair employment practice acts; nineteen states had fair housing laws; and ten states had fair education acts. More important than these state enactments, however, are the federal statutes enacted in the 1960s and 1970s: the Civil Rights Act of 1964, the Fair Housing Act of 1968, the Equal Employment Opportunity Act of 1972, and the Equal Credit Opportunity Act of 1976.[69]

This network of federal and state laws, providing the most comprehensive protection against racial, ethnic, or religious discrimination by government officials or private persons, implements the ideal of equality and serves as a model for democratic countries throughout the world.

Equally important have been decisions of the United States Supreme Court, especially since *Brown v. Board of Education*[70] in 1954. Although the cases have involved racial rather than religious discrimination, there can be no doubt that their spirit serves to protect minorities exposed to persecution on account of religion or creed.

While Jews share, with other religious and ethnic and with racial minorities, the benefits of these statutes and court decisions, Jews were among the leading proponents of these developments. In every important civil rights or civil liberties struggle in the twentieth century, American Jews and their organizations—notably the American Jewish Committee, the American Jewish Congress, the Anti-Defamation League of B'nai B'rith, the Jewish Labor Committee, and the Synagogue Council of America—have been in the forefront as lobbyists, propagandists, financial supporters, organizers, and legal activists or defenders. Indeed, often these organizations pioneered with path-breaking legislative and litigation approaches, and with a demonstration of courage and determination to fight back, to resist, and to vindicate their rights and liberties. True enough, the Jews had allies, but often the initiative came from Jewish organizations, and often they were *primus inter pares.*

VIII

The world being what it is, we can hardly expect that the America in which our children and grandchildren will need to live and make their life will not have its quota of misanthropes, anti-Semites, and men and women whose passions are fired by envy and suspicion. In the Talmud it is stated that God speaks to the children of Israel and says: "My children, I created the evil desire [*yetser hara*], but I also created the Torah as its antidote."[71] So, too, we must think that though there will be some Americans who will scheme and plot against American Jewry and against Judaism and Jewish life, culture, and aspirations, the Constitution and laws will stand as an antidote.

But no sooner have we said this than we are confounded by the bitter words of James Madison that bills of rights are only "parchment barriers" against the will of "overbearing majorities." A government, he wrote to Jefferson, will invade private rights when its acts are supported by the people.[72] The record of American history shows, I believe, that Jewish immigrants attained liberty and equality during the scores of years when America was a land of unprecedented opportunity. In his speech accepting the Republican Party nomination for President, Gerald Ford, referring to the pioneer vision of our revolutionary founders and immigrant ancestors, said: "Their vision was of free men and free women enjoying . . . unlimited opportunity."[73] But we can well ask whether anyone can speak responsibly of today's or tomorrow's unlimited opportunity. For what we see are millions of young people with wants unsatisfied and with feelings that their satisfactions may be beyond their reach because for them the promise of opportunity will remain unfulfilled. There is grave danger when millions of young people are led to think that their future is dependent on their education and training, but who find themselves educated and trained for a world that does not need their skills and knowledge. As David Potter cautioned us, society "must not hold out the promise of opportunity unless there is a reasonable prospect of the opportunity's being fulfilled."[74] When promises and expectations remain frustrated, envy—the sixth of St. Gregory's deadly sins—takes over, and breeds suspicion, hate, and violence. A society in which there is widespread disenchantment with the economic race, in which the work ethic is obsolete, in which there is limited opportunity and a diminution of mobility, in which the normal processes and institutions of government are distrusted, in which the voices of morality and religion tend to be discredited, in which the foundations of family life are shaken, such a society offers fertile soil for the breeding of demagogues and rabble-rousing racists. American Jews would find life in such a society difficult if not intolerable. We therefore face a future that may be menacing. But fortunately the menace will be not only to American Jews but to all Americans who stand committed to our nation's basic ideals and values. While up to the present this country's material conditions were preeminently congenial to the fostering of our ideals and values, in the future we will need to reverse the order: give priority to the ideals but at the same time *compel the material conditions to conform to them.* It will be a case of mind or spirit over matter. We must struggle with the angel until it will bless us. All of us, Jews and non-Jews alike, will need to be guided by the saying of Theodor Herzl, "Wenn ihr wollt, ist es kein Märchen"—"If you will it, then it is no fairy tale."

The uniqueness of the Jewish experience in America probably would not have happened were it not for the pluralistic character of American society from its very origins: we were Jews among Presbyterians, Episcopalians, Baptists, Catholics, Quakers, Mennonites, and scores of other religious denominations and sects. There could be civil peace only if each religious group followed the principle of live and let live. Should religious pluralism disappear through the ultimate succes of ecumenism or of secularism, or both, then Jews, marked off as a religious group, would be exposed to grave dangers. Ironically, it is in our self-interest that we should wish to see the Christian denominations and sects continue and flourish, for the life of Christianity will insure the life of Judaism.

Nor would the uniqueness of the Jewish experience in America have happened were it not for ethnic pluralism: we were Jews among Italians, Poles, Irish, Swedes, Germans, and scores of other ethnic or national groups. There could be civil peace only if each ethnic group followed the principle of live and let live. Should assimilation succeed to the point where ethnic consciousness and pride would become too feeble to be reckoned an important aspect of American culture and life, then the Jews, marked off as an ethnic group, would be exposed to grave dangers. It is, therefore, in the self-interest of Jews to do all they can to sustain and foster the idea of ethnic heritage, ethnic consciousness and pride, for the Irish and the Poles, the Italians and the Hungarians, no less than for themselves; for their ethnic survival will help insure the survival of American Jews as a distinctive people.

The security and prosperity of American Jewry require one other material-social condition, one that we have already noted; i.e., that America should become again and remain a land of unlimited opportunity. Where there is no opportunity, or equality of opportunity, the have-nots will demand equality of results, equality of actual economic and material conditions. For the twentieth century has aroused colossal expectations which will not be denied. If there is to be no equality of opportunity—both in law and in fact—then there will be a demand for equality of status. It is, therefore, in the self-interest of American Jews to work for a legal and social order in which the demand for jobs will not exceed the supply, in which reasonable goals of people for a good life will be attainable, in which essential human needs will be met, in which human attainments will be within every American's reach.

The English poet Edward Thomas wrote that "The past is the only dead thing that smells sweet." To Americans—and especially to American Jews—America's past smells sweet. It is up to us, the living and future generations, to see to it that America's past is not a dead thing but a living, meaningful, continuing presence.

NOTES

1. Quotation in E. E. Urbach, *The Sages* (Jerusalem, 1975), vol. I, p. 547.
2. Aviva Zuckoff, "For Making Bricks without Straw, Etc.," *Israel Horizon,* June 1969, p. 14.

3. See Bertram W. Korn, *American Jewry and the Civil War* (Philadelphia, 1951), chap. 6.
4. Henry L. Feingold, "The Condition of American Jewry in Historical Perspective: A Bicentennial Assessment," *Amer. Jewish Year Book*, Vol. 76 (1976), p. 3.
5. John Higham, *Send These to Me: Jews and Other Immigrants in Urban America* (New York, 1975), p. 182.
6. Feingold, op. cit. (supra n. 4), p. 28.
7. As one recalls the action of General Grant, one cannot help but compare it with the action of General George S. Brown, Chief of Staff, when he made his disparaging remarks about Jewish influence before an audience at Duke University on October 10, 1974. This incident involved no action but only speech. Brown was called to the White House and rebuked by the President, and he was also severely criticized by members of the U.S. Senate and House of Representatives and by other prominent Americans and by editorials in newspapers throughout the country. Milton Ellerin, "The Brown Affair—Reactions and Aftermath," American Jewish Committee, December 20, 1974; Hyman Bookbinder, Washington Letter, American Jewish Committee, January 1, 1975.
8. Jacob R. Marcus, *Early American Jewry* (Philadelphia, 1951), vol. 1, chap. 2; A. V. Goodman, *American Overture* (Philadelphia, 1947), chap. 5.
9. Marcus, op. cit., p. 31.
10. Ibid. p. 32.
11. Quoted by Urbach, op. cit. (supra n. 1), vol. 2, p. 934, n. 89.
12. Feingold, op. cit. (supra n. 4), p. 6.
13. Andrew M. Greeley, *Ethnicity, Denomination and Inequality: A Bicentennial Report to the Ford Foundation* (Chicago: Center for the Study of American Pluralism, National Opinion Research Center, October 1975).
14. The Census Bureau survey was of 45,000 households in 50 states and the District of Columbia. Persons were asked to identify themselves as belonging to one or another of eight listed ethnic groups: English, German, Irish, Spanish, Italian, French, Polish, and Russian. The Census Bureau listed only Yiddish as the original language of the Russian group. Almost all scholars in the field have correlated "Russian" with "Jewish." Father Greeley, in his report to the Ford Foundation, cited in note 13 supra, belittles ethnic surveys and rightly says that "It is possible that if a religious question is asked before an ethnic question, a Jewish respondent whose family came from Poland will not describe himself as Polish. If, on the other hand, an ethnic question is asked, and a Jewish answer rejected, a Jew with a Polish family background may have no choice but to answer 'Polish'" (p. 14).
15. Greeley, op. cit. (supra n. 13), table 4, p. 58.
16. Ibid., p. 19 and table 6.
17. Ibid., pp. 20, 21, and tables 9, 10, and 11.
18. Ibid., p. 27, and tables 12, 13, and 38.

19. Ibid., p. 26, and table 18. Only about 40 percent of non-Jewish youth attend college. *Newsweek,* March 1, 1971, p. 63.
20. Andrew M. Greeley, *Ethnicity in the United States* (New York, 1974), table 4, pp. 42–43.
21. Ibid., p. 112.
22. Nathan Glazer, *American Judaism* (Chicago, 1957; 2nd ed. 1972), p. 108.
23. Nathan Glazer, "Social Characteristics of American Jews, 1654–1954," *American Jewish Year Book* vol. 56 (1955), pp. 12, 13.
24. Ibid., p. 17.
25. Ibid., p. 29.
26. Sidney Goldstein, "American Jewry, 1970: A Demographic Profile," *American Jewish Year Book,* vol. 72 (1971), p. 85.
27. The Carnegie study is summarized in detail by Seymour M. Lipset and Everett C. Ladd, "Jewish Academics in the United States," *American Jewish Year Book,* vol. 72 (1971), p. 89.
28. Before World War II, when one tried to think of Jews who were professors, one could recall the names of Morris R. Cohen, Harry A. Wolfson, Isaac Husik, Felix Frankfurter, Morris Jastrow, and Franz Boas.
29. See *American Jewish Year Book,* vol. 73 (1972), p. 570; *New York Times,* "These Panthers Wear Yarmulkes," Review of the Week Section, May 31, 1971.
30. *New York Times,* January 23, 1973; Jack S. Cohen, "Jewish Poverty and Welfare," *Congress Bi-Weekly,* May 24, 1974.
31. Bertram H. Gold, introduction to *The Other Jews: Portraits in Poverty,* by Dorothy Rabinowitz (American Jewish Commitee, 1972), p. 7.
32. Ibid., p. 8.
33. *New York Times,* September 14, 1971. For other materials on poverty among Jews, see *The Jewish Poor: A Brief Bibliography,* leaflet published by American Jewish Committee, July 1973. For the special problem of old age among Jews, see "A Rationale for Synagogue Programming with the Jewish Aging," *Anaylsis,* no. 50 (March 17, 1975), Synagogue Council of America.
34. According to the Bureau of Census figures, in 1971, 12.5 were poor; in 1974, 11.6 percent, or close to 25 million people, including 7,467,000 blacks—31.4 percent of blacks were poor.
35. *New York Times,* September 28, 1975, Sec. E, p. 3. The per capita income for Sweden was the highest in the world—$5,596; the United States was a close second with $5,523. The countries with the lowest incomes were Mali, $50; Rwanda, $61; Upper Volta, $62; India, $93.
36. Greeley, *Ethnicity, Denomination and Inequality* (cited supra, n. 13), p. 44, and tables 38, 39, 40.
37. Ibid., p. 46.
38. Ibid., pp. 51–52.
39. Ibid., p. 49.

40. Ibid., p. 46.
41. Op. cit. (supra n. 23), pp. 30–33. What is set forth in the text is part quotation from and part paraphrase of Glazer's article.
42. Ibid., p. 32.
43. Ibid., p. 33.
44. Op. cit. (supra n. 22), p. 80.
45. Joseph L. Blau, *Judaism in America* (Chicago, 1976), p. 113. Cf. Blau, "The Spiritual Life of American Jewry, 1654–1954," *American Jewish Year Book*, vol. 55 (1956), pp. 99 ff.
46. Blau, *Judaism in America*, pp. 114–15.
47. Ellis Rivkin, "A Decisive Pattern in American Jewish History," in Jacob R. Marcus, ed., *Essays in American Jewish History* (Cincinnati, 1958), pp. 39–41.
48. A. J. Toynbee, *The Study of History* (London, 1934), vol. 2, p. 393.
49. *Ethnicity in the United States* (cited supra n. 20), p. 28.
50. John Clive, *Macaulay: The Shaping of the Historian* (New York, 1973), p. 117.
51. Isaac Herzog, *Judaism: Law and Ethics* (London, 1973), p. 148.
52. Cf. Oscar Handlin and Mary F. Handlin, "The Acquisition of Political and Social Rights by the Jews in the United States," *American Jewish Year Book*, vol. 56 (1955), p. 48.
53. Mass Jewish immigration did not begin until toward the end of the nineteenth century. In 1880 there were 300,000 Jews in the United States. By the end of the century the Jewish population was about a half-million. From 1900 to 1914, the beginning of World War I, another 1,500,000 were added; from 1914 to 1924, another 350,000 came. From 1899 to 1914, Jewish immigration averaged 90,000 persons per year.
54. David M. Potter, *People of Plenty* (Chicago, 1954), pp. 91–92.
55. Ibid., p. 95.
56. Glazer, "Social Characteristics of American Jews" (cited supra n. 23), p. 17; Potter, op. cit., p. 73.
57. See Jacob Katz, "Religion as a Uniting and Dividing Force in Modern Jewish History," in J. Katz, ed., *The Role of Religion in Modern Jewish History* (Cambridge, Mass.: Association for Jewish Studies, 1975).
58. See Daniel J. Elazar, *Community and Polity* (Philadelphia, 1976).
59. Blau, op. cit. (supra n. 46), pp. 19–20.
60. See Will Herberg, *Protestant, Catholic, Jew* (New York, 1955).
61. *Sanhedrin* 44a. In the Brother Daniel case, however, the Supreme Court of Israel, in 1966, held that Brother Daniel, despite his valid halakhic claim to be a Jew, had lost his Jewish status by having chosen to remove himself, by conversion to Christianity, from the Jewish community, and so did not qualify under the Law of Return.
62. Cf. J. G. Herder, "Essay on the Origin of Language," in F. M. Barnard, ed.,

J. G. Herder on Social and Political Culture (Cambridge, 1969), pp. 117 ff.
63. Deut. 5:3.
64. See Konvitz, *Fundamental Liberties of a Free People* (Ithaca, N.Y., 1957), pp. 345–61.
65. Hugh Trevor-Roper, ed., *Critical and Historical Essays: Lord Macauley* (New York, 1965), pp. 116, 127; John Clive and Thomas Pinney, eds., *Thomas Babbington Macaulay: Selected Writings* (Chicago, 1972), pp. 181, 187. Jews were barred from Parliament by an act of 1701 which required an oath "on the true faith of a Christian." Stat. 13 Wm. III, c. 6, 1.
66. See Richard B. Morris, "Civil Liberties and the Jewish Tradition in Early America," lecture delivered in 1954 and 1955, reprinted in A. J. Karp, ed., *The Jewish Experience in America* (New York, 1969), vol. I, pp. 404, 417.
67. Konvitz, op. cit. (supra n. 64), p. 346.
68. Morris, op. cit (supra n. 66), p. 423.
69. See Konvitz, "Legislation Guaranteeing Equality of Access to Places of Public Accommodation," *Annals of the American Academy of Political and Social Science,* Civil Rights in America (vol. 274, 1951), 47; M. R. Konvitz and Theodore Leskes, *A Century of Civil Rights* (New York, 1961), pp. 155 ff.; Emerson, Haber, and Dorsen, *Political and Civil Rights in the United States* (student's ed., 1967), vol. 2, pp. 1407, 1512, 1618, 1673, 1680; Civil Rights Act of 1964, 78 Stat. 241; Fair Housing Law, Title VIII of Civil Rights Act of 1968, 82 Stat. 82; Equal Employment Opportunity Act of 1972, 86 Stat. 103; Equal Credit Opportunity Act of 1976, 90 Stat. 251.
70. *Brown v. Board of Education,* 347, U.S. 483 (1954).
71. *Kiddushin* 30b.
72. Konvitz, *Fundamental Liberties of a Free People* (cited supra n. 64), p. 346; Saul K. Padover, ed., *The Complete Madison: His Basic Writings* (New York, 1953), p. 243.
73. *New York Times,* August 20, 1976, p. A–10.
74. Op. cit. (supra n. 54), p. 114.

MOSES RISCHIN

The Jews and Pluralism: Toward an American Freedom Symphony

If American Jews have been especially identified, and readily identified themselves, with a tradition of cultural pluralism, it hardly comes as a surprise. Broadly disseminated as an American challenge for nearly two generations, cultural pluralism became virtually a climate of opinion and a mystic formula for harmonizing all our diversities in a world consciously or unconsciously bent on their dissolution. Despite its patent inadequacies as a theory of group relations even for American Jews, and perhaps just because of its imprecision, the philosophy and rhetoric of cultural pluralism continues in varying degrees to inform American society at every turn.[1] Over thirty years ago, at the close of the most devastating war and holocaust in world history and the impending end of Europe's colonial dominance of the world, Margaret Mead proclaimed cultural, racial, and religious democracy as our nation's universal mission in terms that have become so familiar as to verge on a national litany.

> It remains to be seen whether the sheer spiritual challenge of developing a culture in which the age-old distinctions between different racial and cultural groups can be orchestrated into a pattern where each is given dignity, combined with the task of developing our place in a world society, may give new impetus to religion in America.[2]

For American Jews in the early years of the twentieth century, cultural pluralism was a response to the universal trauma of modernization. By transvaluing their historic religious traditions, they were able to assimilate America to their own secularized modes of expression and to legitimate an American Zionism in particular. It became, in effect, a general theory of cultural modernization that emerged, it would seem, almost inevitably, out of Jewish history.

Harking back to the Middle Eastern crossroads of the three continents where the world's peoples first converged and the West's religions had their origins, the Jews of the Diaspora, in the course of their repeated migrations, continually refined their heritage into a spiritual and ethnic amalgam that Salo Baron has called "Jewish ethnicism."[3] Two millennia of stateless and landless survival amid diverse societies conditioned the classic minority of the Western world to perceive the pluralistic realities of the modern United States, where all mankind was predestined to be free and equal, in terms imbued with its own messianic predispositions. In a nation that was a world becoming a world nation, "Jewish ethnicism" was to attain its freest expression. As the American world nation came to accept the full implications of its role, the explicit recognition of a pluralistic ethic fortified the profound American loyalties of Jews, renewed their age-old Jewish affirmations, and legitimated their historic experience as a viable model from which others might also learn.

The creative durability of "Jewish ethnicism," in defiance of the taxonomy devised some years ago by the once fashionable historical philosopher Arnold J. Toynbee, which classified the Jews with a number of "fossilized relics of similar societies now extinct," is vividly illustrated in a story told by Harold Isaacs.

Some years ago that distinguished scholar of international relations gained admission to a meeting of the new American Society for African Culture, despite its restriction of membership to "persons of African descent," on the grounds that the children of Israel had sojourned in Egypt for some generations, thus giving him a more plausible claim to ancient African ancestry than the Society's president. Although he was admitted only as an observer,

Isaac's *chutzpah* (read, "gate-crashing") is symptomatic of the historic persuasiveness of "Jewish ethnicism" in a free and democratic pluralistic society.[4]

For a time, in the wake of the racial, social, and cultural upheavals of the 1960s, pluralism appeared to have become boundless, atomizing American society beyond belief and casting doubts on the ability of so fragmented a nation to hold together in any meaningful fashion. Yet, although ethnic and other group identities were syncretized, rediscovered, extrapolated, morselized, and legitimated in ways entirely unanticipated, and at a pace and on a scale without previous parallel, a new equilibrium seemed to be emerging. In 1976, two historic events appeared to herald the onset of a new consensus that a distinguished historian has aptly called "pluralistic integration."[5]

An unprecedented Independence Day Observance incorporated the American heritage of ethnic diversity into the promise of the Declaration of Independence, paying tribute to an overarching tradition of ethnic pluralism as if it had been inseparable from the pursuit of individual rights and immanent from the time of the nation's founding. In an address before one hundred newly naturalized citizens from China, Cuba, Egypt, Korea, Chile, England, Scotland, and Sweden, standing on the tree-lined greensward in front of the Monticello home of the third President of the United States and the author of the Declaration of Independence, the thirty-fourth President of the United States linked the spirit of '76 to the nation's classic tradition of immigration, which made "America unique among nations and Americans a new kind of people." Furthermore, Gerald Ford insisted, "The sense of belonging to any group that stands for something decent and noble so long as it does not confine free spirits or cultivate hostility to others is part of the pride every American should have in the heritage of the past." This new fullness of vision, extending to the whole spectrum of mankind, reaffirmed a new democratic esthetic that no longer denied the reality of color for the sake of justice but proclaimed the positive beauty of all colors in the name of equal justice for all. "'Black is beautiful' was a motto of genius," exclaimed the President "which uplifted us far above its intention. . . . Once Americans had thought about it and perceived its truth, we began to realize that so are brown, white, red, and yellow beautiful . . . The beauty of Joseph's coat was its many colors. I believe Americans are beautiful—individually, in communities, and freely joined together by dedication to the United States of America." "Above all," declared Ford, "we need more encouragement and protection for individuality. The wealth we have of cultural, ethnic, religious, and racial conditions [is a] valuable counterbalance to the overpowering sameness and subordination of totalitarian societies."[6]

In our time, *Omnia in pluribus* (the all in the many) might appropriately serve along with the familiar *E pluribus unum* (one out of many) as a motto for a pluralistically integrated America, where a regard for the paramount rights of all individuals and a regard for the claims of all groups seems central to the recognition of the liberties of all Americans.[7]

As if to doubly commemorate the full coming of age of a consensual American pluralism, ethnic and regional awareness came full circle in 1976, when for the first time in the nation's history a colonial native son of the deep South, and the first southerner since the Civil War, was elected President of the United States. To certain sectors of the electorate, the earnest, small-town, Anglo-Saxon, Southern Baptist seemed as much threat and enigma as urban Irish Catholics who had aspired to the Presidency appeared to other Americans in 1928 and 1960. Seeking to neutralize these sentiments, on October 21, 1976, in an address at the Alfred E. Smith Memorial dinner in New York City, Jimmy Carter, in his opening remarks, struck a note of comparison between his own campaign and the 1928 smear campaign against Smith, a Governor, who also had never served in Washington and who was "criticized . . . for his religion and his accent."[8]

To an eminent historian of the South, the high visibility of "ethnic southerners" in the second half of the twentieth century, as earlier, has been self-evident. As a matter of fact, insisted C. Vann Woodward, the declining distinctiveness of European ethnics contrasted with the conspicuous persistence of "the most indigenously American minorities of all," the Southern-Americans and the Afro-Americans, "the oldest and the latest of the 'hyphenates.'" In adverting to the once highly charged hyphenate usage that crested during World War I, Woodward reminded non-Southerners that Southerners, both white and black, were ethnics too, that hyphenism was a venerable American tradition and not an anachronism, and that most Americans are, to some degree, also something else.[9]

Significantly, the classic era of hyphenism in the first two decades of the twentieth century generated the first formal full-scale colloquy over the nature of the identity of the peoples of modern America. Out of that colloquy, in which American Jews were notably engaged, emerged a theory of cultural pluralism formulated by America's first Jewish philosopher.

In a nation more diverse than ever and less patient with its diversities than at any other time since the 1850s, the problems of culture and society acquired a new urgency. With 3,000 to 5,000 predominantly Southern and Eastern European immigrants passing through Ellis Island daily, the greatest volume of newcomers to throng onto American shores in the nation's history added a menacing new immigrant presence to the old. Their coming activated popular racialist nativism, aroused social anxieties, and induced a sense of crisis. When the everyday hyphenism of a nation of immigrants, inflamed by cultural confrontation, was set ablaze by World War I, the country became bitterly divided along European lines as it had never been divided before.[10]

American Jews seemed faced with an especially tragic identity crisis, for these were the peak years of Jewish migration, which saw the arrival of one and a half million Jews from Eastern Europe, with many more on the way as hopes for reform in Tsarist Russia were dashed. These vast numbers not only threatened to overwhelm and to recast American Jewish life but appeared to heighten nativist, anti-immigrant, and anti-Semitic sentiment as well. Given a double edge by the new popularity of the melting pot image on the one hand, and the growing belief in ineradicable racial differences on the other, extreme nationalism appeared to endanger the foundations of an already sorely tried Jewish integrity being shaken by the most rapid and the most revolutionary transformation in Jewish history.

In 1914, the collapse of nineteenth-century Europe would find

American Jews especially vulnerable. Strenuously American, they also knew themselves to be trans-European and trans-Atlantic in their responsibilities. They felt personally implicated in the fate of their fellow Jews massed in the battle-ravaged East European Jewish heartland from which the majority of America's Jews had only recently migrated to the United States.

To counter the forces of inner dissolution and outer catastrophe, a handful of young American Jews came to espouse a new American ideology that, in American and democratic terms, for the first time advanced a culturally pluralistic vision of American society of which Zionism was to be an integral component. In a world that was to become progressively democratic in pursuit of the American model and where all historic peoples were becoming recognized claimants to cultural freedom and parity, the pluralistic vision was to inspire American Jews to identify their best selves with the highest values of two dynamic civilizations, the new American Zion and the renascent ancient one.

This emergent ideology reflected the modern identity needs of the new generation of America's Jews—as Americans, as Jews, and as Progressives, flushed with the democratic impulses of the early twentieth century. It aimed to transcend the dividers that isolated Jews from one another and alienated them from their obsolescent Jewish pasts by revitalizing their ancient Hebraic traditions along modern American lines. In effect, this ideology would bridge the gap between a nineteenth-century America and the problematic new one, between Jewish and American habits of mind, and between older and newer Americans who were equally in search of a viable way to rejuvenate their twentieth-century world nation. It would become central to the thinking of some of the most influential Americans of the early twentieth century.

Most suited to welcome a vision of a new America and a new world inspired by American example were purposeful young American Jews, primarily of Central European origin, who were detached from rival Russian and German camps and eager to help define the parameters of a new age. Most notable among them were New York's Stephen S. Wise; California native sons Judah L. Magnes and Julian Mack; the people's attorney and budding elder statesman Louis D. Brandeis; his disciple, Felix Frankfurter; and, most especially, the philosopher and key architect of cultural pluralism, and "the outstanding intellectual in the American Zionist movement," Horace Kallen.[11] These remarkable rabbis, judges, and public men of the Progressive era, dedicated to lifting up the common cause in their own cause, would fully emerge when the cataclysmic events of World War I thrust the United States and its Jews into roles of world leadership. As a handful of older and newer Americans began to glimpse the dilemmas of American society in fresh ways, cultural pluralism and Zionism would find their first American spokesmen.

Yet the Progressive era, especially productive in democratic stratagems and ideas in politics, economics, and education, proved less than congenial to the formulation of a theory of cultural democracy. In familiar sectors of governmental policy, where formal, long-established public institutions piloted by trusted old Americans prevailed, a profound American faith in the capacity of both for reconstruction and innovation was rooted in the mandate of the eighteenth-century republic and the mission of nineteenth-century New England schoolmasters and reformers. No such links seemed apparent, however, between a hallowed old *American* America of pilgrims and pioneers and the profane new *un-American* America of alien industrial hordes who appeared to defy familiar categories and who looked ominous. In 1904, the reissuance, for the first time in over a century, of Crevecoeur's *Letters from an American Farmer* by an enterprising young New York publisher might have provided the occasion for examining afresh the Crevecoeurian question, "What then is the American, this new man?" But it did not. No correspondence was detected between the new Americans of the revolutionary era and the Americans, old or new, of the twentieth century. In a lackluster preface, Columbia Professor William P. Trent found it a "propitious season" for the revival of the "pioneer poet-naturalist" whose "observations of primitive Americans and their institutions" had with the passage of time acquired "historical value." In an equally perfunctory introduction, young Ludwig Lewisohn, later a fervent Zionist, merely credited the correctness of literary historian Barrett Wendell's genteel strictures that "Crevecoeur's American is no more human than some ideal savage of Voltaire."[12]

Yet four years later, the image of the melting pot, first suggested by Crevecoeur, was given popular currency by a Jewish melodrama, originally called *The Crucible,* that catapulted a nineteenth-century image of gradual assimilation into an embattled popular symbol of instant Americanization. Opening on October 5, 1908, in a Washington, D.C., theater, to the acclaim of first-nighter President Theodore Roosevelt, a supreme antihyphenate to whom *The Melting Pot* was dedicated on publication, it would elicit assent, outcry, and incredulity, as the destiny of millions of new Americans, as well as old, seemed to be resolved summarily to the total disregard of historical realities. Recently, a young historian has lucidly argued, in an admittedly radical reinterpretation, that Israel Zangwill's play can be read as a problem statement by a deeply divided man rather than as a paean to instant assimilation. And it can. In rejecting "sectarian" Judaism as obsolete, Zangwill is seen as proclaiming the message of universal Hebraism, of a Judaism divested of ethnic parochialism and destined to be the universal American religion, perhaps the Judeo-Christianity of our own philo-Semitic post-Holocaust era.

But so broad and so retrospective a reading of *The Melting Pot* fails to take account of the spirit of other times; of Zangwill's apocalyptic desperation, fed by the specter of impending doom, if not holocaust, in Tsarist Russia; of mounting nativist and anti-immigration passions in the United States; and of extreme nationalism everywhere. Zangwill's "melting pot" alternative to a homeland on ancient Judaean soil or a provisional Zion in some British territory, viz., Uganda, to which the spectacular July 4 Entebbe Airport incident contributed an ironic fillip, could only be regarded by most of his Jewish contemporaries as a cry of despair rather than a counsel of hope.[13] At best it seemed a tactic to gain time and asylum. But it failed to address itself to the cultural dilemmas of modernization, which called for new perceptions of the American scene in the twentieth century that would be genuinely reflective of the social and cultural realities that were shaping and reshaping new American identities.

Yet if Zangwill sensationalized a simplistic view of the Americanization process, he also injected a secondary motif, the "symphony of America," composed by the violinist hero David Quixano in tribute to the melting pot, that was to be casually appropriated by Rabbi Judah L. Magnes and soon transformed into the key metaphor of an emergent cultural democracy. In 1909 at New York's cathedral synagogue, in a sermon censuring Zangwill's play, the young rabbi, who was to become the first president and chancellor of the Hebrew University, called for "the symphony of America" to "be written by the various nationalities which keep their individual and characteristic note and which sound this note in harmony . . . not the harmony of the Melting Pot." But not until Horace Kallen, in his notable article of 1915 in the *Nation,* "Democracy versus the Melting Pot," sized upon the symphonic image, to the delight of John Dewey, who deplored the melting pot idea, was it launched as the central musical metaphor and symbol of an ethnically pluralistic America, where "each ethnic group may be the natural instrument, its temper and culture . . . its theme and melody and the harmony of its dissonances and discords . . . the symphony of civilization." But unlike a "musical symphony," continued Kallen, "written before it is played; in the symphony of civilization the playing is the writing, so that there is nothing so fixed and inevitable about its progression as in music." The following year in New York City, in his famous address, "Nationalizing Education," before the National Education Association, Dewey affixed the symphonic image upon American education. "Neither Englandism nor New Englandism . . . any more than Teuton or Slav, can do anything but furnish one note in a vast symphony," he declared.[14]

In the midst of World War I, the major advocate of the American freedom symphony spoke with the voice of a resurgent old America. Called by Milton Konvitz the philosopher of "the Hebraic-American idea," and America's "most hyphenated thinker," Horace Kallen drew exclusively on American democratic scriptures in formulating what he called interchangeably, "the American idea," Hebraism, Zionism, or cultural pluralism. "My ideas regarding cultural pluralism have a strictly American derivation. . . . This pluralism has an entirely different philosophical and political intention than . . . the . . . isolationist political thinking that is indigenous to Europe," he would everlastingly reiterate. This latter-day Emersonian, chiefly responsible for proclaiming the nation's first trans-ethnic declaration of cultural interdependence was, above all, an ardent American nationalist. "I am not an American through the mere accident of birth and through having grown up on American soil. I am an American by considered choice."[15] Kallen's philosophical integrity, impeccable academic credentials, felicitous advocacy, and passionately American outlook were to enable him to play a singularly creative role in illuminating twentieth-century America's ethnic and cultural dilemmas.

Kallen's original relationship to the American universe was forged at the philosophical vortex of early twentieth-century America. Emanating from the depths of a fierce confrontation with his inner self, it led to the making of a new American, the undivided, loosely hyphenated American of our time. Born in Silesia in 1882, the son of an unbending Orthodox, East European rabbi against whom he rebelled completely, he had the special good fortune to be brought as a five-year-old to turn-of-the-century Boston, the shrine of nearly three centuries of self-conscious American history, culture, and a heroic tradition of religious dissent. In the first year of the twentieth century, young Kallen entered Harvard on the threshold of the final decade of the forty-year presidency of Charles W. Eliot. In that heady era, which saw the flowering of an adventurous, great twentieth-century university at the hub of nineteenth-century American culture, everything seemed possible. "It was a fresh morning in the life of reason, cloudy but brightening," and much more.[16]

In these years, America was to become uniquely available to the imagination of a poor immigrant lad in "Another world." In Harvard Yard, in categories and in ways that were to make uncommon sense, the mutually exclusive and discordant worlds of his rejected Judaic past, the old North and West End urban immigrant frontier, and historic Boston classroom ideals were to be simultaneously transvalued and given new sanctions and dimensions. They were to be pluralized, Anglicized, melted, Hebraized and reconstructed with the aid of the university fathers of Kallen's rarefied new America. Personifying entirely disparate responses to the world, George Santayana, Barrett Wendell, and William James, all at the height of their powers, were to become his mentors, confidants, and lifelong friends, honing his philosophical and literary intelligence to a fullness that is rare in any time but that seemed almost commonplace in Harvard's golden age, when the university bubbled with the widest array of hot-living philosophers in academic captivity. They thickened the atmosphere like "so many religions, ways of fronting life . . . worth fighting for," exulted James in 1900, and had the capacity to turn Harvard into "a genuine philosophic universe" where, that "Irishman among the Brahmins" believed, "the world might ring with the struggle, if we devoted ourselves exclusively to belaboring each other." Even Josiah Royce, "the mightiest spokesman of the Genteel Tradition," James's philosophical adversary and dear friend, by inciting young Kallen's dissent, "enhanced the feelings of release and adventure that came from my studies with his colleagues."[17]

Almost as if by design, in Kallen's three undergraduate years, Santayana, the European outsider; Wendell, the American insider; and James, the mediator between continents and centuries, were successively to become his Harvard patriarchs and the dominant influences in his self-education. In his freshman year, he encountered the quiet exile, announced atheist, and spiritual alien in genteel Protestant Cambridge, George Santayana. With that serene and elusive outsider the youngster established almost immediate rapport and identification. A question after a philosophy lecture extended to a conversation and lengthened into a dialogue that was to last for decades. "He was," reminisced Kallen, "an atheist who rejected Catholicism without alienating the Catholic ways of thought, just as I rejected Judaism without rejecting the Hebrew Jewish ways of thought." Ironic, detached, a lifelong Spanish subject with a Spanish passport, the elegant Santayana was a kindred Spinozistic spirit, Emersonian in his quest for harmony, with a moral and historical imagination shaped by a repudiated religious tradition as cleaving as Kallen's own antique heritage. In 1912, upon resigning from Harvard at the age of forty-nine and departing for his beloved historic Europe, Santayana, as a farewell gesture, left young Kallen his doctoral cap and gown, the ceremonial regalia of the secular humanist for whom there would be no direct successor but for whom the eclectic Kallen might become a kind of American heir.[18]

In his second year at Harvard, a chance meeting with Barrett Wendell, the genteel spokesman of Anglo-American cultural retrospection and fervent assimilationist, initiated a second enduring dialogue and apprenticeship which "freed my surprised mind," recalled Kallen, "for ways of perceiving the American Idea and for the art of saying anything that I saw which gave a new turn to my appraisal of myself as a free man among other men." Wendell's innovative course in the history of American literature, celebrating the central influence of New England nonconformity in "the single traditional democracy now existing," proved to be sheer revelation. The seminal influence of the biblical prophets, Kallen learned, had shaped the "strongly Hebraic" character traits of the Puritans and, by extension, of the American republic, where Wendell saw the promise of "a growing world democracy." As John Higham has so perceptively observed, Wendell enabled Kallen to find his "own people enshrined within the self-image of New England's founding fathers." Judaism spurned might now become Hebraism regained, inseparable from the American core tradition with its intellectual intensity and its universalistic and unique democratic mission. "In the world's count of it," Kallen wrote a few years later, "the culture of the Jews appears as no mere religion . . . It is called Hebraism, not Judaism, and . . . covers the total biography of the Jewish soul."[19]

If Wendell opened the way back for Kallen to a usable Hebraic and Puritan past, in Kallen's third year at Harvard William James opened the way to the future, to psychic self-knowledge, and to a problematic, pluralistic universe that was to energize and shape Kallen's vision of himself as a *ganzer mensch.* In 1902, *The*

Varieties of Religious Experience provided "unexpected confirmation of the heart's vision which the mind could accept," validating and authenticating young Kallen's secularized religious impulses, although he did not then recognize that James's disguised discussion of the "sick soul" was autobiographical. But like James, who had been invalided by melancholia for four agonizing years in his youth, that "very remarkable fellow," as Josiah Royce characterized young Kallen, "barring his rather doubtful health . . . of the familiar and pathetic variety," was in the throes of "religious despondency" as he sought to find appropriate living expression for his religious emotions. James's radical probing into the psychology of religious experience, it would appear, provided a vindication for the "subliminal" reality of Kallen's own psychic malaise, releasing him to heal himself permanently, as had the young James, by "a self-accomplished psychological reintegration." Over seven decades later, Kallen vividly recalled his conversion in 1903 to Zionism, "a channel in which I became again a whole person," emancipated "from a rebellious attitude which shut out the operational working of my Jewish past." In the life and writings of James, Kallen saw mirrored the universal rites of emotional and intellectual passage from the genteel nineteenth into the uncharted twentieth century. "If we except Spinoza," wrote Kallen in 1910 in his memorial tribute, James was one of the few philosophers "whose philosophy and life were . . . absolutely at one" and whose "extraordinary and infectious joyousness . . . seemed woven into the warp and woof of his philosophic vision as well as into the routine of his daily life."[20]

In the contrarieties of the life and thought and commitments of the philosopher-psychologist, Kallen saw the self-made pragmatist, whose "direct immediate intuition into the character of reality" was the modern American response to experience. "The perspectives and appreciations that a sensitive and highly cultured immigrant might have," remarkably close to Kallen's own, James "concentrated and transfused," wrote Kallen, into "the philosophy of America . . . what is inwardly most untraditional and modern in the whole of white civilization. . . . The private experiences of William James and the public experiences of Europeans making a home in the American wilderness . . . coincide. . . . Each comes to be as the slow throwing-off of traditional conventions of the habit of life."[21]

The most ardent and original disciple of the nation's first universally acknowledged philosopher was to compose a pluralistic American social philosophy that affirmed a complex American identity. In simultaneous revolt against "the closed, stifling atmosphere of late-nineteenth century culture"[22] oozing genteel pieties and a chill abstract Judaism as comfortless as the rigid ghetto Orthodoxy of his father, Kallen identified with a more distant American and Jewish past and the cultural promise of American life. Once launched upon the charting of a new America, he persisted in that quest into his ninety-second and last year. By then Kallen's "America idea" had become pervasive.

The general theory of cultural pluralism was initially implemented by Kallen in the Harvard circle of his Jewish contemporaries and aspired to "the free cultivation of a full Jewish life" in all its diversity "orchestrated to modernity." During his six years as graduate student, teaching assistant, and lecturer in philosophy at Havard, having overcome his "dumb anxiety" over his Jewishness, he placed his imprint on the first Jewish college-student organization dedicated to the promotion of Hebraism as the sum total of the cultural and religious expression of the Jewish people. The Harvard Menorah Society, a declaration of "reverence for the sources of one's being," in Santayana's definition of piety, was to become "a landmark in the Jewish renaissance" in the view of Louis Brandeis, and the cornerstone of the Intercollegiate Menorah Society. Committed to pride in ethnic roots rather than shame and concealment, to expansive Jewish knowledge in place of Jewish sectarianism and ignorance, and to a catholic inclusiveness and open door to all, it represented Kallen's social application of Jamesian-pragmatism and pluralism to the university milieu.

Young and impetuous Kallen could prove overly eager to appropriate Jamesian principles. In the last year of his life, an overworked and ailing James was unable to attend Kallen's lecture on Zionism, but cautioned his disciple against making absolutist distinctions between "Hebraic pragmatism" and "Hellenistic perfectionism" in his overzealous effort to identify the Hebraic tradition with the pragmatic, the modern, and the American. Curiously, even the premier Jewish scholar-to-be of the twentieth century could not resist the eloquent persuasiveness of his young mentor, the translator of his nationalist poems from the Hebrew, and lifelong friend. In his first published prize-winning article, Harry Wolfson, to Kallen's subsequent amusement, portrayed the Spanish Hebrew poet and philosopher Judah Halevi as a forerunner of Hebraic pragmatism, by contrast with Maimonides, whom he depicted as a medieval Hellenist.[23]

But despite his tendency to magnify distinctions, the iconoclastic, romantic young philosopher was ever receptive to the views of sympathetic others in the open marketplace of ideas. Had not James repeatedly exhorted him to beware of the pitfalls of vicious abstractionism? Had not his doctoral dissertation, "Notes on the Nature of Truth" (1908), celebrated the tentativeness of all truths? When, in 1915, John Dewey detected implications of segregation in Kallen's call for cultural democracy, he promptly modulated his terms to suit the sensibilities of the nation's philosopher of democracy and successor to James in his affections. Despite their common pragmatic outlook, Kallen was keenly aware that he and Dewey were conditioned by different backgrounds and perspectives, that Dewey "treated problems in terms of the total situation," whereas he started from "comparatively independent individual components." In January 1916, in response to Dewey's demurrer, Kallen refrained from renewing his appeal for "a federation or commonwealth of national cultures" or "federal republic" of nationalities. Instead he defined culture as "nothing more than spiritual hyphenation . . . humanism in the best sense of the term." In "The Meaning of Americanism" he wrote, "Americanism as a social ideal" was identical with "the idea of culture." Dewey's commitment to diversity, to individuality, and to holding people together "in immediate community of experience," in conversation, neighborhood, town meeting, and face-to-face local association, as the first stage in transforming the Great Society into the Great

Community, made him receptive to Kallen's pluralistic vision. In 1924, the Dewey influence was discernible when Kallen introduced the term *cultural pluralism* into print for the first time and defined it as a "fellowship of freedom and cooperation" animated by a "spirit of cooperative liberty" that would eventuate in a "national fellowship of cultural diversities."[24]

If the rhetoric of cultural pluralism was moderated by Kallen in response to Dewey's criticism, it was raised momentarily to new heights of eloquence by Dewey's most fervent and most meteoric student, Randolph Bourne. No one more elegantly interpreted the intimate relationship between Americanism, cultural pluralism, historic Jewish ideals, Zionism, and internationalism than did the radical "intellectual hero of World War I," who gratefully acknowledged that he "was set working on the whole idea of American national ideals by the remarkable artcles" in the *Nation* by Kallen. Indeed, Bourne credited the term *trans-nationalism,* which he first employed in 1916 in his renowned *Atlantic Monthly* article describing a multicultural America, to a Jewish classmate at Columbia. This "Jewish idea," he insisted, must be the basis for a long overdue "new spiritual internationalism" and American cosmopolitanism, for the World War had made it all too apparent that "the age-long problems of Jewish nationalism have become the problems of other dispersed nationalities." To Bourne it was clear that "the adjustment which the Jew has had to make throughout the ages" was "a pattern of what other nationals have to make today" in a nation that had become "a vast reservoir of dispersions." Bourne hailed "the current Jewish ideal of Zionism" as "the purest pattern and the most inspiring conception of trans-nationalism." Others, like Norman Hapgood, saw Zionism as "a symbol of the democratic universe—a universe free without being uniform, monstrous, or oppressive of the less numerous." For John Dewey, Zionism was the pragmatic guarantor of cultural freedom for Jews and others in a world where competing claims to complete sovereign rights vitiated the hope for peace among nations.[25]

However inadvertently, no one more ardently assured Kallen of the co-extensiveness of Zionism with Americanism and of the momentousness of that relationship than did Barrett Wendell, who continuously provided a sounding board for the buoyant new American as he ventured forth into an America and a world that seemed more forbidding than ever to the older man. For the elegaic Yankee, the outbreak of World War I tolled the collapse of European civilization and of his whole nineteenth-century world. Buzzing through Kallen's mind in December 1914, when he spoke for the first time on "Democracy and the Melting Pot" before the American Philosophical Association, and early in 1915 as he refined his thoughts for publication in the *Nation* and in the newly founded *Menorah Journal,* were passages from two letters in which Wendell confided his apprehensions, finding his only consolation for the "miseries of national life" in the "spiritual energies of the Jews." Wrote Wendell,

> Your Jewish race is less lost than we, of old America. For all [its] sufferings . . . it has never lost its identity, its tradition, its existence. As for us, we are submerged beneath a conquest so complete that the very names of us means something not ourselves. . . . I feel as I should think an Indian might feel, in the face of ourselves that were.

Clearly implied in Wendell's anguished declaration of faith in the spiritual vitality of the Jews was the charge to Kallen to carry forth the American democratic tradition, which had been inspired by Old Testament prophets and was unique to America and to their common heritage. "We are the only living people . . . to whom democracy has been confided, not as a philosophical abstraction, but as an ancestral practice," insisted Wendell. "Hebraism and English nationality—these are the spiritual background of the American commonwealth," echoed Wendell's heir.[26]

The "tory-like" stance of Wendell's "protesting spirit" in defense of the past, their curiously common if bifurcated past, cemented a friendship, recalled Kallen, that "stood the test of radical divergences in outlook and aspiration to the end." It was in fact the corresponding "tory-like stance" of Kallen's own "protesting spirit" that enabled him to sustain lifelong friendships with such notable adversaries as Wendell, T. S. Eliot, Santayana, and many others, and to encompass seeming paradoxes in life-style and opinion with that empathy that uniquely defined his pluralistic horizon. "Preserve your own individuality," his mentor had counseled young Kallen, and do not "shut out understanding of different ones." In his last letter to Kallen, in 1920 just before his death, Wendell pithily summed up their affectionate dialogue of nearly two decades. "After all, the difference between a reactionary and a radical, at heart, is only that one longs to retain whatever is good and the other to destroy whatever is evil."[27]

As unapparent to contemporaries as Wendell's unflagging influence on Kallen was Kallen's profound impact on Louis Brandeis, whom he converted to cultural pluralism and to active Zionism (as Sarah Schmidt has so clearly established) by demonstrating their compatibility with Americanism. Almost overnight in 1913 and 1914, in letters and conversations, the messianic progressive and philosophy and psychology instructor, then at Wisconsin, the nation's most outstanding state university, helped his fellow New Englander to perceive the intimate relationship between Americanism, Hebraism, and Zionism and so freed him to assume the leadership of the American Zionist movement and to affix his stamp upon it. In the lead article in the inaugural issue of *The Menorah Journal,* Brandeis submitted that twentieth-century American ideals had been the ideals of Jews for twenty centuries, that indeed, among Jews, democracy was not "an ideal merely. . . . It was a practice." In Brandeis's notable address, "Zionism and Patriotism," his classic syllogism invariably drew as much upon Wendell as it did upon Kallen. "Practical experience and observation convince me that to be good Americans, we must be better Jews, and to be better Jews we must be Zionists."[28]

In an era that saw the shattering of the world's dominant continent after a century of peace, the polarization of America's ethnics along European lines, and the virtual closing of the gates to Europeans of the "new immigration" because of their alleged racial inferiority, Kallen inevitably focused his sights on the American ethnics of European origin. But his theory of cultural pluralism extended to all Americans. In 1918, in collaboration with James

Weldon Johnson, he wrote the booklet *Africa and the World Democracy.* Elsewhere he argued that the case for a Jewish homeland in Palestine had its parallel for Liberia, no less than for England, France, and Italy. In 1924, his collection of occasional essays, *Culture and Democracy,* written in the course of the previous decade, opened ominously with a preface entitled "Postscript—To Be Read First: Culture and the Ku Klux Klan," but left no doubt that American culture was the expression of the "many, gathered upon the American scene from the four corners of the earth and taking root and finding nourishment, growth and integrity upon its soil." The oppressed blacks of the South, Kallen asserted, were but the extreme example of ethnic difference exacerbated by economic stratification and a warning to the nation of the tragic price of ethnic suppression.[29]

Indeed, the term *cultural pluralism,* recalled Kallen, was first crystallized in 1906 in the course of discussions with his student, Alaine Locke, when Kallen was serving as a teaching assistant to both James and Santayana. Locke insisted that he simply was a human being and that his color was of no consequence. When, two years later at Oxford, the first black Rhodes scholar was excluded from Thanksgiving Day festivities, Kallen, then a Sheldon fellow, declined to attend. Forty years afterward, Locke reminded Kallen that in 1908 they had attended ceremonies together at Oxford where James had been awarded an honorary degree after delivering a series of lectures, published the following year, entitled *A Pluralistic Universe.*

The most striking evidence of the impact of Kallen's theory of cultural pluralism upon any ethnic group was in fact exemplified in the career of Alaine Locke, who became the father of the New Negro and the champion of the Harlem Renaissance. In 1925, a year after the publication of *Culture and Democracy,* Locke edited the landmark volume, *The New Negro,* convinced that Negroes could achieve recognition in American terms only through cultural and artistic expression rooted in an African cultural consciousness, part of a universal "racial awakening," comparable to the coming of age of Europe's "emergent nationalities" and of a "renascent Judaism" in Palestine. Published posthumously in

1956, *The Negro in American Culture*—based on materials left by Locke—paid singular tribute to Kallen's vision of cultural democracy.[30]

By then, what in the 1920s and 1930s had appeared to be the rarefied ideas of a Harvard- and Oxford-educated social philosopher had become self-evident truths, ever more complex and unpredictable in their unfolding.[31] In a post-immigrant and post-World War II world-conscious America, an eminent American historian offhandedly sketched the patterns of group life that were a pragmatic consequence of a pluralistic nation whose people were shaped by the variety of their ethnic antecedents, sectional origins, and other associations. By 1963 a panoramic commentary on ethnic New York of the 1950s even argued that "ethnicity" was "commonly the source of events." By 1970, in an updated edition of *Beyond the Melting Pot,* where race and especially ethnicity were given added emphasis, the term *ethnicity* appeared in the index, and great pains were taken by the authors to explicate this phenomenon. Two years later, "ethnicity" became the theme of a major exploratory conference, global in scope, at the American Academy of Arts and Sciences. In the subsequently published volume, the editors concluded that ethnic groups could no longer be seen as "*survivals* from an earlier age. . . . [We] now have a growing sense that they may be *forms* of social life that are capable of renewing and transforming themselves."[32]

Appropriately, *Ethnicity* opened with a discussion of "Basic Group Identity" by the most wide-ranging veteran scholar of contemporary group identity patterns. By contrast with the father of cultural pluralism, who developed his ideas out of his own inner turmoil, Harold Isaacs was an early modern China expert, whose ideas emerged out of global turbulence. Yet while Isaacs appeared at the periphery of the American, the Jewish, and the European experience, he has been ever aware that all that he has written on international politics and human relations might be read as autobiography as well. "Every man shares his individual identity in some inescapable measure with the group of which he is inescapably a part," he asserted.[33] Perched at the threshold of the first world-scale revolution in history ever since becoming a young foreign correspondent in China in 1930, he has looked to new patterns of social and economic relations as the only means of redressing the imbalance of centuries between Eastern and Western civilizations. "We will either transform our paretic world and cast a global society in which Asia and Africa can thrive with us, or else they will, out of intolerable frustration create a new set of tyrannies, of which Russia's will have been the first, and China's the second," he warned in 1951 in a revised edition of his classic study and first book, first published in England in 1938, *The Tragedy of the Chinese Revolution.*[34]

In his lifetime, conditioned by two world wars, civil wars, and post-colonial revolts, unitary nations and empires everywhere appeared to be disintegrating. Isaacs experienced firsthand the universal shaking out and atomization of virtually all group and power relations and the ubiquitous emergence of the ethnic, the tribal, and the primordial as enduring and central social realities.

As a matter of course, Isaacs would project a decisively world perspective back upon the American scene. His second book, *No Peace for Asia* (1947), reporting on the attitudes of American soldiers, those "unwilling exiles," toward the native peoples, opened the way to a full-scale inquiry into the nature of group identity and perception on a global scale. As senior research associate at the Center for International Studies at the Massachusetts Institute of Technology, Isaacs undertook a series of imaginative background and case studies in which he probed the identity problems of people pitched into the maelstrom of modernization in a politically and racially realigning world. Whether Asians, Africans, or Americans, all were members of the first generation to enter a new egalitarian universe where Western whites were no longer the masters and non-Western non-whites no longer the subjects. In less than a decade there appeared *Scratches on Our Minds: American Images of China and India* (1958); *Emergent Americans: A Report on Crossroads Africa* (1961), based on American college youth contacts; *The New World of Negro Americans* (1963), a study of the impact of the new Africa on blacks of America; *India's Ex-Untouchables* (1965); and *American*

Jews in Israel (1967). Studies of Chinese in Malaysia and of Filipinos and of Japanese in the process of acquiring new identities were also completed.[35] And in 1975, culminating Isaac's long-term scrutiny of basic group identity patterns came *Idols of the Tribe: Group Identity and Political Change,* an analysis of the wider implications of his findings. A terse opening statement, apocalyptic in its starkness, set the tone of the book: "We are experiencing on a massively universal scale a convulsive ingathering of people in their numberless grouping of kinds . . . only the latest and by far the most inclusive chapter of the old story in which after failing again to find how they can co-exist in sight of each other without tearing each other limb from limb, Isaac and Ishmael clash and part in panic and retreat once more into their caves." Contrary to the prognostications of elitists and perfectionists, "our tribal separatenesses" concluded Isaacs, "are here to stay."[36]

Yet all said, after insisting in chapter upon chapter on the persistence of our "tribal separatenesses," Isaacs in his closing chapter, "What New Pluralisms?", even more emphatically affirmed the dynamism of "basic identity" in a rapidly changing world of uprooted peoples. Nowhere, declared Isaacs, was this more dramatically so (not surprisingly) than in the United States, "where all group identities, all ethnicity, especially all the American varieties, are made in melting pots and always have been." The result, in its current phase, he concluded, was the production "not of a second-class Wasp but what is becoming . . . a one-class American who is often also something else at the same time." Pressures and counterpressures to redefine and to revise the relative positions of the group and the individual in the society, despite some merits, seemed questionable. Isaacs had no doubts that American pluralistic theory and most Americans placed a premium on the basic rights of the individual in the public domain while leaving open a great private domain where individuals associated freely in groups "embracing all measures of assimilation and of sustained differences on the basis of a shared common culture, a shared set of institutions, and a shared set of rights and opportunities," A representative American and Jew, Isaacs, like Horace Kallen, the architect of cultural pluralism, reasserted the classic American tradition of the primacy of the individual.[37]

By all counts, the past quarter century was providential for Jews. In a self-consciously pluralistic yet increasingly homogeneous and egalitarian-minded nation, an ease and spontaneity in group expression, an openness in personal relations, and an enhanced access to all sectors of society enabled Jews to realize themselves as Americans, as Jews, and as complete human beings to a degree that had never been quite possible earlier. They experienced the most unqualified public acceptance and the greatest degree of self-fulfillment in all of American and of Diaspora history. Under these circumstances,[38] even the genuine dilemma of Jewish survival in the face of almost total secularization, an unprecedented incidence of intermarriage, and the crumbling of social barriers aroused as much hope as it did anxiety. Illustrative of this underlying mood was a profile of Jewish organizational life by an ingenious political scientist in which contemporary American Jewry was sketched with unparalleled indulgence. There was not a trace of a familiar earlier indictment. The charge that Jews knowingly or unknowingly were in flight from "Judaism as Disaster," dispersing centrifugally in response to mutual repulsions induced by anti-Semitism and self-hate was without point. On the contrary, a nuclear core of "integral Jews (living according to a Jewish rhythm)," which accounted for from 5 to 8 percent of the Jews of the United States, was portrayed as a magnet acting upon a series of wide open concentric rings of diverse American Jews. Successive circles of "Participants," "Associated Jews," "Contributors and Consumers," as well as vaguely or latently Jewish "Peripherals," "Repudiators," and "Quasi-Jews," to use Elazar's terms, with tenuous and vestigial Jewish predilections at best, were all seen as centripetally drawn to the magnetic Jewish core. Where group, associational, and family ties were eroded, an "individualistic pluralism" with little more than transient attachments was given ready sanction. In the post-modern era, a receptivity to quasi-Jewish and even more marginal and enigmatic residual identities had become symptomatic of a diffuse new Jewish pluralism that was no longer shaped by loyalty to immediate forebears, ideologies, or a community of culture or religion but by the irrevocable need to be.[39]

It could not be otherwise. For over a generation an irreducible

Jewish presence had been projected by the world-encompassing mass media from which there has been no escaping. The delayed impact of the Holocaust, the increasingly perceived implications of the creation of the State of Israel, the virtual demise of a once vital and pervasive immigrant Jewish culture, and the sudden reappearance out of the mists of Eastern Europe of the lost Jews of Soviet Russia registered conspicuously in the most out-of-the-way places. Creating ever audible and visible waves of Jewish self-consciousness, merging public and private voices came to serve as permanent and vivid reminders of a transvalued "Jewish ethnicism," manifestly unequivocal in its apotheosis as a bulwark of a free America and a free world. In the strategic Middle East, Israel, so intimately dependent on the good will of the United States, has come to be recognized as an outpost of democracy crucial to the survival of liberal civilization, an earnest of the American idea, even as the interplay of many factors may make clearer someday "what it signifies to be a *Jew,* an *Israeli,* an *American.*"[40]

If there has been no return to the innocent optimism of the Progressive years in the post-modern era, there has been a new perception of the value of Jewish historic continuity as a source of strength, meaning, and cultural regeneration for Jews as well as for others. The increasing ascription of the term *Diaspora,* so uniquely associated with the Jewish past, to diverse peoples reflected the need, in a modern world of contracted personal horizons, of culture and growing ethnic self-consciousness for a breadth and depth of experience extending beyond national borders. As other continents and times acquired a new contemporaneity on a contracting globe, the Jewish dimension of civilization acquired an enhanced universality. In the wake of the revolutionary Catholic transformation of the 1960s, the emergence of the "communal Catholic" clearly found a parallel in the great Jewish awakening of the late nineteenth and early twentieth centuries, which led to the making of the "communal Jew." In that same decade, the rediscovery of ethnic America, variously called "the new ethnicity," "ethnic pluralism," or "the new pluralism," was attributed to the capacity of Jewish intellectuals to anticipate a universal need.[41]

No group in twentieth-century America has been so consistently and clinically concerned with the problems of human identity, its relation to group morale, psychology, personal fulfillment, intergroup relations, and inevitably to group survival as have America's Jews. In an era when all patterns of personality and culture have been fractured and all modernist formulas made problematic as well, Jews have seen their own dilemmas as part of the common plight. They have sought to identify, to define, and to conceptualize perceptions heightened by their own personal and collective autobiographies in universal terms. "The lonely crowd," "belongingness," "self-hatred," "identity," "alienation," "uprootedness," "ethnicity," "the new pluralism," and others are all terms devised or given currency by American scholars to describe a condition or problem symptomatic of the vast social and cultural change that has come to challenge all group and personal individualities. On the American scene, "cultural pluralism" emphasizing human individuality, "the most precious and indefeasible yet the most precarious value in the world," was the first such term to be applied to the total society. It may also be the most inspired and the most seminal. It has certainly been the most overarching and ambitious in its commitment to embrace without exception all persons and peoples, voluntary no less than natural groups. In the final decades of the twentieth century, it continues to serve as the archetypal inspiration for giving renewed meaning to the vision of a pluralist and integrated America dedicated to cooperative freedom.[42]

In the years ahead, continuing efforts will be made to balance the claims of group as opposed to individual rights. New strategies will be improvised in response to problems identified in politics, law, education, culture, employment, multilingualism, and other sectors of the society. The original theory of cultural pluralism implicitly assumed that the individual pursuit of excellence and the group aspiration for cultural recognition, once legitimated, would be co-extensive with one another and mutually supportive. Clearly such an assumption failed to take account of the enormous disparities and inequities among groups that were inadvertently fortified by the universalistic imperatives of technology, bureaucracy, and a mass society. Hopefully a multi-group fellowship, imbued with a trust in fair play for all and committed to imaginatively ameliorating ongoing inequities, will insure the open pluralism to which the huge majority of Americans are committed. Increasing opportunities for the less advantaged by uplifting their quality individually will keep the way open to all. As long as this seems attainable, those nursing a real grievance will not be driven by desperation, apathy, or isolation to turn to authoritarian or nihilistic nostrums out of a pained hatred of themselves or of others or of the world for denying them opportunities of advancement, expression, and fulfillment. The fragility and interconnectedness of all our group and personal hopes and identities make the assurance of that dignity inseparable from the maintenance and protection of all our rights.

In a time of pulling together at the beginning of the third century of American independence, the symphony as musical metaphor for a free and culturally pluralistic America seems more resonant than ever. In an age when the metaculture of music contests the cultural primacy of the written and spoken word,[43] the fiddles may be tuning again. The new world symphony, where "the playing is the writing, so that there is nothing so fixed and inevitable about its progression as in music," its harmonies inseparable from its dissonances, may yet become, in ways not quite anticipated, the irresistible symbol of a nation, the like of which the world has never seen—one committed to freedom, to equality, and to diversity, and to their simple practice.

NOTES

This paper is an expansion of the Judith R. Herman Memorial Lecture, which was given on October 21, 1976 in New York. I am particularly indebted to the splendid analysis of ethnic pluralism by John Higham. See especially chapters 10 and 11 in *Send These To Me: Jews and Other Immigrants in Urban America* (New York, 1975). Sarah Schmidt, in addition to alerting me to her fine articles on Horace M. Kallen and Zionism, has been especially generous in sharing with me her knowledge of the Kallen Papers. Miriam Kallen, Rachel Kallen, and Milton R. Konvitz responded graciously to my queries, for which I am also most grateful.

1. See especially John Higham, "Ethnic Pluralism in Modern American Thought," in *Send These to Me: Jews and Other Immigrants in Urban America* (New York, 1975), pp. 196 ff.; Milton M. Gordon, *Assimilation in American Life* (New York, 1964), pp. 148 ff.
2. Willard Sperry, *Religion and Our Racial Tensions* (Cambridge, Mass., 1945), p. 81.
3. Salo Baron, *Modern Nationalism and Religion* (New York, 1947), pp. 213 ff.; cf. Hans Kohn, *The Idea of Nationalism* (New York, 1944), pp. 27 ff.
4. Maurice Samuel, *The Professor and the Fossil* (New York, 1956), pp. 18 ff.; Harold R. Isaacs, *American Jews in Israel* (New York, 1967), pp. 39–40.
5. Higham, "Another American Dilemma," in *Send These to Me*, pp. 240–43 and 246; and "Hanging Together: Divergent Unities in American History," *Journal of American History* 61 (June, 1974): 5–28.
6. *Weekly Compilation of Presidential Documents* (July 5, 1976), XII, 1132.
7. I am indebted to Richard Hoffman and Frank Kidner, Jr., of San Francisco State University for their counsel on Latin usage. See Daniel Boorstin, *The Americans: The Democratic Experience* (New York, 1973), p. 248, for the suggestion of the alternate motto, *E pluribus plura*, which does not quite convey the condition that I would like to suggest.
8. *New York Times*, October 22, 1976, p. A–17.
9. C. Vann Woodward, *American Counterpoint* (Boston, 1971), pp. 4–5. See also George B. Tindall, "Beyond the Mainstream: The Ethnic Southerner," *Journal of Southern History* 40 (February 1974): 3 ff., and *The Ethnic Southerners* (Baton Rouge, 1976).
10. Moses Rischin, "The Jews and the Liberal Tradition in America," *American Jewish Historical Quarterly* 51 (September 1961): 11–12; Frederick C. Luebke, *Bonds of Loyalty: German-Americans and World War I* (DeKalb, 1974), pp. 57 ff.; Higham, *Strangers in the Land* (New Brunswick, 1955), pp. 195 ff. See also Oscar Handlin, "A Twenty-Year Retrospect of American Jewish Historiography," *American Jewish Historical Quarterly* 65 (June 1976): 308–9.
11. See Melvin I. Urofsky, *American Zionism from Herzl to the Holocaust* (New York, 1975), pp. 75 ff., and *Letters of Louis D. Brandeis;* Vol. 3, *Progressive and Zionist*, ed. David Levy and Melvin I. Urofsky (New York, 1973), p. 226.
12. Thomas Philbrick, *St. John De Crevecoeur* (New York, 1970), p. 163; H. St. J. Crevecoeur, *Letters from an American Farmer* (New York, 1904), XX, p. viii.
13. Joseph Leftwich, *Israel Zangwill* (London, 1957), pp. 251–59; Neil L. Shumsky, "Zangwill's The Melting Pot: Ethnic Tensions on Stage," *American Quarterly* 27 (March 1975): 29 ff. Cf. I. Zangwill, "The Jewish Race," *Papers on Inter-Racial Problems Communicated to the First Universal Races Congress Held at the University of London July 26–29, 1911*, ed. G. Spiller (London, 1911), pp. 276–79; Philip Gleason, "The Melting Pot: Symbol of Fusion or Confusion?" *American Quarterly* 16 (Spring 1964): 24–29: Higham, *Send These to Me*, pp. 203, 238–39.

14. Quoted in Arthur Goren, *New York Jews and the Quest for Community* (New York, 1970), p. 4. See also Horace Kallen, *Culture and Democracy* (New York, 1924), pp. 124–25; John Dewey, "Nationalizing Education," National Education Association of the United States, *Addresses and Proceedings* 54 (1916): 185; and John Dewey to Horace Kallen, March 31, 1915, "Kallen Papers," American Jewish Archives. (Hereafter, all Kallen letters cited are from the American Jewish Archives, unless otherwise indicated.)
15. Milton R. Konvitz, "Horace M. Kallen (1882–1974): Philosopher of the Hebraic-American Idea," *American Jewish Yearbook* (1974–75), vol. 75, pp. 55, 67; H. M. Kallen to Moses Rischin, December 4, 1953; H. M. Kallen, *Individualism: An American Way of Life* (New York, 1933), p. 5.
16. S. E. Morison, *Three Centuries of Harvard, 1636–1936* (Cambridge, 1936), pp. 365 ff., 417; Henry F. May, *The End of American Innocence* (New York, 1959), pp. 54 ff.; Hutchins Hapgood, *The Spirit of the Ghetto*, ed. Moses Rischin (Cambridge, 1967), p. xv; George Santayana, *Character and Opinion in the United States* (New York, 1920), p. 38.
17. H.M. Kallen, "Journey to Another World," in *College in a Yard*, ed., Brooks Atkinson (Cambridge, 1958), pp. 115–117; Horace Kallen to John Dewey, October 10, 1949. Kallen's earliest surviving letters from his mentors are dated: June 21, 1902 (Barrett Wendell); January 31, 1903 (George Santayana); and December 5, 1903 (William James). See also Gay Wilson Allen, *William James* (New York, 1967), p. 414; Santayana, *Character*, p. 58; *The Letters of Josiah Royce*, with an introduction by John Clendenning (Chicago, 1970), pp. 503–4.
18. Kallen, "Journey," pp. 117–18; Kallen, *Culture and Democracy*, pp. 255 ff.; Kallen, *What I Believe and Why—Maybe*, ed. Alfred J. Marrow (New York, 1971), p. 181; George Santayana, *The Middle Years* (New York, 1945), pp. 6–8, 122–23, 152 ff.; George Santayana to Horace Kallen, December 12 and 27, 1911.
19. Kallen, "Journey," p. 118; Laurence R. Veysey, *The Emergence of the American University* (Chicago 1965), p. 187–88; Barrett Wendell, *Liberty, Union and Democracy: The National Ideals of America* (New York, 1900), p. 530; Higham, *Send These to Me*, pp. 204–5, 211; Kallen, *Judaism at Bay* (New York, 1932), p. 39; Kallen in *Menorah Journal* 1 (April 1915): 130; cf. Sacvan Bercovitch, *The Puritan Origins of the American Self* (New Haven, 1975), p. 186.
20. William James, *The Varieties of Religious Experience* (New York, 1902), pp. 160–61; Introduction by H. M. Kallen in *The Philosophy of William James* (New York, 1925), pp. 23, 30; Ralph H. Gabriel, *The Course of American Democratic Thought*, 2nd ed. (New York, 1956), pp. 340–43; H. M. Kallen, *Individualism*, p. 8; *The Letters of Josiah Royce*, p. 503; Sarah Schmidt, "Horace M. Kallen and the Americanization of Zionism, In Memoriam," *American Jewish Archives* 28 (April 1976): 61–63; Sarah Schmidt, "A

Conversation with Horace M. Kallen: The Zionist Chapter of His Life," *Reconstructionist* 41 (November 1975): 33; H. M. Kallen, "William James," *Nation* 91 (September 8, 1910): 210–11.

21. Kallen, "William James," *Nation* 91 (September 8, 1910); 210–11; *The Philosophy of William James,* pp. 32–34; cf. Thomas C. Cochran, *Social Change in America; The Twentieth Century* (New York, 1972), pp. 21, 35.
22. John Higham, *From Boundlessness to Consolidation: The Transformation of American Culture 1848–1860* (Ann Arbor, 1960), p. 28.
23. Horace M. Kallen, "On Being Jewish Today," *Studies and Essays in Honor of Abraham A. Neuman,* ed. Meir Ben-Horin, Bernard D. Weinryb, and Solomon Zeitlin (Leiden, 1962), p. 327; Sarah Schmidt, "Horace M. Kallen," *American Jewish Archives* 28 (April 1976): 60; *Menorah Journal* 1 (January 1915): 4; Henry Hurwitz and I. L Sharfman, "The Decennial of the Menorah Movement," *Menorah Journal* 1 (October 1915): 253 ff.; William James to Horace M. Kallen, June 14, 19, 1909; Lewis Feuer, "Recollections of Harry Austryn Wolfson," *American Jewish Archives* 28 (April 1976): 60.
24. William James to H. Kallen, June 19, 1909; George Santayana to H. Kallen, November 13, 1914; John Dewey to H. Kallen, March 31, April 16, 1915; Kallen, *Individualism,* p. 4; Kallen, *Culture,* pp. 43, 64, 232; Morton White and Lucia White, *The Intellectual Versus the City* (Cambridge, 1962), pp. 177–94; cf. Merle Curti, *The Roots of American Loyalty* (New York, 1946), pp. 214–19; Corliss Lamont, ed., *Dialogue on John Dewey* (New York, 1959), pp. 15–16); J. Christopher Eisele, "John Dewey and the Immigrants," *History of Education Quarterly* 15 (Spring 1975): 71–72.
25. Randoph Bourne, "The Jew and Trans-National America," *Menorah Journal* 2 December 1916): 280–81; Norman Hapgood, "The Future of the Jews in America," *Harper's Weekly* 61 (November 27, 1915): 512; John Dewey, "The Principle of Nationality," *Menorah Journal* 3 (October 1917): 207–8; also see Randolph Bourne, *War and the Intellectuals: Essays by Randolph S. Bourne, 1915–1919,* ed. Carl Resek (New York, 1964), pp. xi–xiii, 107 ff., and statement by Kallen in *Menorah Journal* 1 (October 1915): 258. Cf. David A. Hollinger, "Ethnic Diversity, Cosmopolitanism and the Emergence of the American Liberal Intelligentsia," *American Quarterly* 28 (May 1975): 142.
26. Barrett Wendell to H. M. Kallen, December 6, 30, 1914; H. M. Kallen, "Democracy and the Melting Pot," *Journal of Philosophy* 12 (February 18, 1915): 94–95; Kallen, *Culture and Democracy,* p. 93: Barrett Wendell, *Liberty, Union and Democracy,* p. 325; Kallen, "Nationality and the Hyphenated American," *Menorah Journal* 1 (April 1915): 82–83. Cf. Bruce Catton, *Waiting for the Morning Train: An American Boyhood* (New York, 1972), pp. 18–19, for contemporary echoes of Wendell.
27. Kallen, "Journey," pp. 118–19; Corliss Lamont, ed., *Dialogue on George Santayana* (New York, 1959), pp. 38–39; Higham, *Send These to Me* pp. 212–13; M. A. DeWolfe Howe, *Barrett Wendell and His Letters* (Boston, 1924), pp. 183, 273, 330.

28. Sarah Schmidt, "The Zionist Conversion of Louis D. Brandeis," *Jewish Social Studies* 37 (January 1975): 26–27; Sarah Schmidt, "Messianic Pragmatism: The Zionism of Horace M. Kallen," *Judaism* 25 (Spring 1976): 220–22; Veysey, *The Emergence of the American University,* pp. 107–8; Louis D. Brandeis, "A Call to the Educated Jew," *Menorah Journal* 1 (January 1915): 13; Brandeis, "Zionism and Patriotism," in Moses Rischin, ed., *Immigration and the American Tradition* (Indianapolis, 1976), p. 234.
29. Kallen, *Judaism at Bay,* pp. 119–20; Kallen, *Culture and Democracy,* pp. 42, 165.
30. Horace M. Kallen, *What I Believe and Why—Maybe,* ed. Alfred J. Marrow (New York, 1971), pp. 129, 173; Sarah Schmidt, "A Conversation," *Reconstructionist* 41 (November 1975): 29; Alaine Locke to Horace M. Kallen, June 6, 1948 (Horace M. Kallen Papers, YIVO Institute of Jewish Research); Alaine Locke, ed., *the New Negro* (New York, 1925), pp. ix, xi; Margaret J. Butcher, *The Negro in American Culture* (New York, 1956), pp. 227–28; cf. J. L. Magnes, "A Republic of Nationalities," February 13, 1909 (A copy of this sermon was made available to me by Arthur Goren); B. Joyce Ross, *J.E. Spingarn and the Rise of the NAACP, 1911–1939* (New York, 1972), pp. 28, 82; Moses Rischin, "The Jews and the Liberal Tradition," pp. 9–10.
31. Oscar Handlin, *Adventure in Freedom* (New York, 1954), pp. 159, 244–46; S. P. Fullinwider, *The Mind and Mood of Black America: 20th Century Thought* (Homewood, Ill., 1966), pp. 115–16; Nathan J. Huggins, *Harlem Renaissance* (New York, 1971), pp. 57–58, 304; Handlin, *The American People in the Twentieth Century* (Cambridge, 1954), pp. 161–62; Nathan Glazer, *American Judaism* (Chicago, 1957), pp. 89, 120; Higham, *Send These to Me,* pp. 211–12.
32. Handlin, *The American People,* pp. viii, 230–32; Nathan Glazer and Daniel P. Moynihan, *Beyond the Melting Pot: The Negroes, Puerto Ricans, Jews, Italians, and Irish of New York City,* 2nd ed. (Cambridge, 1970), pp. 310, 353; Nathan Glazer and Daniel P. Moynihan, eds., *Ethnicity: Theory and Experience* (Cambridge, 1975), p. 4. In 1974 the Immigration History Society co-sponsored a conference on American ethnicity with the Center for the Study of Democratic Institutions. See *Center Magazine* 7 (July–August 1974): 18–73.
33. *Ethnicity,* pp. 29 ff.; Isaacs, *American Jews,* pp. 38–39.
34. Isaacs, *The Tragedy of the Chinese Revolution,* 2nd ed., rev. ed. (Stanford, 1961), p. xi.
35. Isaacs, *Idols of the Tribe* pp. x–xi, 112–14, 130–36.
36. *Ibid.,* pp. 1, 216.
37. *Ibid.,* pp. 211–213; Isaacs, *New World,* p. 326; cf. Kallen, *Individualism,* pp. 235 ff.
38. In 1946, Sidney Hook, in his address to the American Jewish Committee at its annual meeting, reported that the results of his polling of students in

philosophy on whether they would choose to become Jews were clear-cut: "No Jewish student ever wanted to be born Jewish." See Horace M. Kallen, *Of Them Which Say They Are Jews* (New York, 1954), p. 112.

39. Daniel J. Elazar, *Community and Polity: The Organizational Dynamics of American Jewry* (Philadelphia, 1976), pp. 41, 55–56, 70 ff.; Kallen, *Of Them Which Say They Are Jews,* pp. 42 ff.; cf. Marshall Sklare, *America's Jews* (New York, 1971), pp. 180 ff.; Charles S. Liebman, *The Ambivalent American Jew* (Philadelphia, 1973), *passim.*

    The late Joseph Levenson of Berkeley, a distinguished scholar of Chinese history, had his vision of himself as a believing Jew illuminated by his perception of modern China. In his file of notes on "Judaism," he recorded the following: "Modern situation (empirically grounds for pessimism) reanimantes Jewish potential: choice (possibility of dissolution creates possibility of choice)." See Joseph R. Levenson, *Revolution and Cosmopolitanism: The Western Stages and the Chinese Stages* with a Foreword by Frederick E. Wakeman, Jr. (Berkeley, 1971), xxv.

40. Henry Fairlie, "Epistle of a Gentile to Saul Bellow," *New Republic* 177 (February 5, 1977): 18 ff.; Eugene V. Rostow, "The American Stake in Israel," *Commentary* 63 (April 1977): 33 ff.; Isaacs, *Idols,* p. 197.

41. See Richard D. Brown, *Modernization: The Transformation of American Life 1600–1865* (New York, 1976), especially chap. 8, "Epilogue: The Experience of Modernization during the Past Century"; Glenn Hendricks, *The Dominican Diaspora* (New York, 1974); Lawrence J. McCaffrey, *The Irish Diaspora in America* (Bloomington, Ind., 1976); Martin L. Kilson and Robert I. Rotberg, eds., *The African Diaspora* (Cambridge, 1976); Andrew M. Greeley, *The American Catholic* (New York, 1977), p. 270; Michael Novak, *The Rise of the Unmeltable Ethnics* (New York, 1971), pp. 193 ff.; Richard Gambino, *Blood of My Blood* (New York, 1974), pp. 357, 368; *Jednota Annual Furdek 1977,* 16 243–44; Moses Rischin, "The New American Catholic History," *Church History* 41 (June 1972): 225 ff.; Irving M. Levine and Judith M. Herman, "The New Pluralism," in *Overcoming Middle Class Rage,* ed. Murray Friedman (Philadelphia, 1971), pp. 269 ff.

42. Kallen, *Judaism,* p. 255; *The Philosophy of William James,* pp. 53–54; Kallen, *Cultural Pluralism and the American Idea: An Essay in Social Philosophy* (Philadelphia, 1956), pp. 97–98; Konvitz, "Kallen," pp. 66–67.

43. See George Steiner, *In Bluebeard's Castle: Some Notes Towards the Redefinition of Culture* (New Haven, 1971), pp. 115–24; Yehudi Menuhin, *Unfinished Journey* (New York, 1977).

IRVING HOWE

The East European Jews And American Culture

Two extremes cry out to be avoided. First, the one that many of us recall from school: a view of American culture as the unsullied emergence of native voices, to which immigrants brought no discordant sounds or subversive notes. The second, a pathetic boasting that we too—we Jews, we Greeks, we Poles—have made our "contribution" to America. In certain kinds of Jewish periodicals there is a naive harping on distinguished people who happen to be of Jewish birth: Jascha Heifetz on the violin, Louis Brandeis in legal thought, Saul Bellow in literature, and, since what presumably counts is the origin of the distinguished person rather than the nature of his work, Hank Greenberg in baseball and Mickey Cohen in crime.

Somewhere there must be a more serious way of asking how the influx of East European Jews over the past century affected the styles, values, outlooks of American culture, and how, in turn, the immigrant Jews were changed by their exposure to the culture of the West.

I

Anyone who approaches a segment of Jewish history must sooner or later confront the question: Is that history to be studied essentially through the categories of modern historiography—categories of national emergence, social class, economic interest, etc.—or is it to be seen as a unique strand in Western history?

The belief in a unique Jewish history has large dangers. It gets blown up too easily into national mysticism or, in America, into a self-congratulatory sentimentalism comforting Jews precisely insofar as their "Jewishness" grows vaguer. And yet . . . try as one may to analyze Jewish history through the categories of modern historical study, insist as one should that Jews are neither better nor wiser than other peoples, it is difficult to ignore the shared perception that the Jewish past *is* different. An Israeli writer, A. B. Yehoshua, provides an unpretentious statement: "Our uniqueness comes to the fore in one thing only: the ability to preserve our identity while in exile." To which must be added: preserve that identity under conditions of the most extreme adversity, so that Jewish history becomes at many points almost indistinguishable from Jewish martyrdom.

The will to survive—whether in some distant villages of Iraq or in the major centers of Western civilization—remains a factor of profound moral weight. It cannot simply be explained by any of the usual socioeconomic categories. Jews have wanted—apparently as a value-in-itself—to remain Jews, and at least until recently that has been the dominating fact in their history.

Not, to be sure, that this has always led to pleasurable consequences or been celebrated as a blessing by those who experienced it. The great Yiddish writer Sholom Aleichem has a passage in one of his stories enumerating an all-but-endless list of Jewish woes and then concluding with high irony: "But for that we are reckoned the chosen people, the wonder and envy of the world." And in the early years of the twentieth century, almost every significant secular Jewish movement, from the nationalists on the right to the socialists on the left, and including the many strands of Zionism, shared a goal of wanting to make Jewish life "normal," that is, put an end to that state of wandering and exile which they regarded as "abnormal"—though you might suppose that an "abnormality" existing since the fall of the Second Temple could itself come to be seen as a norm.

What that state of "abnormality" was I can squeeze into a ruthless phrase: it consists of having been a pariah people, regarded by the dominant religious power of the West,

Christianity, as a stubborn denier of God's will and therefore meriting persecution. This condition has persisted through extraordinary changes of historical circumstances. And if today, in America, that sense of "abnormality" has waned, its residual power is still enough to make Jews feel insecure. They are endowed—this is virtually intrinsic to being a Jew—with a haunting historical consciousness. Indeed, the central myth of Jewish life can be regarded as *the experience of memory,* a shared burden or obligation to remember the lashes and fires of the past.

Precisely this consciousness controls or at least colors the East European migration to the United States. It helps to make that migration different from all other migrations.

Some years ago, in an essay I wrote for the catalogue of an exhibit organized by the Jewish Museum of New York, I suggested a little fancifully that the migration of the East European Jews resembled a collective utopian experiment. There had, after all, been systematic discussions among the East European Jews on whether they should migrate to America, with the rabbinical authorities usually saying no, since salvation could come only from on high, and the secularist Jews usually saying yes, since the only salvation they could foresee was the one they forged for themselves. For suggesting that the migration of the East European Jews to America resembled a collective utopian experiment, I was amiably rebuked by Prof. Robert Alter, who wrote that most of the immigrants had barely been literate, they had come here for personal reasons, to escape the Tsar's army or in search of bread, and it was grandiose to speak of these simple people as coming to America in behalf of a shared, indeed, an exalted Jewish end. Well, I accepted my chastisement . . . but I was not convinced.

For what I have come to believe in the course of writing *World of Our Fathers* is that the distinction between collective enterprise and personal goals was not, for the Jews, nearly so clear or precise as we may suppose. I have become convinced that when your barely literate Jew, with his few scraps of Hebrew and his kitchen Yiddish, ran away from pogroms to sweat and sometimes starve in New York and Chicago slums, he was indeed thinking of himself—but he was thinking of himself *as a Jew,* which is different from simply thinking about himself. It was characteristic of Jewish life that a sense of collective fate should become implanted in almost every Jew's personal experience, no matter how ignorant he might be or how commonplace that experience. One could not grow up a Jew, at least until the last few decades in America, without having some sense of occupying a distinctive place in the scheme of things.

In the memoirs of Abraham Cahan, the Yiddish writer and editor, I found a confirming passage:

> Each new wanderer, ruined by a pogrom or seeking to improve his lot or caught up in the excitement of the exodus, thought he was trying to better his own condition only. . . . But soon every emigrating Jew moving westward realized he was involved in something more than a personal expedition. Every Jew . . . came to feel he was part of an historical event in the life of the Jewish people. Ordinary Jews became as idealistic and enthusiastic as intellectuals. Even Jewish workers and small tradesmen who had managed fairly well [in the old country] sold their belongings and joined . . . the move westward to start a new Jewish life. They did so with religious fervor and often with inspiring self-sacrifice.

Cahan, I believe, is entirely right. Jewish intellectuals like Dubnow and Zhitlovsky spun their theories; Jewish workers sang, *vos mir zenen zenen mir, aber iden zenen mir,* "whatever we may be we may be, but Jews are what we are." Theory and folk sentiment came together.

I cannot say that this sense of a special, even unique history was a direct *cause* of the migration of the East European Jews and, somewhat later, their entry into the culture of America. Let me just say that it was a major condition. . . . It made the Jews self-conscious, it made them ambitious, it made them wary, it made them eager, and it also made them wonder whether those goods of the alien world they were so eager to conquer were worth conquering. In short, it enabled them to go. Once in America, the immigrant Jew would want to adapt to its ways, but he would also want to keep some portion, some saving fragment, of his identity as a Jew.

The sociologist W. I. Thomas has remarked, in a brilliant phrase, that the process of Americanization was devoted to "the destruction of memories" among the immigrants. Now, with peasants from the Balkans or even farmers from Scandinavia, this may not have been too difficult a task, since some of these people had already been excluded from the cultures of their home countries. But the Jews, though already subject by the late nineteenth century to the shocks of the European Enlightenment and no longer the religiously unified people they had been for centuries past, still wanted, in their deepest persuasions, to resist that "destruction of memories." An Italian or a Pole might submit to it and retain his religion, even a fair portion of his received customs. But a Jew who submitted to the "destruction of memories" ceased to be a Jew. This in fact did happen to an undetermined number of Jews in America; but not to the Jews as a whole, or at least not yet.

How then did this peculiar historical self-consciousness affect the encounter of the immigrant Jews with American culture? No other immigrant group was as eager as the Jews to penetrate that culture yet none was as stubborn in hanging on to essential fragments of its tradition. Reaching the American schools and colleges, then becoming writers, artists, and intellectuals, the children of the immigrants brought more of "Jewishness" with them than the Italians, say, brought of "Italianness." Often unwittingly, sometimes in corrupted and vulgar ways, the Jews transported Jewish accents, values, tones, stories, myths, complaints. They carried more cultural baggage than other immigrant groups, simply because they had been less able to store it back home. And because the immigrant generations created here a rich Yiddish culture, partly drawn from the old country but partly improvised in response to new conditions, the Jews—that is, the children of the immigrants—who became our writers, actors, poets, and artists brought with them not just an awareness of historical distinctiveness—at the very least that meant, *we are not Christians and we know it*—but also a rich hoard of cultural materials: a separate language, a distinctive outlook, a wonderful heritage of folk stories, legends, and jokes.

Now, the irony of all this is that just as the immigrant Jews were, so to say, exporting elements of their culture to America, they were rapidly losing it themselves. Perhaps the loss was a precondition for the export. In any case, the children of the East European immigrants, those children who would grow up to become writers, artists, and critics, steadily lost touch with the sources of the Jewish past. The immigrant experience stamped them forever, but this was already a thinned-out residue of the complex religious culture that had been built up over the centuries by the East European Jews. A process of loss was being enacted here—first, the immigrant culture was estranged from its old-world sources, and second, its children were estranged from the immigrant culture.

All depends on what perspective you take. Look at the problem from the perspective of American culture, and it seems clear the immigrant Jews contributed heavily. Look at it from the perspective of Jewish life, and it seems clear that the immigrant Jews lost heavily.

Let me put the matter in more concrete terms. The Jews were different from all other ethnic groups in America in that they brought with them their intellectuals. By and large, the others did not. The Jews did not bring them all at once: in the first great wave of immigration, during the 1880s and 1890s, the Jews who came over tended to be ill-lettered, the social flotsam and jetsam of the *shtetl,* the adventurers and adventurous. But after the turn of the century, when, for example, the major Yiddish writer Abraham Reisen comes to America and, a few years later, the gifted poets who call themselves *Di Yunge* also come, there occurs a gradual reunification between the Yiddish-speaking intelligentsia, both religious and secular, and the masses of Yiddish-speaking immigrant workers. Out of this reunification come the golden decades of Yiddish literature and theatre in America.

This point about the intellectuals can hardly be overstated. An Italian professor of art in Florence or history in Milan seldom had any reason to come here; those who came were the dispossessed, the landless peasants of the South, who barely had any contact with Italian high culture in the first place. But among the East European Jews there were hardly any professors—the Tsar had made sure of that. The Yiddish-speaking intelligentsia consisted of journalists, teachers, party spokesmen, and plain *luftmenshen* who had no more reason to remain in Eastern Europe than the Jewish masses did. So they came here also, often working in the same shops as the ordinary people and living next door in the same tenements. This meant that immigrant Jewish life was to be remarkably enriched. The new freedom of America enabled the Yiddish intelligentsia to express, to "live out," the ideologies and visions it had accumulated in Eastern Europe. It enabled the Yiddish intelligentsia to fulfill itself in the arts, with such poets as Mani Leib, Leivick, and Moishe Leib Halpern. So those among the next generation, children of the slums, who were ambitious to become novelists or artists or playwrights, came not from a deprived immigrant milieu cut off from its old-world cultural sources; they came from a thriving and feverishly brilliant immigrant milieu which had kept its culture, indeed, had brought it to flowering.

But still more. The Yiddish culture the immigrant Jews brought over—that unstable, idealistic mixture of religious memory and custom, newfound secular notions, radical theories, etc.—was itself in a state of extreme ferment, what might be called creative decomposition. A boy or girl growing up on the East Side didn't, as a rule, receive a fixed or rigid heritage; he or she was not often subject to the kind of strict Orthodox upbringing that Isaac Bashevis Singer has described in the memoirs of his youth; here everything was in flux, open to debate, so that such youngsters encountered a touch of rabbinic Orthodoxy, a smattering of socialist ideology, a smidgin of Yiddish culture, all mixed up into a stew of excitement. Cultures sometimes reach their peaks of creativity just when they are starting to come apart. The talmudic quickness of debate, the ferocious intensity of belief, the preference for openly expressed feeling over repressive gentility—all these strains of Jewish life would be carried over into American culture, sometimes elevated, sometimes misshapen.

One concrete sign of this was a quite extraordinary, perhaps even appalling, tendency toward verbalism. What had Jews done over the centuries in their helplessness? They had thought and written, but above all, they had talked. You argued with God, whether or not He listened; you whispered to your neighbor in the House of Study; you talked to the old commentators upon sacred texts as if they were still alive and could answer back. The word became the great Jewish defense against the alien world, just as it was also the great Jewish illusion. The word became the Jewish mode of magic, so that those of us who came later would literally shower the country with words. About the writers this is obvious. But look at your Jewish taxi-cab driver: what is he but a crude and rudimentary version of the word-obsessed intellectual? *M'redt*—one talks. We talked our way into the gentile world.

II

What then, we may now ask, did the Jews contribute to American culture? The simplest but fundamental answer is: *they contributed Europe, they brought the old world back to a country which had fled from it.*

American culture had taken pride in its distinctiveness, had made of its physical and spiritual distance from Europe the claim to a special destiny. It had seen the new world as a paradise giving humanity a second chance, and sometimes, in consequence, had made of its provincialism a badge of pride. To this new world there now came a people that also claimed a special destiny, but one deriving from ancient times. The Jews brought a rich sense of the past to a nation that had found virtue in denying the past, and they brought a persuasion that the life of mankind was unified, to a nation that had seen itself as exempt from the common burdens of mankind.

Now all this may seen an odd thing to say about immigrants jabbering in Yiddish, locked into the slums of the East Side of New York or the West Side of Chicago, immigrants who themselves barely knew anything about the range and variety of Western, that is, European culture. Yet I think that what I am suggesting here is the truth. The early American settlers, especially the New England Puritans, had cultivated a sense of the past; but a main thrust of American cultural history—through the Emersonians, through Twain's contempt for Europe, through the popular belief, virtually a national myth, that America would be spared the blood and torment of Europe—had been to weaken, deny, shake off the sense of the past.

For the Jews, such an outlook was simply impossible. Insofar as they retained Jewish consciousness, they lived in proximity with the events of the Bible; for the more religious Jews there was barely any sense of historical time at all, there was only the biblical yesterday and the exile of today.

The Jews came with a rich supply of stories, legends, myths: stories about *kiddush hashem,* sanctification of the name, enacted by endless generations of martyrs; stories about contests in the medieval era between Catholic hierarchs and cautious rabbis, in which the latter, though obviously more clever, allowed themselves to be bested in order to avoid bloodshed; stories about Jewish children of twelve or thirteen being drafted into the Tsar's armies for twenty-five years; stories about Hasidic sages who yoked joy and wisdom into a fresh union; stories about later Jews, Socialists or Zionists, who no longer bowed under the whip of oppressors but fought back with their fists.

The Jews brought legends, songs, jokes. Legends about Hershel Ostropolier, the ne'er-do-well scamp; jokes about Chelm, the town of fools that served to mock the excessive rationality of the Jewish mind; songs about matchmakers, rabbis, loving mothers, raisins and almonds, the charms of the accursed old country. The resonance of these elements of folk culture went far and deep. I take as an example not some high-flown piece of poetry or rhetoric but a little folk story, the merest anecdote, about Chelm, the town into which the Jews wisely packed their foolishness:

> They asked a Jew of Chelm: "What would you do if you found a million rubles in the marketplace and knew who had lost them? Would you resist the temptation and return the money?"
>
> The Jew of Chelm answered, quick as a flash: "If I knew the money was Rothschild's I'm afraid I couldn't resist the temptation and would not return it. But if I knew the million rubles belonged to the poor *shammes* [sexton] of the old synagogue, I'd return it to the last penny."

Part of what it meant to be a would-be American Jewish writer, or even painter, was that a fragile anecdote like this one offered a rich store of implications: it meant being able to see a whole cultural style, indeed, a whole cultural fate, in this one little story; and it meant being obliged to respond to it through the eyes of one's father, even if one were devoting one's deepest energies to battle against him.

Very quickly, the process of cultural migration began. The tunes of Yiddish folksongs leapt, sometimes in debased form, into American theatre and vaudeville; the comic routines of the *badkhn,* or marriage entertainer, found an unexpected home on the stage in eastern and midwestern cities; the multiple ironies of the Jewish joke were wrenched, sometimes with backs broken, into American popular culture.

But it was not only their own folk culture—which, I need hardly remind you, still contained a major component of religious belief and feeling—that the immigrant Jews brought to America. It was also a version of Russian culture, the nineteenth-century humanist Russian culture which some East European Jews had so eagerly appropriated. The more literate among the immigrant Jews felt that together with the old bedclothes, pots, and pans they had brought across the ocean, they had also kept a special claim on the moral idealism of the great Russian writers. Tolstoy, Turgenev, Chekhov—though not the sensationalist and anti-Semite Dostoevsky—were very close to them.

In many complex ways, then, the Jews brought a *new past* to America. By now almost everyone knows those enchanting if eerie memoirs of Jewish peddlers down south who would be approached by fundamentalist whites or pious blacks as if they, the peddlers, had just stepped out of the Old Testament and could bring news of Abraham and Isaac. Up north, the impact was greater still. For the first time, a significant number of Americans had to bear the impact of a non-Christian culture. Some accepted this with generosity, others as if they were being mauled by agents of Satan. Henry Adams snarled at the thought of "four-hundred-and-fifty thousand Jews now doing Kosher in New York alone," but William Dean Howells took the trouble to visit the immigrant streets and admire "the splendid types of that old Hebrew world which had the sense if not the knowledge of God when all the rest of us lay sunk in heathen darkness."

What such serious writers said in trying to cope with the influx of strange materials from an alien culture, the popular entertainers matched or mimicked in rougher terms. The "Jew comic" entered upon the American stage, sometimes done by gentiles, sometimes by Jews. Frank Bush said, "Oh my name is Solomon Moses, I'm a bully sheeny man," and "I keep a clothing store 'way down on Baxter Street / Where you can get your clothing now I sell so awful cheap." Weber and Fields brought dialect jokes to the American stage, David Belasco heavy melodramas with heavy Jewish accents and noses. Joe Welch introduced the *shlemiehl* to gentile Americans, who found him a brother under the skin.

Helping American culture reconnect with the past soon meant enabling America to connect for the first time with the modernist culture of twentieth-century Europe. The immigrants brought to both tasks a rich, sometimes overrich, infusion of energy. Among the "common" unlearned Jews who came to America, there was a sense of opportunities opened, long-suppressed inclinations now free to be released. The streets were crucial. Forming each day a great fair of Jewish life, the immigrant streets became a training-ground for Jewish actors, comics, singers. Ill-lettered Jews, long held in check by the caste system of the old country and its repressive moralism, now discovered their turn had come. Full of sap, excited by the sheer volume of street noise, letting loose sexual curiosities beyond the reach of Jewish shame, the children of the streets erupted with an outburst of vulgarity. It was a vulgarity in both senses: as the urgent, juicy thrust of desire, intent upon seizing life by the throat, and as the cheap, corner-of-the-mouth retailing of Yiddish obscenities.

A shrewd critic of the 1920s, Gilbert Seldes, remarked on the "daemonic" abandon of the Jewish entertainers, their heat and fury; he called them "possessed." People like Al Jolson, Fanny Brice, George Jessel, Sophie Tucker, wrote Seldes, "give something to America which America lacks and loves—[they] are out of the dominant class. Possibly this accounts for their fine carelessness about our superstitions of politeness and gentility . . . and their contempt for artificial notions of propriety."

It helps, at this point, to see the culture of the East European Jews as resembling a tightly coiled spring, held in for centuries by external pressures, straining always to break loose, and now suddenly, in America, uncoiling with a joy of surprise. What was true for the popular entertainers was equally true for the serious painters who began to appear in the immigrant Jewish quarters at about the turn of the century. These painters came from poor working-class homes. There was little tradition regarding canvas, easel, and paint among East European Jews. For a Jewish boy somehow yielding himself to this strange world of art, it was necessary to make an enormous leap, straight across the centuries, into kinds of knowledge and experience his own culture could not give him. The popular entertainers released energies and traditions they barely knew were available to them; the painters and sculptors hurriedly appropriated energies and traditions they were just starting to encounter. Yet, in both cases, they helped bring Europe to America.

Taking lessons from the fine but essentially minor artists of New York in the early 1900s, from men like Robert Henri and John Sloan, the Jewish apprentice artists soon recognized—just because they themselves had so little of an artistic tradition behind them, just because they carried so little esthetic baggage—that they had to make a bold leap across conventional American art, the very art they had gotten to know only yesterday and still knew very imperfectly. They went directly to Paris. Young artists like Abraham Walkowitz and Max Weber left behind the narrowness of the immigrant subculture, discarding whatever frail ties they had with American artistic conventions and moving straight to the heart of the new—Paris, the home of modernism. Weber became a friend of Matisse, Picasso, and Vlaminck; Walkowitz immersed himself in the work of Cézanne. Perhaps because they had started from "nowhere," that is, from the wildly pulsing heart of immigrant desire, some of these American Jewish painters could speed past the earnest limits of American art much more readily than their native contemporaries. So it was that boys from the East

Side played a crucial role in bringing modernist art to America.

To a lesser extent, the same was true in literature. Literary modernism came to the United States only after the First World War and, by and large, Jewish writers had little to do with it. The major American modernists in literature—Hemingway, Stevens, Crane, Williams, Fitzgerald, Faulkner—had come into relation with the great European masters during and shortly after the war, and they had managed on their own to fuse the innovations of Joyce and Proust, Eliot and Yeats with the traditions of Emerson, Whitman, and Melville. The immigrant Jewish writers came onto the scene only later, during the thirties and afterward, and their role in the triumph of literary modernism was not so much as poets and novelists but as critics. The critics around *Partisan Review*—figures like Meyer Schapiro, Lionel Trilling, Philip Rahv, Harold Rosenberg—made their mark through an effort to bring together an anti-Stalinist radicalism in politics with a combative defense of cultural modernism and an equally fierce assault on middlebrow philistinism. One of the great contributions of this group of writers, most of them sons of immigrant Jews, was to help complete the *internationalization* of American culture. They helped make Kafka known among us; they helped bring pre-Stalinist Russian literature of the twentieth century, in all its brilliance, to America; they created a new kind of essay—sharp, polemical, brittle, free-swinging, full of bravado, sometimes insolence. If, in twentieth-century literature, the role of the Jewish writers, mostly critics, was a secondary one, it was also important in validating modernism on the American scene.

There is another kind of contribution the immigrant Jews made to American culture. For better or worse, hopelessly, irremediably, Jewish culture was a plebeian culture. The kind of separation between inert masses and aristocratic intelligentsia that characterized so much of European culture was impossible in Jewish life. Consider the major Yiddish writers of the early years of this century: Leivick, Mani Leib, Moishe Leib Halpern. All, at one time or another, were workers: a laundry man, a house painter, a pants presser. These were men of high literary achievement, but they lived in the same tenements, they worked in the same shops, they went for a bit of air to the same parks, as did the masses of immigrant garment workers.

More than social circumstances can be observed here. The world outlook of the Jews, no matter through which political opinion it revealed itself, insisted upon the need to educate, to elevate the consciousness of, the *folksmassn*. If the Haskalah intellectuals, Hebrew-speaking enlighteners of the nineteenth century, wanted to reach those whom they proposed to enlighten, they had first to master the Yiddish language. In turn, the Yiddish writers looked toward those American writers, like Whitman and Melville, whom they felt to be plebeian in origin and outlook, writers with whom they could readily identify.

So it was that one contribution of the immigrant Jews to American writing was a certain roughening of voice, a street skepticism, a street poetry. The gentility against which writers like Dreiser had rebelled was quite beyond the reach of those of us who clawed and scratched our way out of the immigrant quarters. It simply made us laugh. The immigrant Jewish writers, ranging from Henry Roth to Saul Bellow, brought a bracing street realism to American fiction—sometimes a good healthy dose of the better kind of vulgarity, full of the juices and delights of common life, and sometimes an unhappy quotient of the kind of vulgarity that would flourish in the Borsht Belt and come to rest in Hollywood and Broadway.

But the most important element of feeling or sensibility that the immigrant Jews brought to American culture is, by definition, the hardest to specify. Self-consciously or by mere routine, many of the American Jewish writers started with the assumption that there remains a body of inherited traditions, values, and attitudes that we call "Jewishness." Jewish belief and custom may have become attenuated, and the writers themselves only feebly connected with these; yet the persuasion remains that "we" (whoever that "we" might be) must live with a sense of differentness and perhaps even draw some sustenance from it. That sense of differentness may, at its best, constitute a rich moral perspective upon the ways of the outer world: for which serious man or woman wants entirely to feel at home with this world? And even at its least, it comes to occasional encroachments of memory, bouts of sentiment regarding food, holiday, customs.

The immigrant Jews introduced a new voice into American culture: ironic, complex, querulous, haunted: a voice, perhaps, of *menshlichkeit.* How hard it is to describe this voice, how certain many of us are that we can recognize it!

> *Saul Bellow:* In the stories of the Jewish tradition the world, and even the universe, have a human meaning. [In Jewish stories] laughter and trembling are so curiously intermingled that it is not easy to determine the relations of the two. At times the laughter seems simply to restore the equilibrium of sanity; at times the figures of the story . . . appear to invite or encourage trembling with the secret aim of overcoming it by means of laughter.

> *Philip Rahv:* A "Jewish" trait in Bernard Malamud's work is his feeling for human suffering on the one hand and for a life of value, order and dignity on the other. Thus he is one of the very few contemporary writers who seems to have escaped the clutch of historical circumstance that has turned nihilism into so powerful a temptation.

In one respect, at least, the tradition—not of classical Judaism but of immigrant Jewish culture—still operates strongly in the work of American Jewish writers. To feel at some distance from society; to assume, almost as a birthright, a critical stance toward received dogmas; to recognize oneself as not quite at home in the world—these assumptions continue to inform the work of a good many American Jewish writers. Nay-sayers, shoulder-shruggers, eyebrow-raisers, American Jewish writers keep some portion of their parents' and grandparents' irony, skepticism, sometime rebelliousness. For how much longer? Who knows?

It would be a large mistake to suppose that the movement from immigrant Jewish to American culture was always smooth and fruitful. The truth is that there was a good deal of waste: talents unrecognized or declining into obscurity in the immigrant neighborhoods, features of Jewish experience and culture that never were to be absorbed into American life and soon came to be discarded. The greatest waste took the form of neglect, shared about equally by the host American culture and the immigrant Jews. I refer to the fate that befell Yiddish literature and theatre in this country. What extraordinary talents, what brilliant achievements, flared up in the few decades during which *Yiddishkeit* flourished in this country—and how little of it has survived either in the literary consciousness of America or in the memories of the Jews themselves. That the dominant gentile culture should have been indifferent to the special genius of the Yiddish-speaking immigrants is perhaps to be expected; that the Jews themselves should have turned their backs on their own achievements is cause for shame.

In the end, America made a far deeper impact on the immigrant Jews than they did on America. It was inevitable: that is the price America exacts for its blessings. Historically, the migration of the East European Jews can be seen as one step in a long process of the modernizing of Jewish life, a gradual acceptance of the Enlightenment, the West, modern history and culture. What began timidly when the first Haskalah writers suggested there might be sources of knowledge and wisdom other than the traditional pietistic ones, ended with American Jewish writers, artists, and professors in a rush for universality. And as they came here, the immigrant Jews discovered that there was more in the world than their grandfathers had dreamt of, more than the rabbis had denounced, more, even, than the socialists and Zionists had invoked. The world was deeply *interesting;* it was a greatly tempting place. The world had rich traditions, extraordinary achievements, that could not simply be dismissed as "goyish" diversions and corruptions, though it had plenty of those too.

There were the riches of the world, its sensuous and sensual attractions, its beauties created through the arts of man, created by that very culture which the Jews had been taught to regard with suspicion, contempt, and fear. There were the glories of architecture; there were the vast accumulations of paintings devoted to the pleasures of the eye; there were the endless achievements of Western culture, from literature to science. There was a world to enter, to conquer. How brilliantly the Jews made this entry is one of the most remarkable facts of modern history. Whether they would remain Jews . . . that is still a question.

So we come back to the mystery with which we began: the mystery of Jewish distinctiveness. What was it that made the Jews so ready to break into Western culture, so receptive to its charms and delusions, its glories and its scandals? We know some portion of the answer—we know that the dialectical training of talmudic study readied young Jews for the logical acrobatics of modern thought, that the messianic hungers streaking East European Jewish life readied them for the heady strivings of modern ideology, that precisely the costly disciplines of suppression to which they had subjected themselves made them eager for breakthrough, distinction, sometimes even pleasure. Yet something of a mystery remains, some core of restlessness, eagerness, perhaps even madness, some thread of difference which has made us what we are and for which we have paid with oceans of blood.

ELI GINZBERG

Jews in the American Economy: The Dynamics of Opportunity

When I was first invited to prepare this paper under the auspices of the American Jewish Committee, it was suggested that I deal with the role American Jews have played in the development of business and labor in the United States. I did not need much time to reflect on the fact that given their small numbers, and the fact that most of them were descendants of immigrants who arrived on these shores less than a century ago, their role was considerable. I began to match names with fields of endeavor. In retailing, Strauss, Rosenwald, Lazarus came quickly to the fore. In investment banking, Schiff, Seligman, Andre Meyer, Gustave Levy; in mining, Guggenheim, Lewisohn, Hochschild; in motion pictures, Loew, Fox, Zukor; in communications, Ochs, Sarnoff, Paley. The ease with which these major contributors could be identified pointed to the probability of doubling and quadrupling their number.

And much the same was true for the role of Jews in the American labor movement: among the former leadership the names of Gompers, Hillman, Dubinsky came readily to the fore, followed by Finley, Wurf, Shanker among the current leadership.

But when I thought further about my proposed assignment, I became restive to the point of making a counter-suggestion. I was unable, on quick reflection, to see what was particularly "Jewish" about the contribution of these and other leaders. What they brought to their work and the mainsprings of their success did not seem to be deeply rooted in Jewish thought, ethics, experience.

With one or two exceptions they were Jews primarily in terms of family origin and affiliation but not in terms of deep knowledge and special commitment.

The more I considered the matter, the more it appeared to me that the preferred approach was to turn the subject around and to broaden the angle of inquiry from the few to the many. Accordingly I chose the present theme, which, in colloquial terms, is how did it happen that the American economy did so well for the Jews.

Before we focus on the American economy and the Jews, let me quickly establish that other ethnic groups as well as the Jews fared well in the United States, and that belatedly and slowly, this is turning out to be the case even for the blacks. While the first three centuries of black experience in this country left a great deal to be desired—I am reminded of Myrdal's finding in the early 1940s that upward mobility for blacks was to escape from sharecropper status on a southern farm to a WPA job in the North—since 1940 the rate of progress has been as fast, if not faster, than that for any other group in our history. Admittedly a disproportionate number of blacks remain in the lower occupational groupings at or close to the poverty level. But the point worth making in the present context is the sizable proportion that have moved into the middle class since the end of World War II.

But our concern is with the Jews, not the blacks. The critical question is how it happened that within four to five generations, the descendants of largely impoverished immigrants from Eastern Europe, without knowledge of English or the ways of the West, were able to create the largest, most affluent, and secure community in the recorded history of the Jewish people. The tale that I will seek to reconstruct would be more convincing if my data base were broader and deeper. In point of fact it is unbelievably shallow. I am reminded of an exchange between Henrietta Szold and my father (Professor Louis Ginzberg) in 1905, when Miss Szold was editing the *American Jewish Year Book* and complained about the paucity of reliable data. My father's comment was that he knew more about the Jews of Sura and Pumbedita than he did about those in New York City. If it is not out of place for a speaker to lobby, I would urge the leadership of the American

Jewish Committee to take urgent and strong action to fill the information gap about the characteristics of American Jews, their major institutions, and their patterns of life. It will take, at best, considerable time to accumulate the building blocks and erect a sound structure of facts and figures.

I would have had literally no tale to tell, except one made out of whole cloth, were it not for the fact that some years ago, when Louis Finkelstein was preparing his major work on *The Jews,* he sought my help in getting a chapter prepared on the economic history of the Jews. I quickly disabused him of the idea that I was his man, but I did put him on the track of Professor Simon Kuznets, whom Finkelstein fortunately was able to persuade to take on the assignment. Since that time Kuznets has made two further contributions, and it was his three pieces that provided me with a jumping-off place for today's presentation. I might add that Kuznets, Nobel Prize winner in economics, was himself a relatively late immigrant from Eastern Europe to these shores.

With these not unimportant introductory remarks back of us, let me proceed directly to my analysis. To simplify matters I will divide it into four periods: from 1880 to World War I; World War I to World War II; World War II to 1976; and a look ahead until the end of this century.

There is a reason for my picking 1880 as my point of departure. In that year the Jewish population in the United States numbered 250,000. Today it stands at just under six million. Kuznets has estimated that eight out of ten Jews in the United States are of East European origin. The large inflow started in the eighties and continued right up to World War I. These thirty to thirty-five years can be looked upon as the era of "Getting Established." What happened was, first, that the Jews who came intended to stay. What is more, most of them did remain—only one in fourteen left. This is a sharp contrast with other immigrants, about one in three of whom sooner or later returned to their country of origin. Many Southern Europeans, especially Italians, came with the idea of working hard for some years, saving their money, and returning home to set up in business. The East European Jews sank their roots in their country of adoption. They saw their future, and more importantly their children's future, in the United States.

They came to stay in a country which had jobs for them, not always good jobs, but jobs. There were exceptions, of course—the major depression in the mid-nineties; recurrent seasonal unemployment in the clothing industry, where so many Jews had obtained employment; and periodic strikes which, when they lasted for any length of time, brought severe hardships to the workers and their families.

The next point can be most readily illuminated by reference to a term popular in economic development literature—the *demonstration effect,* which refers to the fact that change is facilitated when people have concrete examples that they can follow. The success of many Spanish and German Jews encouraged the new immigrants to think that with work and luck they too could make it in the United States. The demonstration effect helped them to realize that the potential for Jews was much greater in the United States than in Eastern Europe.

Certain demographic, family, and personal characteristics also contributed to speeding the assimilation of the newly arrived masses of East European Jewry. As Kuznets has uncovered, they had a smaller than average number of children than their neighbors in the Old World, and this continued to be true after they arrived in the New World. With fewer children to support, they could make their limited family resources stretch further. Moreover, the Jewish family was not only intensely child-centered but had a strong sense of family obligation; successful relatives were willing to help the younger generation of both sexes stay in school or acquire a skill.

The final characteristic of this period of getting established relates to the fact that the Jews settled in large urban centers which offered better than average public educational opportunities. There is a lot of nonsense bruited about concerning how smart the Jews are. There is something to this, but not nearly as much as most people believe. I have spent the last sixty years of my life in the public and private schools of New York City as student and teacher. I attended and graduated in 1927 from what was then the largest boy's high school in the United States. The performance record of the Jews was somewhat better than for other groups but not conspicuously so. And that is also my impression after four decades of teaching at Columbia.

The second stage, "Moving Up," divides into two distinct periods—from 1915 to 1929, followed by the depression years up to 1940. What happened? First, the children of blue-collar workers did not remain blue-collar workers. The sons of painters, clothing workers, mechanics moved into white-collar occupations. Not all of them by any means, but a high proportion of the total. We forget that even among the third and fourth generation there remains a distinct minority of Jews in blue-collar jobs.

Next, since many Jews came to the United States with some background in trade and commerce, significant numbers found it relatively easy to get started in business and, by working hard and accumulating modest savings, to speculate in real estate and in stocks during the prosperous 1920s, when everything was booming.

The extent to which the Jews are overrepresented in business is indicated by the fact that if one looks at a later generation of Jewish youngsters entering college in the 1960s, one finds that businessmen are almost twice as likely to be fathers of the Jewish freshmen than of the non-Jewish entrants (55 vs. 20 percent).

There are a great many differences as well as parallels between Jews and blacks in their processes of integration into the economic mainstream, but among the important differences is the lack of prior experience of blacks in small-scale entrepreneurship. The blacks came out of a subsistence economy; the Jews have been prominent among the world's traders for a long time.

To return to our major theme, the depression wiped out many Jews: some became despondent to the point of suicide. Were it not for the fact that I once wrote a book on the depression—*The Illusion of Economic Stability* (Harper, 1939)—I would probably not have remembered that manufacturing wages in North Carolina dropped to five cents an hour, day help was obtainable on the Concourse in the Bronx for fifty cents for a ten-hour day and meals; and fertile farm land in Iowa sold for twenty-five dollars an acre.

The depression years also help to illuminate some of the important relations between education and occupational mobility. A considerably higher than average number of Jewish youth were college graduates, and when the private job market went into rapid decline, many succeeded in entering public employment as schoolteachers, local and state civil servants, and as federal employees after Roosevelt went to Washington. I received my Ph.D. in economics at Columbia in the spring of 1933, and shortly thereafter I had job offers from Washington paying four thousand dollars, which at the time was a splendid opening salary. In fact, anyone who took his doctorate in economics from that date to this has had the good fortune to be in a constantly expanding field.

But employment dragged badly throughout the thirties. The country never got below 10 percent unemployment throughout the entire decade. Many young Jews prolonged their stay at the university and even pursued training in physics, engineering, and mathematics, fields they had eschewed earlier. This turned out to be a lucky move for Jews, since when the war economy got under way in 1940–41, there was a high demand for people trained in the hard sciences.

This brings me to my third period, "Making It"—from World War II to 1976. During these three and a half decades, the American economy has escaped a serious depression. We have had recurrent recessions, and we are still emerging from the most severe of all the post–World War II setbacks. But let's face it: we have escaped any major period of economic hardship. As a result, it was a propitious time for people to begin to make it, and many Jews did just that.

Secondly, favorable demographic trends assisted the upward mobility of Jews further. A brief story involving AJC staff will help to make the point. In the late forties or early fifties, one of the AJC staff (Bloomgarden) came up to talk to me at Columbia about discrimination against Jewish applicants seeking admission to medical school. He knew of my ongoing research work in the medical field and was therefore shocked when I told him that the problem had largely disappeared. Any good Jewish student could gain admission. The explanation lay in the shrinkage of the total pool. The much reduced birth rates of the depression years were being reflected in a much reduced number of applicants.

Since Bloomgarden was a man in search of a subject, I suggested he explore anti-Semitism in the executive suite, a suggestion based upon my perceptions as a consultant to one of the nation's largest chemical companies, which I knew had no Jews in upper management. The democratization resulting from the war, reinforced by demographic trends and rapid economic growth, helped to reduce religious discrimination. It was reported that only after the war did the great Mellon empire, headquartered in Pittsburgh, allow Catholics into senior management. All non-Protestants were benefited, and among these the Jews were well positioned to move into fields and levels formerly closed to them.

The postwar era saw a rapid expansion and absorption of scientific, professional, and technical manpower. Large governmental contracts for R&D, the explosive growth of the university system, and the expansion of science-based industry, such as computers, set the stage. The high proportion of Jews attending college created a jumping-off base for them to move rapidly into these expanding areas. By 1970 the figures reveal that with one out of six in the nation's labor force classified as belonging to this highest occupational category, the proportion of Jews is about one out of three, or close to double the national average.

Finally, note must be taken of the contribution that many wives made to improving the income of their family. American Jews, following the national pattern, encouraged their daughters to seek a higher education, and as the barriers against working married women were lowered, increasing numbers pursued careers in teaching, social work, and business.

Five strands run through this story from 1880 to 1976. Firstly, Jews had the good fortune to be in the right place at the right time. They came to New York, and those who moved on settled in other large East Coast and Middle West cities—Boston, Philadelphia, Baltimore, Chicago—at a time when these large cities were in their heyday. In 1930 Jews accounted for one out of every three persons in New York City.

By contrast, consider the blacks. In addition to being the victims of racism, they had the misfortune to be locked up in the South, which after 1865 was the wrong place to be since there was a shortage of jobs even for whites.

Jews had a second advantage due to the value they placed upon education, including higher education, which, as we have seen, yielded large rewards, especially after 1940. In fact the breakthrough of Jews into the executive suite is closely linked to their antecedent breakthrough into the higher technical ranks of large corporations.

Thirdly, the shift of the economy from agriculture and manufacturing to services was a positive development as far as the Jews were concerned. They had acquired, as noted earlier, considerable experience in trade and commerce, which stood them in good stead as these fields expanded rapidly.

Fourthly, the lowering of the barriers against religious minorities proved a major boon. Let me call attention to what happened in the academic world, which I know best. In my undergraduate days at Columbia in the latter twenties, the number of Jews on the faculty could have been counted on one hand. My class had a 10 percent quota for Jewish students, not for New York City but for the entire country. The Graduate School of Business at Columbia, established in 1916, had no tenured Jewish professor until I achieved that rank at the end of World War II—thirty years until the first appointment! Today an informed count suggests that about half of the tenured faculty is Jewish.

To supplement the above: a few years ago the deans of the major law schools on the East Coast—Harvard, Yale, Columbia—were Jewish. Jews have been elected president of such Ivy League institutions as Dartmouth, Brown, Pennsylvania. And Professor Lipset's analysis in the early seventies revealed that Jews accounted for over 20 percent of all faculty members at elite institutions of higher education. What these selected data suggest is a major revolution within the last quarter century.

In sharp contrast, I recall warning the trustees of the National Urban League, in 1952, that with discriminatory barriers being lowered in the labor market, it was essential for more blacks to seek higher education and professional training if they wanted to take advantage of the new job situation.

The fifth and final strand that should be identified as contributing to the rapid economic gains of the Jews relates to the significant growth in the not-for-profit sector, that is, in government and nonprofit employment. A recent article of mine on "The Pluralistic Economy" (*Scientific American,* December 1976) estimates that one out of every three, or possibly as many as two out of every five, jobs are in this sector. And it has been relatively easier for minorities—Jews, blacks, women—to obtain jobs and pursue careers in the public than the private arena, especially since the 1930s.

Now for a brief look ahead. I suggested earlier and now repeat that it would be a serious error to see American Jews as a wholly distinctive group with experiences that have no counterpart among other ethnic and racial groups. That would be as false a postulate as the alternative, which argues, for instance, that there is nothing distinctive about the way in which Jews climbed up the job and income ladder. Among the many interesting phenomena that have been little studied is the ethnic replacement cycle. I am struck with the increasing replacement in New York City of Jews by Italians in dentistry as the Jews moved in larger numbers into medicine. And the AJC has recently published an account of the replacement of Jews by blacks in the Philadelphia school system. But we have all too few such studies.

On a related front, there has been an approximately threefold increase in the percentage of blacks admitted to medical schools, from 2 to 6 percent of the entry class. Unless the Supreme Court rules the public interest does not justify the use of special criteria for training and employment, those at the end of the queue are likely to continue to receive some special consideration, which will have a slightly adverse effect on those further front in the queue.

Since the future is always uncertain, let me speculate about the likely decline in the relative incomes of scientists, professionals, and technical personnel, an arena where Jews have done very well till now. In the future the American economy may pay off a little less handsomely for educated manpower now that so many more Americans are becoming educated. It does not follow that every physician at the end of his residency will be able to earn $50,000 and at the end of a decade of practice over $100,000.

Thirdly, I am impressed with the probability that fourth-and fifth-generation Jewish youngsters may be less hungry, less competitive, less inner-directed. The people who try the hardest seldom start at the top. When I think back to the Columbia troubles of 1968, there were almost as many Jewish youngsters working strenuously to unmake American society as there were Jewish youngsters out to make it for themselves.

A fourth clue to the future may be revealed in the new President's cabinet appointments, which include two women, one of whom is black, and one an unaffiliated Jew. Women are over 50 percent of the population, blacks about 11 percent; Jews, with less than 3 percent will command less attention. As we become increasingly sensitized to the claims of other ethnic groups, Jews may recede from their earlier position of prominence.

Another point worth stressing is the shift in the locus of economic expansion from the usual areas of Jewish concentration. Let us consider the following figures. Approximately 60 percent of all the Jews in the United States are on the East Coast, in contrast to less than 20 percent of the total population. The South, with about a third of the nation's population, accounts for only one-sixth of the Jewish population. Only in the West is there an approximate balance: 18 percent of the nation's population, 13 percent of the Jewish population.

To sharpen the focus: Jews account for 0.6 percent of the total population of Texas, 6 percent of New Jersey's population, and 12 percent of New York State's. That means that proportionately there are twenty times more Jews in New York State than in Texas, and we are told that the Northeast is in decline and Texas is still on its way up. Although I wrote a book a few years ago entitled *New York Is Very Much Alive* (McGraw-Hill, 1973), and I still hold to that thesis, I do believe that the Jewish population is poorly distributed to take full advantage of the next cycle of the country's expansion. Jews, both as individuals and as members of a distinctive community, have been adversely affected by the rapid transformation of neighborhoods where they earlier had made large private and communal investments. I will do no more than mention the Bronx and Brooklyn, although similar instances can be found in all the large northern cities with substantial Jewish populations.

The final point relates to the characteristics of some of the new Jewish immigrants and their descendants. Orthodox, frequently ultra-orthodox, they keep themselves at arm's length from the economy and society. They discourage their children from attending college. And they look askance at married women working out of the home. In fact their women, with four, five or six children, couldn't find the time to work for pay if they wanted to. These new immigrants may not require public assistance, but they have positioned themselves in a manner which is likely to keep most of them in the lower range of the income distribution. They do so because they have values more important than "making it."

What does the future look like, then, for American Jews, postulating as I do that the economy will not seriously falter, and that the club of Rome is wrong in its dire predictions of a world of scarcity?

- The relative rate of progress of Jews will be slower, among other reasons because other ethnic and racial groups are likely to move faster.
- The retardation in the rate of growth of Jewish economic well-being may be speeded if a significant proportion of young Jews opt out of the competitive race, as they are likely to do.
- Jews are poorly located when it comes to the spatial aspects of future economic development.
- But all of the foregoing factors added together are still likely to leave Jews at or close to the top of the economic heap as the United States ushers in the twenty-first century.

NAOMI W. COHEN

Responsibilities of Jewish Kinship: Jewish Defense And Philanthropy

America posed a new kind of challenge to the waves of Jewish immigrants who landed on these shores. Subscribing to the ideals of Locke and Jefferson which glorified the individual, the nation never mandated or recognized the legal existence of ethnic or religious groups. Jews, like other immigrants who had experienced prejudice and disabilities in Europe just because they were members of a particular class, responded with more than gratitude. They swore fealty to the American ideology and became the foremost defenders of the idea that individual merit above all determined a man's destiny. Some went further. Intoxicated by the freedom they enjoyed, they eagerly threw off the bonds of Jewish community control under which they had lived in the Old World and chose the path of total assimilation into the American mainstream.

But while the United States, in theory at least, afforded the Jew the option of discarding all Jewish associations, most Jews could not purposefully cut themselves off from their roots. Moreover, their needs as Jews necessitated some form of group organization. Religious law and practices—certainly Jewish burial, which was always paramount in the minds of the new immigrants—could not be carried out by individuals alone. Jewish schools, and the care of the Jewish needy, as long as the government did not provide for them, similarly exceeded the capabilities and resources of individuals. Finally, if Americans, despite the benign neutrality of the federal government and the inclinations of the Jews themselves, persisted in defining Jews as a separate group or subjected its members to any form of discrimination, who was there to defend the vast aggregate of Jewish individuals? Thus, desire to hold on to Jewish traditions and pride in an ancient heritage merged with the practical realities into a counter-thrust to America's challenge of assimilation.

From colonial times on, those who opted to live both as Jews as well as Americans were forced to find ways of insuring the survival of the group, its religion, and the security of fellow Jews in an individualistic and voluntaristic society. The very first were pioneers in community planning,[1] for they had few guidelines to follow. The closed structure of the pre-modern ghetto, although it served as the model for the colonial synagogues, and even the more advanced Jewish communities of Western Europe had little relevance in nineteenth-century, expanding America, where social lines were fluid and where Jews lived in all states and territories, spoke different languages, and followed different practices. But hardly conscious that they were breaking new ground, American Jews developed a ramified communal structure built of voluntary organizations. And, the multiple associations and projects which they fashioned attested to their basic acceptance of the responsibilities of Jewish kinship.

In the maze of pluralistic endeavors which have characterized the American Jewish communal structure, several common threads emerge. First, since Jews were ever a minority, much of their activity included the element of defense. Defense had a double thrust, to strengthen the group's internal resources, its viability, its "lastingness" and to strengthen its position with respect to the outside majority. Admittedly, defense is a broad rubric; it can be read into areas as diverse as education, religious reform, the struggle for the separation of church and state, and Zionism. Even the project for a Jewish Publication Society, which was originally discussed before the Civil War, aimed for more than the dissemination of Jewish classical or modern writings. In point of fact it was prompted by the hope that the availability of Jewish classics in English to both Jews and non-Jews would serve to refute the charges leveled by the missionaries about Jewish beliefs and would generate Jewish pride in, and Christian respect for, Judaism.[2]

Secondly, whether the voluntary activity was cultural or charitable or social, it had to be American in form. Thus, for example, a nineteenth century Jewish newspaper urged that German Jewish immigrants discard the German language and German customs in their social clubs in order to show their Americanism and their disdain of clannishness.[3] More important, Jewish organizations, like other voluntary associations, learned in the twentieth century (as did the AJC) that they could not survive for any length of time if their organizations did not conform to the *democratic* or American mold.[4]

Thirdly, while voluntary activity reflected age-old Jewish values, Jews labored to show how they could fit the values to modern problems and how those values harmonized with American ideals. For example, the traditional yearning for a restoration to Palestine was the base upon which modern Zionism built, but in the United States, early Zionists likened their movement to the pioneering era of America and compared the Palestinian settlers with the Pilgrims. More recently, Zionists point out how Israel shares the American commitment to world democracy.[5]

In our discussion of certain facts of American Jewish philanthropy—charity, care of the immigrant, and activity on behalf of foreign Jews—we will see how Jewish values were articulated to ring true in American ears and how Jewish defense was a paramount concern of the minority community.

I

Both Jews and non-Jews have given frequent lip-service to the statement "Jews take care of their own." So ingrained has that byword become that many were rudely surprised in recent years to discover that Jews too had their pockets of poverty. Nevertheless, it is true that Jewish charity did not begin in America. It was part of the Jewish heritage which the immigrants brought over with them and which could not be discarded along with their alien garb or alien language. It testified to the almost unconscious acceptance of the Talmudic precepts "All Israel is responsible for one another" and "All those that feel not for the distress of others are not of the Abrahamic seed." Unlike many in Christian America, Jews were not led to philanthropy, in the first instance, by the dream of refashioning the universe or proving the inexorable march of progress or by any evangelical crusade to win souls for their faith.[6] They accepted the need to give to the unfortunate—a duty incumbent upon all Jews irrespective of wealth—as a fact of life.

America reinforced that acceptance, first because Protestantism, at the root of the American ethic, preached similar values[7] and made charity a responsibility of the churches. Secondly, the very first Jews who landed on the shores of New Amsterdam were taught a lesson they never forgot. In 1655 Governor Peter Stuyvesant and the directors of the Dutch West India Company grudgingly allowed Jews to settle in the colony on condition that they care for their needy ones and keep them from becoming public charges.[8] The Jews and their descendants after them renewed their agreement to those terms generation after generation. Failure to comply, they feared, could shut America's gates to future immigrants and might even spark anti-Jewish outbreaks in the United States.

In colonial times charity was an offshoot of the synagogue, or as it was called more correctly, the *kahal*, which serviced social and cultural as well as religious needs. Although the New World (except in the case of Georgia[9]) was not used as a dumping ground for the Jewish poor, the Jewish communities had their own indigent as well as the widow and the orphan, the sick, the aged, and the dead. Shearith Israel, the first synagogue in New York, allocated close to 25 percent of its budget between 1730 and 1745 to charity.[10] The earliest constitution we have of that synagogue, dating back to 1728, spoke in matter-of-fact terms about the transient and native poor:

> If any poor person should happen to come to this place and should want the assistance of the Sinagog the Parnaz is hereby impowered to allow every poor person for his maintenance the sum of Eight

> Shillings pr Week and no more Not Exceeding the term of twelve weeks. And the Parnaz is also to use his utmost endeavours to despatch them to sum othere place as soon as Possible assisting them with necessarys, for their Voyage . . . those poor of this Congregation that shall apply for Sedaca shall be assisted with as much as the Parnaz and his assistants shall think fitt.

It is interesting to note that while the community unquestioningly assumed the burden, it made no pretense of giving scientifically or, on the other hand, of clamoring for social reform. Nevertheless, when we remember that at that time an unskilled laborer earned about two shillings a day, we see that the charity rates were fixed so as not to undermine the value of free labor or the status of the worker.[11] Furthermore, the fact that private philanthrophy—i.e., direct aid from an individual donor to a suppliant—was frowned upon meant that the community recognized the importance of at least elemental controls over charity.

Even in the pre-Revolutionary era charity transcended local needs. American Jews responded to the messengers who came to collect on behalf of the Jews of Palestine. And, just as the American congregations had received help from fellow Jews in Europe and in other New World settlements, so did they in turn contribute money and religious articles to younger communities in America seeking to establish themselves.

The causes which American Jews supported in colonial days persisted, and in the nineteenth century, as soon as there was a Jewish press, the problems of the needy were more effectively advertised. The editors of the early periodicals often acted as the Federation and defense agencies of their day, and they mobilized their readers on behalf of the chronically unfortunate, the new Jewish communities, and those victimized by plagues, fires, and floods.[13] American Jews also rallied on numerous occasions for the relief of non-Jews, a fact which in the opinion of two newspapers was laudatory albeit unreciprocated.[14] Jews took justifiable pride in their benevolence, and Christians too added their praise.[15] Madison C. Peters, eminent Protestant minister, commented in 1902: "If the bigoted authorities of New Amsterdam who gave their permission to a few Hebrews to settle in their city upon condition that they should always support their own poor could see how well they have kept the promise . . .those old burghers would open their eyes in surprise at the many and magnificent benevolent institutions, covering every conceivable case of need, which testify to the inborn kindness of the Hebrew's heart."[16] As one New York periodical, the *Jewish Messenger,* saw it, benevolence had another value—it kept alive Jewish communal vitality. For that reason some Jews argued against government subsidies to private charitable institutions.[17]

After 1840 charities were generally separated from their earlier base in the synagogue. Secular organizations sprang into existence to cope with the needs of the poor, the sick, the orphaned, the immigrant.[18] The change weakened the synagogue, but it afforded an opportunity to Jews who were succumbing to the powerful forces of secularization and religious apathy to retain some form of Jewish identity and communal participation. Perhaps, as some commented even then, philanthropy was becoming a surrogate for religion,[19] but irrespective of whether that was good or bad, it shows that American Jews were more creative in their handling of secular communal problems than in religious or cultural productivity.

Toward the end of the nineteenth century, trends that were current in American philanthropy generally reverberated in the Jewish community. There were the beginnings of consolidation and interagency cooperation, the glimmer of the federation movement (in which Jews were the pioneers), and the first steps to treat cases according to scientific guidelines and with a professional staff. Social gospel, the movement which activated Protestant churches to fight the evils of rapid industrialization, also echoed within Jewish circles. In their Pittsburgh Platform of 1885, Reform rabbis resolved "to participate in the great task of modern times, to solve on the bases of justice and righteousness the problems presented by the contrasts and evils of the present organization of society."[20]

Not until World War I did the role of the lay donor, usually a community-minded successful businessman or professional, fade noticeably. The directors of a philanthropic agency (and the same people served more than one agency in what was really a philanthropic interlocking directorate) gave time as well as money. They decided the allocation of funds according to their own investigations and knowledge; some, like Jacob H. Schiff, visited the unfortunates regularly or entertained them on annual outings.[21] Such benevolence reaped more than divine rewards. Philanthropists gained the admiration of Jews and non-Jews, and certainly a position of leadership within the Jewish community. Since Jews were generally barred from posts of command in old established civic causes—charity organizations, museums, private libraries—that were the purview of the American elite, they could satisfy their ambitions in Jewish areas. And, because of the weakened position of the synagogue, the philanthropic maze became increasingly the locus of Jewish communal power, where decisions and policies could and did shape the course of American Judaism for years to come.

Philanthropists also had the satisfaction of generating independence and pride in the group to which they belonged. As Schiff once said, a Jew would rather cut his hand off than apply for relief from non-Jewish sources. The other side of pride was fear—fear for the image of the Jew in American society, and philanthropic activity contributed to the salutary picture of the sober, ethical, responsible Jew.[22]

Not least important, the philanthropist also proved his Americanism by his communal labor. Like his non-Jewish counterpart, he too worked through voluntary associations, and he too subscribed to the doctrine of stewardship popularized at the end of the nineteenth century by Andrew Carnegie. (Stewardship, however, had separate Jewish roots in the person of the court Jews, or intercessors, of pre-modern times.)[23] Indeed, the uninterrupted growth of Jewish philanthropic agencies, particularly those pioneering efforts like the federation movement which were adopted by American philanthropy generally, was largely assured because of the essential harmony between the timeless Jewish teachings on charity and similar American values.

II

Between 1880 and 1914 close to 2,000,000 Jewish immigrants arrived in the United States. Most were victims of Tsarist repression, which, in addition to sporadic physical annihilation, was systematically crushing the Jews economically and culturally. They had no options but escape and few material resources but for the assistance they would receive from their brethren in the New World.

American Jews faced this problem of mammoth proportions with grim determination. They did not like the new arrivals, who in Western eyes appeared shabbily dressed, downright dirty, unhealthy, and vulgar. They did not understand the immigrants' language, *shtetl* customs, or religious practices, which differed so markedly from Western Jewish usage. (On one occasion, when a neighborhood gang attacked a group of Russian Jews on New York's Lower East Side, who had walked down to the river on Rosh Hashanah in observance of the *tashlich* custom, a Jewish newspaper admonished the ruffians for their lack of tolerance but admitted that *tashlich* was inherently outlandish.)[24] Nevertheless, the immigrants were still Jews, and by the 1890s, when it was clear that Russian conditions would not improve, American Jews had no recourse but to respond to the dictates of conscience, humanity, and Jewish tradition.[25]

True, they were involved too. At a time when heightened nationalism and currents of racist thinking were turning the nation to ever greater rejection of the unpalatable foreigner, they feared that Christian America might equate them, the established Jews, with the unwanted East European Jews. But the determination to welcome and clean up the immigrants and their life-style in order to protect their own image was but a secondary motive. It would have been far simpler for them, particularly when the United States was tightening up its regulations on immigrant entry, to have joined the ranks of the restrictionists and mouthed the latter's rhetoric about preserving the purity of American institutions. But not only did American Jews choose to defend open immigration, a function which they filled from then until 1965, and not merely on behalf of Jews, but they plunged into a variety of new tasks on behalf of the immigrants—from tuberculosis care, to settlement houses, to instruction (in Yiddish too) on how to run a farm.[26] In responding to immigrant needs, the American Jewish community reached new heights in the volume of philanthropic agencies and a climax in innovative thinking with respect to the tasks of philanthropy.

As was the pattern which we traced regarding charity, the formula for helping the immigrants added American forms and values to the underlying Jewish base. The very fight to counter the restrictionist cause invoked the ideal articulated by the Founding Fathers that part of America's mission was to serve as the haven for the world's oppressed. From that vantage point, the restrictionists, and not the immigrants or their supporters, were un-American.[27] Moreover, philanthropists linked their help to the immigrants with the doctrine of Americanization. In settlement houses and adult education classes, they taught the newcomers English and civics. The spokesmen of the community warned the immigrants to behave properly as citizens—not to fall prey to the bosses who would pay for their votes, and certainly not to support the dangerous and un-American practices of the socialists and anarchists. The handful of benefactors who revived the Jewish Theological Seminary in 1902 planned for an institution which would provide stable and conservative leadership for the East Europeans, one which could counter radical and secular trends as well as foreign habits with an American-trained rabbinate.[28]

Immigrants could and did resent their benefactors, who imposed their values in high-handed fashion, who often did not hide their personal aversion for the East European, and who did not appreciate how the cultural baggage of the newcomers served the emotional needs of the uprooted. Some demanded a voice in the agencies which were plotting their destinies, and the Russian Jews, as soon as they were able to, began erecting a new philanthropic structure parallel to the older one.[29] That in the eventual process of consolidation the East Europeans were accorded increasing recognition testifies not only to the strength of their numbers but also to the fact that their demand for representation, a kind of early neighborhood control, fitted the logic of American democracy more readily than the older paternalistic form.

Community defense was also an integral component of the work for the immigrant. It was bad enough, the communal leaders muttered, that American Judaism would become Russianized. But worse still were the dire prospects in store for all Jews if the new arrivals remained unacculturated or spawned radical movements. Such behavior would surely feed the currents of anti-Semitism which were becoming more apparent at the turn of the century. In lecturing and tutoring their brethren, the leaders adopted the posture of non-Jewish critics, and they too railed against the evils of the ghetto and of Jewish clannishness. Simultaneously, however, they labored unceasingly to defend the immigrants against repeated slurs and charges from the larger community—how immigrants brought disease, poverty, crime, political corruption, and factory evils.[30]

The reasons of defense were chiefly responsible for propelling the Jews to the forefront of the movement to distribute the immigrants from the congested city areas along the mid-Atlantic seaboard to the interior of the country. If the new arrivals were settled in the South and West, the "leprosy of the ghetto walls" would be wiped out and Americanization hastened. In this way, the visibility of the Jew as alien, the most troubling factor to Christians and hence to the established Jews, would be lowered. Edward Freeman, British historian, had written in the 1880s that nations disliked Jews because they were strangers and a nuisance. By emptying the conspicuous enclaves through proper distribution, the Jews hoped to reduce the alien and nuisance quotient. Finally, and here the Jews had the approval of numerous government officials, distribution could prove the best and perhaps the only way of undercutting the restrictionist drive. The National Liberal Immigration League, organized in 1907 by two Jews, had as its motto: A Stream That Is Dangerous When Unchecked Will Prove a Blessing to the Land When Well Directed.[31]

No wonder then that Jews experimented with different forms of distribution. The Baron de Hirsch Fund erected the Industrial

Removal Office, whose job was to gather information on employment opportunities in interior regions and, with the help of local Jews in those areas, move immigrants there from eastern cities. (The IRO, we should point out, served as the model for the Division of Information, a distribution agency set up as a federal bureau in 1907 in the Department of Commerce and Labor.) Individual Jews had talked as early as the 1890s about moving industrial enterprises to suburban areas and building cheap housing there for the immigrant workers, and this too was attempted by the Hirsch Fund. For a few years before World War I, Jacob Schiff virtually alone underwrote the Galveston project, a scheme to land the Europeans directly at the Gulf port, thus avoiding the need to uproot and relocate a second time, and distribute them from Galveston throughout the Southwest. The thinking was innovative, the goals eminently patriotic. Hardworking immigrants, acculturating rapidly, would contribute of their talents to building up new areas of the nation. Taught manual and agricultural skills in schools established by the philanthropists—a leaf from Benjamin Franklin's ideas on self-help—the Jewish immigrants would repay, through their economic productivity, the debt which they owed the United States for having admitted them.[32]

Agricultural colonization was also widely discussed in the Progressive era as a method for ameliorating urban and therefore immigrant problems. Progressives added an idealistic flavor by associating colonization with the agrarian myth—a doctrine which taught that social virtue and a nation's very moral fiber derived from the work of the yeoman farmer. In point of fact, however, the physical and moral advantages of colonizing the East Europeans in farming settlements had been raised in Jewish circles over fifty years earlier. Isaac Leeser, rabbi of Philadelphia's Congregation Mikveh Israel, advocated such a scheme in 1843 in the very first issue of his monthly journal, *The Occident*. Leeser, like others in his and the succeeding generation, talked about the "ennobling pursuit" of agriculture in contrast to the bad effects of huckstering and petty trade on Jewish character. Leeser was not prompted so much by the agrarian myth as he was by the European statesmen and critics who, since the days of the French Revolution, had been pointing out the deficiencies of the Jews and their "unproductive" economic roles. Leeser and indeed other Jewish defenders were thereby adopting the measuring rod and values of their critics when urging the community to enhance its image in the eyes of the world. When Americans took up the colonization issue around 1900 and debated questions like "Can the Jew be a farmer?" the Jews had already sustained numerous failures at colonizing new immigrants. Only the colony of Woodbine, New Jersey, supported by the Hirsch Fund, lasted for any length of time.[33] Nevertheless, the criticism of unproductivity continued to rankle within the Jewish community, and attempts to drive the immigrant into respectable pursuits of manual labor lived on in tandem with the concept of distribution.

Distribution as a major palliative to the immigrant invasion failed for many reasons, not least of which was the growth of consumer industries and services in the cities, which attracted not only the immigrants but native farmers. The manufacturing cities were where the action was, the new frontier. Today, with the new burst of ethnicity, it would be quite fashionable to claim that failure was in reality a blessing, for it preserved group cohesiveness, permitted experimentation in Jewish belles-lettres and Yiddish theater, and provided Jews the opportunity for a significant role in the politics of states like New York and Pennsylvania. Be that as it may, the attempts at distribution teach us the response of the community seeking to blend Jewish and American values, the innovative thinking which the pressures of community defense as well as immigrant needs bred, and very importantly, the service that voluntary organizations provide usually ahead of government agencies in meeting social problems.

III

Pre-modern Jewish communities obeyed the religious injunction to ransom captives—fellow Jews taken prisoner by capricious lords or in wars and other forms of conquest. In the nineteenth and twentieth centuries, new captors emerged—the Tsars, the Nazis, the Soviets—along with more sophisticated forms of political and economic captivity, but the responsibility of kinship remained the same. Time and time again American Jews were called upon to help Jews in Europe, Asia, and Africa whom they knew only as the victims of persecution. They, the Americans, responded with money and, where feasible, with diplomatic pressures and public appeals. The breadth of their concern and the magnitude of their response had no parallels in the history of other American ethnic or religious minorities. Jewish efforts joined reform with traditionalist, secularist with socialist, capitalist with laborer, proving how ethnic ties eclipsed theological and economic differences. Indeed, for over 130 years, ever since the Damascus blood libel of 1840, activities on behalf of suffering foreign Jews were the surest means of evoking American Jewish solidarity.

A survey of these activities reveals that American Jews aimed for remediation over and above mere relief. Money was raised on behalf of pogrom victims in Russia, but even greater effort was spent on finding possible ways of stopping the pogroms.[34] Since American Jews had little international leverage (after all, how many could, like Jacob Schiff, threaten to close the money markets to tsarist loans?), they needed allies. Unlike the problems of charity and care for the immigrant, which American Jews shouldered on their own, this facet of philanthropy depended for its success on the collaboration and sympathy of Christian America and the government. If "enlightened public opinion," as the Jewish leaders called it, would condemn the "relics of barbarism," Rumania, Russia, Turkey, and even Hitler's Germany would be forced to end their religious and racial oppression. Therefore, the plan of action called for exposing the persecutions and the perpetrators, enlisting the aid of the secular and Christian press, and soliciting statements of condemnation from prominent public leaders. Where possible American Jews went further and urged that safeguards for their brethren be sanctioned by international agreement, as in the minority-rights treaties at the Versailles Peace Congress. Often, individual Jews, like the court Jews of old, would approach the administration directly and use their friendship with the incumbent President or Secretary of State to ask for American diplomatic intercession. In various instances

Jews and local communities were prodded by the Jewish press, and later by defense agencies, to alert their representatives in Washington, who would then, hopefully, introduce congressional resolutions of protest. Certain critical occasions, like the Kishinev pogrom in 1903 and Nazi terrorism, called for mass protest meetings at which Christians joined Jews in condemning the outrages.[35]

Until World War II this pattern remained fairly constant. Again, not only was the Jewish activity rooted in Jewish values, but it was in harmony with American ideals. During the nineteenth century and into the early part of the twentieth, it was not uncommon for the United States to speak out on humanitarian grounds on behalf of the oppressed in foreign lands. These actions were quite in keeping with the belief that America's mission was to act as the beacon light of freedom for the entire world. In this spirit the Van Buren administration condemned the Damascus libel in 1840 even before the Jews asked for government help. Understandably, American Jews lavished much praise upon humanitarian diplomacy, for that policy justified concern on the part of Americans for the universal values of justice and morality. To plead the cause of Jews, or the cause of any persecuted group, was both proper American as well as Jewish behavior.[36]

Communal defense was also a component of the activity on behalf of foreign Jews. Although not generally articulated until the days of Hitler, there was long an awareness on the part of American Jewry that anti-Semitism was an exportable commodity. The ideas of intellectual anti-Semites—people like Houston Stewart Chamberlain, Goldwin Smith, Edward Freeman—crossed national boundaries, and the theory of racial anti-Semitism was aired in American periodicals in the last quarter of the nineteenth century. American comic weeklies copied, on occasion, directly from the rabble-rousing anti-Semites of nineteenth-century Germany, just as Father Coughlin's *Social Justice* echoed Goebbels' propaganda during the Nazi era. *La France Juive,* Edouard Drumont's monumental contribution to French anti-Semitism a few years before the Dreyfus Affair, reached the American public via a tract published in New York by the name of *The Original Mr.*

Jacobs.[37] Furthermore, anti-Semitism in Europe could and did become part of the life-style of many who later migrated to the United States. Thus, to protect the United States and American Jews from the anti-Semitic virus, it had to be combated in Europe.

Peripheral reasons of defense also contributed to this area of activity. First, if persecution was stopped at its source, it would cut down on the volume of immigration and the hazards to which immigrants exposed the established American Jewish community. Secondly, if communal leaders or agencies did not direct the sympathy and resentment felt by American Jews for their kinsmen abroad, who knew what kind of radical activity a small group might undertake which would tarnish the image of the entire community? It was just that reason, incidentally, that hastened the formation of the American Jewish Committee in 1906.

Unfortunately, the standard methods employed on behalf of foreign Jews had built-in weaknesses. The arguments used to rally Christian support and to condemn the persecutor rested on rationalistic premises—for example, how could modern men believe a blood libel charge? But in a world which grew increasingly irrational in the twentieth century, it was just as easy to believe the myth of the international Jew, the eternal alien who plotted the destruction of Christian civilization, as it was to believe in Aryan supermen. Moreover, American Jewish activity could hope to reach a measure of success only as long as the United States was guided by the dictates of humanitarian diplomacy. However, as the nation became increasingly immersed in world power politics, that policy slowly eroded, and after World War I it was quietly buried. When in the early thirties, the American Jewish Committee reminded the State Department, in a lengthy memorandum, of numerous instances of American intervention on humanitarian grounds, the department replied that those precedents did not make out a convincing case for representations against the Nazi government.[39]

Help for foreign Jews depended not only on a sympathetic government but on public acquiescence as well, and that too could weaken and even paralyze Jewish communal efforts. To plead for

American interference in foreign situations where national interests were not explicitly involved was doomed to failure, if the country was in an isolationist mood. More important, *to plead on behalf of foreigners* could give credence to the suspicion that Jews put higher priority on their Jewish than their American loyalties. Since one of the stock themes in modern anit-Semitism was the international Jew, the alien bound only to his own clan and incapable of true patriotism to the country in which he lived, American Jews felt impelled to weigh their activities on the scale of American anti-Semitism. When anti-Semitism enjoyed greater popularity, they tried to avoid those situations which provided grist for the hatemongers' mills.

All the weaknesses of the American Jewish position were blatantly exposed in the 1930s. Rational and moral arguments had lost their earlier force. The horror with which the Western world received the news of tsarist pogroms gave way to relative indifference and apathy with respect to Nazi policies. In the United States humanitarian diplomacy was long forgotten. Disillusioned and frustrated by the failure of the Wilsonian crusade and by the great depression, Americans buried their heads in the sand and sought immunity from European affairs in neutrality laws. Whereas Theodore Roosevelt had enjoyed the opportunity to chide Russia for its anti-Jewish policies, Franklin Roosevelt kept quiet about Germany. Nationalism and isolationism rode high; the League, the World Court, and former allies England and France were suspect. If those factors were not sufficient to paralyze American Jewish efforts to rescue Hitler's victims, there was also the fear generated by the upsurge in native anti-Semitism. The charges against Jews disseminated in the 1920s by the *Protocols of the Elders of Zion* and Henry Ford's *Dearborn Independent* had become the stock-in-trade of groups like the German-American Bund, William Dudley Pelley's Silver Shirts, and Father Coughlin's National Union for Social Justice. Nor was anti-Semitism limited to the extremists. For example, in three early opinion polls, over one-quarter of the respondents replied that Jews were less patriotic than other citizens. It may be true that

American Jews could have done more in the thirties and early forties for their European brethren, but the forces which inhibited them should not be underrated.[40]

The Holocaust disproved the charge of Jewish power, but in its aftermath American Jews gave greater thought to a better use of the strengths they did have. Like all sub-groups in society—economic, ethnic, religious, or racial—Jews could have directed their strength at the ballot box on behalf of their foreign kinsmen.[41] But while earlier communal stewards like Louis Marshall, Jacob Schiff, and Oscar Straus knew that political favors had to be paid for quietly in votes, they and most American Jews shunned open and organized political bargaining. The traditional posture of Jews, once they became established in the United States, was to maintain a low political profile and to deny the existence of separate, Jewish political interests.[42] Jews differed from their fellow citizens only in matters of religion, they reiterated through the centuries; to set themselves apart politically could evoke the dreaded labels of alien and un-American. Only recently have American Jews become sufficiently confident and assertive to shrug off the insecurities of the first generations of emancipated Jews. Now, in the post–World War II era, since America accepts more readily the different and contending interests which characterize the subgroups in a pluralistic society, Jews appreciate the vote for the legitimate weapon that it is. They are too individualistic ever to vote as a bloc, but they know that they are no less American for their Jewish interests or for any number of them asserting such interests at the polls.

I have deliberately excluded American Jewish activities on behalf of the State of Israel from my discussion. Whereas support of Zionism or contributions for building up Palestine before 1948 were primarily philanthropic causes, efforts on behalf of the State involved more. They reflected, I believe, a more positive commitment and a closer emotional identification than obtained on any other issue. Consciously or unconsciously, American Jews who support the State see it as the Holy Land still, the geographical component of God's covenant with the people of Israel—perhaps the site which in some way can dull the pain of the Holocaust and shore up grace for Diaspora Jewry.[43]

As we look forward, we know that the American Jewish community will continue to face new challenges. It is hard to imagine a time when the need for charity or of the rescue of foreign Jews will fade completely, but it is possible that other aspects of philanthropy—perhaps work on behalf of Jewish education or cultural creativity—will assume greater importance than they have heretofore. In all events, the philanthropic record which American Jews have set so far will provide a stable foundation on which to build. Problems have taken new forms, and methods have changed to suit the times, but a commitment to basic Jewish values has been renewed from generation to generation. As long as there is an American Jewish community, the responsibilities of kinship are likely to be met.

Notes

1. Salo W. Baron, *Steeled by Adversity* (Philadelphia, 1971), ch. 7.
2. *Occident,* II (January–February 1845), 512–513, 517ff.
3. *Jewish Messenger,* December 10, 1880, March 8, 1889.
4. David B. Truman, *The Governmental Process* (New York, 1962), pp. 129–139. On the American Jewish Committee's adoption of the chapter plan see Naomi W. Cohen, *Not Free to Desist* (Philadelphia, 1972), pp. 261–264.
5. Naomi W. Cohen, *American Jews and the Zionist Idea* (New York, 1975), pp. 12, 97.
6. See for example M. J. Heale, "From City Fathers to Social Critics: Humanitarianism and Government in New York, 1790–1860," *Journal of American History,* LXIII (June 1976), 27–29.
7. Robert H. Bremner, *American Philanthropy* (Chicago, 1960), pp. 7–8.
8. Morris U. Schappes, ed., *A Documentary History of the Jews in the United States, 1654–1875* (Third ed. New York, 1971), pp. 1–5.
9. Jacob Rader Marcus, *Early American Jewry* (2 vols. Philadelphia, 1953), II, 279, 281.
10. *Ibid.,* II, 482.
11. David and Tamar de Sola Pool, *An Old Faith in the New World* (New York, 1955), pp. 499–500. I am grateful to Professor Bruce Wilkenfeld of Hunter College for "translating" for me the value of shillings into laborers' earnings.
12. For an overview of Jewish charity in the colonial era see Jacob Rader

Marcus, *The Colonial American Jew* (3 vols. Detroit, 1970), II, ch. 60.

13. Naomi W. Cohen, "Pioneers of American Jewish Defense," *American Jewish Archives,* XXIX (November, 1977).
14. *Jewish Messenger,* August 1, 1884, August 2, 1895; *American Hebrew,* November 18, 1881.
15. For examples of nineteenth century opinions see *Asmonean,* June 8, 1855; *Jewish Messenger,* July 15, 1859, December 21, 1860, February 24, 1871, October 31, 1873, May 14, 1875, January 14, 1887; *American Hebrew,* May 4, 1894, September 20, 1895; Mark Twain, "Concerning the Jews," *Harper's Magazine,* XCIX (September 1899), 534.
16. *Jewish Messenger,* February 7, 1902.
17. *Ibid.,* March 28, 1877, March 28, 1879; *American Israelite,* March 30, 1877.
18. Herman D. Stein, "Jewish Social Work in the United States," in *The Characteristics of American Jews* (New York, 1965), pp. 146–147.
19. *Jewish Messenger,* February 4, 1876.
20. Bremner, *American Philanthropy,* ch. 6; Stein, "Jewish Social Work," pp. 152–153; Nathan Glazer, *American Judaism* (Chicago, 1957), p. 152.
21. Stein, "Jewish Social Work," pp. 147, 155; Cyrus Adler, *Jacob H. Schiff* (2 vols. Garden City, N.Y., 1929), I, ch. 11.
22. American Jewish Committee, Minutes of the Executive Committee, November 7, 1914; *American Israelite,* January 17, 1879; *American Hebrew,* February 13, March 5, 1880.
23. Bremner, *American Philanthropy,* pp. 105–113. The following statement by Schiff echoes the views of Carnegie's "Gospel of Wealth": "The surplus wealth we have gained, to some extent, at least, belongs to our fellow beings; we are only the temporary custodians of our fortune; let us be careful that no just complaint can be made against our stewardship." Adler, *Schiff,* I, 356. For examples of American Jewish stewardship see Naomi W. Cohen, *A Dual Heritage* (Philadelphia, 1969), ch. 4.
24. *Jewish Messenger,* September 22, 1871.
25. Moses Rischin, *The Promised City* (New York, 1964), pp. 95–98; Irving Mandel, "The Attitude of the American Jewish Community Toward East-European Immigration as Reflected in the Anglo-Jewish Press (1880–1890)," *American Jewish Archives,* III (June 1950), 14; Esther Panitz, "The Polarity of American Jewish Attitudes towards Immigration (1870–1891)," in Abraham Karp, ed., *The Jewish Experience in America* (5 vols. Waltham and New York, 1969), IV, 31–62. The German Jewish criticisms of the Russian Jew who was "artful," "intriguing," "indolent," and "inferior" antedated the mass migration. Cf. *Occident,* IV (December 1846), 409.
26. Cohen, *Not Free to Desist,* ch. 3, pp. 137–142, 368–373; Esther Panitz, "In Defense of the Jewish Immigrant, 1891–1924," in Karp, *Jewish Experience in America,* V, 23–63; Stein, "Jewish Social Work," pp. 152–185.
27. John Higham, *Strangers in the Land* (New York, 1973), pp. 124–125; Cohen, *Not Free to Desist,* p. 140.

28. Stein, "Jewish Social Work," pp. 168–178; Samuel Joseph, *History of the Baron de Hirsch Fund* (S. L., 1935), ch. 8; Mandel, "Attitude . . . Toward . . . Immigration," p. 32; *Jewish Messenger*, June 18, July 16, 1886, April 22, 1887, January 10, 17, October 3, 1890, August 28, September 4, 1891; *American Hebrew*, October 24, 1884, August 27, 1886, November 17, 1893, October 26, 1894, November 1, 1895, July 10, October 16, 1896; Glazer, *American Judaism*, pp. 73–75.
29. Rischin, *Promised City*, pp. 103–108; Stein, "Jewish Social Work," pp. 152, 157, 164–165.
30. *Jewish Messenger*, August 13, December 10, 1886, March 27, 1890, April 10, July 10, 24, 1891, September 6, 16, November 25, 1892; *American Hebrew*, August 5, 1881, July 21, 1882, August 20, 1886, November 2, 1888, August 23, 1895; *American Israelite*, November 25, 1887, December 17, 1891; Cohen, *Not Free to Desist*, p. 42. The evils of the ghetto were highlighted in a series of sketches (with accompanying editorial remarks) in the *Jewish Messenger* for August through October 1891. Similar views were expressed by the *American Israelite* and *American Hebrew*.
31. *Jewish Messenger*, September 25, 1891; Edward A. Freeman, "Some Impressions of the United States," *Fortnightly Review*, XXXVIII (September 1882), 333–334. On the concept of distribution and its connection with restrictionism, see Janine M. Perry, "The Idea of Immigrant Distribution in the United States, 1890–1915" (M.A. essay. Hunter College, 1975), pp. 36–45, 68–81, 92–94.
32. Joseph, *Baron de Hirsch Fund*, pp. 25, 44–47, ch. 5; *Jewish Messenger*, August 30, 1878, May 1, 22, July 3, 1891; *American Hebrew*, April 10, 1896. Themes that were aired repeatedly from 1879–1900 in the community and in the Anglo-Jewish press were the values of distribution away from the eastern cities and the importance of farming and mechanical occupations for the immigrant. (The specific references to these subjects in the files of the *Jewish Messenger*, *American Hebrew*, and *American Israelite* are far too numerous to cite.)
33. *Occident*, I (April 1843), 28–30. Other early articles on the advantages of farming and agricultural colonization appeared in the *Occident*, IV (September 1846), XIV (August–September 1856), XV (September 1857), and *Asmonean*, April 20, 1855. For later developments see Joseph, *Baron de Hirsch Fund*, chs. 3, 4; Joseph Brandes, *Immigrants to Freedom* (Philadelphia, 1971), pp. 24–72; Gabriel Davidson, "The Jew in Agriculture in the United States," *American Jewish Year Book*, XXXVII (1935–6), 100–102.
34. See for example Cohen, *A Dual Heritage*, pp. 127–136.
35. For examples of American Jewish diplomatic behavior see *ibid.*, pp. 57–65, 123–136, 195–198, 266–270; Cohen, *Not Free to Desist*, ch. 4, pp. 110–122, 158–159, 165–176; *idem*, *American Jews and the Zionist Idea*, pp. 45, 49–50, 64–69; Allan Tarshish, "The Board of Delegates of American Israelites," in

Karp, *Jewish Experience in America,* III, 134–136.

36. Cyrus Adler and Aaron M. Margalith, *With Firmness in the Right* (New York, 1946), pp. 3–4. Oscar S. Straus, "Humanitarian Diplomacy of the United States" and "John Hay: A Tribute" in Straus, *The American Spirit* (New York, 1913), pp. 19–38, 375–379.
37. Rudolf Glanz, "The Immigration of German Jews Up to 1880," *Studies in Judaica Americana* (New York, 1970), p. 103; Leonard A. Greenberg and Harold J. Jonas, "An American Anti-Semite in the Nineteenth Century," in Joseph L. Blau *et al.*, eds., *Essays on Jewish Life and Thought* (New York, 1959); Cohen, *Not Free to Desist,* p. 216. I discuss the impact of European anti-Semitism on American Jewry in an essay to be published by the American Academy for Jewish Research entitled "American Jewish Reactions to Anti-Semitism in Western Europe, 1875–1900."
38. Cohen, *Not Free to Desist,* p. 8.
39. *Ibid.,* pp. 145, 169.
40. *Ibid.,* chs. 8, 9; Selig Adler, *The Isolationist Impulse* (New York, 1961), ch. 11; Donald S. Strong, *Organized Anti-Semtisim in America* (Washington, D.C., 1941), pp. 36, 49, 59, 73, 95, 130; Charles Herbert Stember and others, *Jews in the Mind of America* (New York, 1966), p. 116.
41. This was suggested by Mark Twain in 1899 in his essay "Concerning the Jews," p. 534.
42. Cohen, *A Dual Heritage,* p. 126; *idem, Not Free to Desist,* pp. 30–32, 57, 60.
43. Cf. Jacob Neusner, *American Judaism* (Englewood Cliffs, N.J., 1972), ch. 4; Marshall Sklare, *America's Jews* (New York, 1971), ch. 7.

NORMAN PODHORETZ

The Rise and Fall of The American Jewish Novelist

Around the turn of the century, Henry James, who had been living abroad, returned to the United States for his first visit in twenty-five years. While James had been away, exchanging America for Europe, millions and millions of people—not, to be sure, of his class—had been exchanging Europe for America, and one of the things that fascinated and troubled him as an "incurable man of letters" was how this "infusion" of aliens would effect the "linguistic tradition as one had known it." It was during a tour of the Jewish ghetto on the Lower East Side of New York—the "New Jerusalem" he called it—that the question aroused his "'lettered' anguish." The East Side cafés, it seemed to him, were "torture-rooms of the living idiom," and they were a "portent of lacerations to come." Given "the extent of the Hebrew conquest of New York" (and "Who can ever tell . . . what the genius of Israel may, or may not, really be 'up to'?"), how would the knightly and embattled English language survive in the United States? In the "ultimate future," said James, "whatever we shall know it for, certainly, we shall not know it for English."

Reading that famous passage from *The American Scene* in 1976, seventy years after it was published, one hardly knows whether to laugh or to cry. Would James have suffered the same "'lettered' anguish" if he had been able to forsee that an absurdly large number of the descendants of these torturers of the living idiom were destined to write doctoral dissertations on, precisely, the novels of Henry James? Or again, how would his "critic's ear," ravaged by the intimations it caught in those East Side cafés of the "Accent of the Future," have reacted to the prose of Saul Bellow, of Norman Mailer, of Bernard Malamud, of Philip Roth? Would he have known such prose for English? And would he have been surprised if he had lived to see what might be described as a Jewish "school" becoming one of the major forces in American letters?

No doubt he would have been surprised, and perhaps dismayed, but there would have been no gainsaying the facts themselves. For thousands of Jewish graduate students *did* devote themselves to the study of Henry James (and Hawthorne, and Melville, and Poe, and Whitman, and Emily Dickinson) in the years after World War II. During the same period, Jews—many of them raised in households where Yiddish was still the main tongue spoken—*did* become an extraordinarily powerful influence in American fiction, American poetry, American drama, American criticism. And so far as the novel in particular is concerned, the British critic Walter Allen was only echoing a standard view when he said, about ten years ago, that the "dominance" of the Southern school deriving from Faulkner had now "largely passed to Jewish writers, through the best of whose work . . . a recognizably new note ha[d] come into American fiction, not the less American for being unmistakably Jewish."

A mere list of names is enough to indicate why the word dominance came to seem appropriate in speaking of the position of Jewish novelists on the American literary scene barely half a century after Henry James's forebodings were expressed. In addition to Bellow, Mailer, Malamud, and Roth, one could point to such novelists of serious literary ambition as (listing them in alphabetical order) Jerome Charyn, Arthur A. Cohen, E. L. Doctorow, Stanley Elkin, Bruce J. Friedman, Herbert Gold, Joseph Heller, Erica Jong, Johanna Kaplan, Robert Kotlowitz, Meyer Liben, Wallace Markfield, Mark Mirsky, Jay Neugeboren, Hugh Nissenson, Cynthia Ozick, Grace Paley, Norma Rosen, Barbara Probst Solomon, Harvey Swados, Edward Lewis Wallant, and a good many others (not to mention writers of wider popular appeal like Meyer Levin, Chaim Potok, Irwin Shaw, Leon Uris, and Herman Wouk; and leaving Isaac Bashevis Singer and Elie Wiesel, both of whom live in America but neither of whom writes in English, out of account altogether).

Now it goes without saying that not all these writers were important; a few of them, I think, were not even very good. It also goes without saying that they differed as much in their interests as they did in stature; some of them did not even deal directly with Jews or Jewish experience as such. Nor, finally, were most of them Jewish in any sense other than the fact of ethnic origin—a fact which itself had an all-encompassing significance for some and very little for others.

Nevertheless, in one way or another, and to a lesser or greater degree, their novels and stories were all colored by the peculiar circumstances of their Jewish origin. It was Henry James himself who said that it is a complex fate to be an American. To be an American Jew, then, must be a doubly complex fate, and it would be incredible if anyone under the sway of this fate could write fiction without reference to it. If I remember rightly, for example, there are no Jewish characters in Heller's *Catch-22*, yet it is hard to imagine anyone but a Jew writing that book—so visibly Jewish is the curious combination of self-pity and self-irony that lies behind Heller's humor, so little whole-hearted is the nihilism to which he aspires. And a similar observation could be made of the work of Norman Mailer: who else but a Jew would be so beset by messianic longings as Mailer is? The Jews, as everyone now knows, are not a race, but there does seem to be such a thing as a Jewish nervous system, or bent of mind, or habit of spirit that persists even after the conditions which produced it are no longer present to the naked eye. And this naturally reflects itself in the fiction of Jews.

But the fact that so many Jews came to write serious fiction in America is only one side of the story. The other side is that so many of them came to be published, read, and acclaimed—not excluding (emphatically not excluding) those who wrote about Jews and Jewish experience in an idiom spiced with Yiddishisms and resounding with the accents of immigrant Jewish speech. The awarding of the Nobel Prize for Literature to Saul Bellow in 1976 was the most vivid sign of this situation, but it was by no means the only one. Literally dozens of works by writers of a similar character had been nominated for lesser literary prizes like the National Book Award in the preceding ten or twenty years, and many—including, of course, some of Bellow's—had won. And what was perhaps even more remarkable, a fair number of these novels had achieved commercial as well as critical success. Which is to say that there was now a large public willing to buy the things the serious Jewish novelist had to offer and to listen to the things he had to say.

This public, I would guess, came into full existence only in the early 1960s. For consider the curious history of a novel entitled *Call It Sleep,* which is about a little boy growing up in the New York Jewish ghettos around the turn of the century (the very world James was describing in *The American Scene*). Published originally in 1934, it went almost entirely unnoticed and sold only a few hundred copies; the author, Henry Roth, retired from literature altogether to become a poultry farmer in Maine. Twenty-five years later, in 1960, a new edition was published which gave several critics an opportunity to complain about how unfairly the book had been neglected, but again only a negligible number of copies was sold. Then a few years later, a paperback publisher decided to give *Call It Sleep* yet another try. In an unprecedented action the reprint was reviewed on the front page of the *Sunday Times Book Review* and very quickly shot to the top position on the paperback best-seller lists. Obviously by the mid-sixties a new receptivity had developed in the reading public to fiction dealing with Jewish experience in America.

To anyone at all familiar with the history of the Jewish group in America, this development was bound to seem remarkable, even breathtaking. Only yesterday Jewish experience had been regarded (and not least by Jews themselves) as at best marginal or exotic and as at worst grubby and rather shameful. Suddenly it was apparently being taken as somehow more meaningful, more interesting, more relevant, more *central* than the experience of most other groups in our society. Only yesterday Jews who wanted to write had assumed as a matter of course that their Jewishness was a burden to be overcome. Suddenly they were all seeing Jewishness as an advantage to be exploited. The exploitation might be genuine, as with Bellow and Malamud, or opportunistic, as with a figure like Leon Uris. But the fact remains that what had once been a disability had now become an advantage.

There is a story behind this development—a story about the Jews and a story about America. Up until the 1930s, Jews played a very minor role in American letters and hardly any at all in the novel. To be sure, there were isolated figures like Abraham Cahan, an immigrant from Russia who wrote several novels in English (*The Rise of David Levinsky,* his best, is still not as well known as it deserves to be), and Ludwig Lewisohn, who was prominent both as a drama critic and as a novelist in the twenties. But the general impression one gets, in looking at the literary culture of the teens and twenties, is that Jews counted for little in it; and to the extent that they counted at all, it was not *as* Jews who had something distinctive to offer, but rather as writers who had learned to "pass"—to operate unobtrusively within the going literary terms. Indeed, one might even go so far as to say that passing was the price they had to pay in order to be accepted as members of the world of American letters. Certainly Lewisohn ceased to be of importance in (was expelled from?) that world after becoming a militant Zionist—in almost melodramatic contrast to what happened to James Baldwin's reputation in the early sixties when he underwent a similar conversion to black nationalism.

The Jewish novelists of the 1930s spoke on the whole with greater assurance than their predecessors, but not great enough to get many people to listen. Henry Roth wrote one very good novel and disappeared into Maine; Daniel Fuchs wrote three very good novels and disappeared into Hollywood; Meyer Levin wrote a tolerable Jewish version of *Studs Lonigan* and disappeared into crudity; Nathanael West (*né* Nathan Weinstein—he was a passer) wrote four highly distinguished novels having nothing at all to do with Jews, and died. Whatever else might be remarked of these writers and other of their Jewish contemporaries, one thing is clear: they did not succeed in imposing themselves on the consciousness of the period, which is to say that they did not succeed in making Jewish experience seem relevant or central. West, of course, never even tried, and the others were all still caught—at least to some degree—in the feeling that Jewish experience was more exotic than real. Reality, they seemed to be saying, is not what happens to me: it is what happens to *them.*

The turning-point came with World War II. The largely native-born generation of Jews which grew to maturity during the depression included a staggering proportion of brilliant literary intellectuals, most of them associated with or nourished by a new magazine called *Partisan Review:* Lionel Trilling, William Phillips, Philip Rahv, Harold Rosenberg, Paul Goodman, Lionel Abel, and (a bit younger) Saul Bellow, Isaac Rosenfeld, Delmore Schwartz, Alfred Kazin, Leslie Fiedler, Irving Howe, Robert Warshow, and Clement Greenberg—to name only the most obvious. Not all of them wrote fiction, but those who did, wrote it with a kind of assurance that was quite new among American Jews: they wrote as though there were no question whatever in their minds of the importance of what they had to tell.

Delmore Schwartz—who wrote poetry and criticism as well as short stories—put his finger on the source of this new assurance: "I understood my own personal squint at experience, and the fact of being a Jew became available to me as a central symbol of alienation . . . and certain other characteristics which are the peculiar marks of modern life, and as I think now, the essential ones." Far from being marginal or exotic, then, Jewish experience embodied the essential characteristics of modern life—not merely of American life, but of life in the contemporary world—as these had been revealed by such great masters as Joyce, Kafka, Mann, Proust, and Eliot. To have been born a Jew was to have been thrust into a condition that all men in our time were destined to enter by a more devious route: the sense of being an outsider, the sense of being homeless and in exile. Why should this be so? Because in a revolutionary era like our own all the old certainties are destroyed, and everyone is forced to ask the questions which are the natural inheritance of the outsider: Who am I? Where do I belong? What is my relation to this weird society in which I find myself? Why am I here? How am I to live?

Surely it was the growth of some such feeling as Schwartz described that dissolved the diffidence which had earlier inhibited the writing of fiction by Jews. Of course the simple passage of time was also a contributing factor. By the mid-forties, the Jews had been in America long enough and were sufficiently "acculturated" to relax about being Jewish. There was, in any case, no point in not relaxing: Hitler had just demonstrated, in horribly irrefutable terms, that Jewishness was a fate not easily to be evaded by anyone born a Jew. Why not embrace it then?

And so it happened that a twenty-five-year-old boy named Norman Mailer, the son of immigrant Jewish parents, came to be the author of the best and most definitive novel about the Second World War. *The Naked and the Dead* is not a book about Jewish experience; nor was Mailer writing in any immediately obvious way out of a recognizably Jewish tradition. Yet the very fact that a second-generation American Jew was able to speak for the American experience of the war in a more authoritative manner than anyone else was in itself enormously significant. It signified that America and the Jews had discovered one another at last; and it turned out that they had come to look remarkably alike after all.

It was, however, in the work of Saul Bellow and Bernard Malamud—and not in the work of Norman Mailer—that the centrality of Jewish experience itself was finally established. Both Bellow and Malamud wrote almost exclusively about Jews, and each forged a prose style which was unashamedly influenced by the rhythms and locutions of Yiddish (yet Henry James would certainly have known it for English). Both, moreover, seemed to take it completely and calmly for granted that everything of any conceivable interest or importance that a novelist might wish to uncover about the human condition could be found in the world of Jewish experience. There was no special insistence on this point: it was not asserted, it was assumed. Neither Bellow nor Malamud was an apologist for the Jews. They both saw the Jews as people, *real* people. Reality, finally, is what happens to me; let them worry for a change about whether what happens to them can possibly be reality too.

Judging by all the attention which came to be paid to Jewish writers, "they" *did* begin worrying for a change. But "they" in this context not only referred to non-Jews; it also meant third and fourth-generation Jews to whom the immigrant world of East European Jewry was approximately as familiar as the War of 1812. Literary critics used to talk a great deal about how important a "usable past" was to the novelist. From the moment Bellow and Malamud discovered such a past in the Jewish experience, an endless parade of younger aspirants to literary fame who never knew any Yiddish, who grew up in highly assimilated middle-class families, and who were educated at schools like Groton and Harvard, began shaking off whatever lingering contempt they might still have felt for Jewish "vulgarity," and started writing novels and stories about life on the Lower East Side.

The wheel, then, was coming full circle, and just as dozens (or was it hundreds?) of young Southern writers in the fifties mechanically followed the example of Faulkner, so did we see scores of young Jewish writers imitating Bellow and Malamud but altogether lacking their intimate feel for Jews and Jewishness. Indeed, by the sixties, for Jews, "passing" was coming to mean the effort to affect a stronger connection with Jewishness than one actually had, rather than the other way around. Certainly it seemed unlikely by then that a novelist named Nathan Weinstein would change his name to Nathanael West, although a Nathanael West might well have changed his name to Nathan Weinstein.

But what about the non-Jewish audience? Why did Jewish writing suddenly become appealing to it? There is, of course, no way of knowing for certain, but I would guess that the explanation largely had to do with the progressive erosion of regional differences in postwar America. Regional conflict was once the basis of American politics, and regional distinctiveness the basis of American culture, but with the pressures of mass communication working to make all parts of the country more and more alike, we began finding a greater and greater emphasis being put on ethnicity as the distinguishing mark among people who might otherwise fade into a boring monolithic gray. The Jews began to fascinate in the same way southerners had a few years earlier and blacks would a few years hence: because they were (or seemed to be) different, because they had (or seemed to have) an individual life of their own, because they retained (or seemed to retain) a pungency and vividness of style as against what was so widely, if simplistically, felt to be the pallor of contemporary middle-class existence.

But there was probably even more to it than that. One of the important reasons for the rise of the Southern school to prominence in the fifties was the fact that its leading themes jibed so well with the conservative temper of the Eisenhower age; and one of the causes of its decline was the change that came over the national mood after the election of Kennedy. I would not wish to press the point too far, but it does seem suggestive to me that it was in this new climate—so unmistakably sophisticated, urban, and cosmopolitan—that so sophisticated, urban, and cosmopolitan a group as the Jewish novelists started coming into its own.

Conversely it is probably no accident that the decline of the Jewish novelists should more or less have coincided with the assault on this ethos which came to be known as the counterculture. For the culture which was being countered by the counterculture was embodied perhaps more saliently in the work of the Jewish "school" than anywhere else. There are, to be sure, complexities here. To the degree that the counterculture was based on the idea of alienation, it represented an extension rather than a repudiation of the tradition of the Jewish novelists. And indeed, several important Jewish writers—Norman Mailer being the most notable—became heroes of the counterculture themselves. But it was not only middle-class society from which the counterculture proclaimed its alienation; it was also established culture in general. And in that establishment, the Jewish novelists had by now earned a prominent place.

So prominent was this place, in fact, that resentment began to be aroused in circles which, unlike the counterculture and its partisans, were not hostile to the values or the tone of the Jewish "school" as such. All through the late fifties and early sixties there was talk, ominously reminiscent of similar grumblings in other periods, of a "conspiracy" between Jewish or (to use the familiar codeword) "New York" publishers and critics to push and puff Jewish novelists. Thus Truman Capote could complain that a "Jewish mafia" had taken over American letters. This, Capote told an interviewer, "is a clique of New York–oriented writers and critics who control much of the literary scene through the influence of the quarterlies and intellectual magazines. All these publications are Jewish-dominated and this particular coterie employs them to make or break writers by advancing or withholding attention. . . . Bernard Malamud and Saul Bellow and Philip Roth and Isaac Bashevis Singer and Norman Mailer are all fine writers, but they're not the *only* writers in the country as the Jewish mafia would have us believe. I could give you a list of excellent writers . . . ; the odds are you haven't heard of most of them for the simple reason that the Jewish mafia has systematically frozen them out of the literary scene."

No matter that the severest critics of the Jewish novelists have always been Jewish critics writing in "the quarterlies and intellectual magazines"—to Henry James's question of 1906, "Who can ever tell . . . what the genius of Israel may, or may not, really be 'up to'?" Capote's answer more than half a century later is: a conspiracy to take over American letters. That this charge should have been made and echoed just at a time when the Jewish "school" began to show signs of creative exhaustion—and just when complaints were being heard about the "overrepresentation" of Jews in other desirable areas of American life—is only one of the many curiosities of a story that Henry James himself might have relished, both for the ironies of its development and the ominous undertones of the chapters yet to come.

I. I. RABI

New Fields to Conquer The Scientific Adventure on the American Scene

My subject is part of the overall concept of "The Jewish Experience in America," specifically the impact of American society on the Jews and the Jewish community as well as distinctive contributions of American Jews to the shaping of our society. I am convinced that the Jews are different. Although man is a very complicated animal and it is hard to tell, but that Jews are different, there's very little question; just common sense shows that; the record shows it.

There were many fields in which the Jews were very important in the shaping of our society. First of all we think of the whole field of labor relations, Samuel Gompers and others who followed, Dubinsky, Potofsky, and so on, who really introduced new things in American society and the organization of labor. The theatre, business, and of course one could go on. But science is something really very special and unique in the Jewish experience. In the first place, I don't think science played any important role in the Jewish community historically. Philosophy, yes, and you can see such a towering figure as Spinoza, and of course all the rabbis who were part of the development of traditional Judaism. But science as we think of it was not part of the Jewish heritage and Jewish thought except as an aspect of philosophy; certainly not as experimental science, because of lack of facilities and everything of that sort. Of course we must remember that science altogether, what we really call science, is not more than four hundred years old, dated, let us say, from the time of Galileo. At that time the Jews had not yet been liberated so there is very little contribution that I know of, although I am not a scholar in this field. There was the famous Golem, but of course that is a beautiful tradition and not quite science. And it took Mrs. Shelley to describe it.

Now as far as science in America is concerned, that too is something quite new. There was very little. It's hard to believe that this country so advanced in technology, which plays such an eminent role in the field of science, does not have an earlier scientific tradition. Science in America can be divided into three periods, from 1876 to 1926, and I take 1876 because it was marked by the establishment of the John Hopkins University and the first Professor of Physics, Henry Roland; and 1926 was the date when I finished my dissertation and got married, but it's important otherwise; 1946, and then from 1946 to the present (postwar). Now let me first give you an idea of how novel this all is. I will read to you some remarks by Henry Roland, the great American physicist, who was a home product. He came from a very good family and was sent to Andover to prepare to go to Yale, where his father, grandfather, and great-grandfather had been before him. He wrote home saying he couldn't stand it. The people at Andover were not interested in science and were persecuting him. His piteous letter asking to be taken out led his mother (his father had died earlier) to consult with a minister in Newark. They transferred him to Rensselaer Polytechnic Institute, from which he graduated as an engineer, to which he later came back as an instructor. During that period he wrote a scientific paper which was rejected by all the American magazines. He sent it to England to James Clerk Maxwell, the nineteenth-century Scottish-born physicst. Maxwell received it enthusiastically, said he was going to read it to the Royal Society and correct the proofs so he could get early publication. This was a tremendous honor, and as a result, when Johns Hopkins was founded, Roland was selected to be the first professor in the first university in the United States in 1876. So you can see how recent this was and what the atmosphere was. The American Physical Society was established at the beginning of the century, in 1899, and I will read you some remarks that Roland, the first president of the American Physical Society, made in his inaugural address.

He examined the history of physics in America, and after mentioning three names, Benjamin Franklin, Rumford, and Joseph Henry, he went on to say: "This is the meager list of those who have earned mention by doing something for the progress of science." The record had been searched for more than one hundred years and came up with three names, beginning with Benjamin Franklin, so you can see that it wasn't a very full record. But Roland ends by saying back in 1899, "But the twentieth century is near, may we not hope for better things before its end." So my story will be, to a large extent, more or less the story of my lifetime because I was born a year before he made this address. But I would like to somewhat broaden the picture of science and how remarkable it is that some people became scientists. I have shown how Henry Roland, who had practically no encouragement, became a great scientist. But I will go back to a contemporary of Henry Roland, A. A. Michaelson, Albert Abraham Michaelson. I will tell you a little bit about him, because he is an honest-to-goodness American scientist in the sense that he comes not only from what you would call Middle America but the West. He was born in Strelno, Poland—at that time Germany. His father had dealt in clothing there but was not doing too well, and when Albert was about four years old they emigrated to America. Extraordinarily they did not stop in New York, but went on right to California. He had heard of the gold strike and the possibilities in that part of the country. So with great difficulty, the Michaelsons crossed the isthmus of Panama and landed in San Francisco. There, as usual, Michaelson's father had a relative, and was outfitted with some goods and went down to a town, a tremendous gold town called Murphy. There he established himself with Albert, and when the gold ran out there he went to Nevada to a town called Virginia City, now a rather considerable place. That is where Michaelson grew up, in a real frontier mining town. After he had exhausted what the school could teach him there, he was sent up to San Francisco to another school. He had a teacher there by the name of Bradley, who taught him the manly art of self-defense as it was called then. After he was through with school the question was "what next?" They heard that you could get an education if you went to the Naval Academy in Annapolis. In 1869 they went to their Congressman, who put him on the list. He was given an examination and he was one of the three highest. But the Congressman, for various reasons, selected somebody else. It wasn't a selection from a scholastic point of view because the man flunked out shortly afterwards. But there was Albert (by the way he got his middle name because of his father's great admiration for Abraham Lincoln), who did not get the appointment. Pressure was put on the Congressman, who said: "I can't give you the appointment, because I have utilized my quota. But President Grant has ten. I'll give you a letter to him and maybe it will get you an appointment to see him." I will read you an excerpt from the letter because it is so beautiful and so typical a picture of America. This is a letter from the Congressman in 1869 to President Grant. He writes: "Had I been at liberty to be governed by considerations of political expediency, I would have selected him. His father is a prominent and influential merchant of Virginia City and a member of the Israelite persuasion who by example and influence to the success of our cause has induced many of his co-religionists to do the same. These people are a powerful element in our politics. The boy, who is uncommonly bright and studious is a pet among them. I do most steadfastly believe that his appointment at your hand would do more to fasten these people to the Republican cause than anything else that could be done. I am sure he would be an ornament to the service and a credit to his nominator." He also had another letter, which Michaelson carried, which did not have these political statements. Well, Michaelson was received by General Grant, who said that his appointments were all filled. But he advised him to go to Annapolis and take the examination, since somebody might drop out. He went; he took the examination, but when nobody dropped out it did not look too good. He was just about ready to go back to Washington to take the train to Nevada, when a messenger arrived, saying that the President had decided to appoint him. Even though he had only ten openings, Michaelson would be the eleventh as a great exception. (Ultimately, Grant appointed two more.) Anyhow, that is how he got to Annapolis and went through the course there. Of course it was very unusual to have a Jewish person at Annapolis. I don't know if he was the only Jewish person, but it was very likely. At one time, in carrying out his duties very strictly, he got into a situation where Bradley A. Fiske challenged him to a fist fight. This was arranged very carefully with all the rules on how to do it, and this is how Fiske describes it in his memoirs: "That I had not the slightest chance became evident in about one minute, but I hammered away as best I could till the referee saw that I couldn't see out of either eye and he declared the fight as finished. I was put on the sick list and stayed on the sick list for eight days." So you see that is how Michaelson became a physicist. Of course, Annapolis, the Naval Academy, did nothing very much for science, but Michaelson was an extraordinarily good student, especially in physics and optics and so on. Some of the superior officers did not like the fact that he did not pay much attention to gunnery, but after sea duty he was assigned, for a time, to teaching at Annapolis. He thought of some experiments, measuring the velocity of light, and he had some other ideas and carried on his experiments for a period of time. He must have been a very charming person because he got very important backing in various places, including getting money from Congress and private persons to carry out these experiments. He met the daughter of an admiral, and after suitable difficulties they were married. I have met his daughter by a second marriage, but I have not been able to ascertain whether the Jewish faith after that point had any influence in his life.

Michaelson made an enormously great discovery in the most beautiful and original experiment which he devised. His experiment showed that the passage of the earth through what was then called the luminiferous ether could not be detected, and Einstein later on showed that one didn't have to suppose it. But that idea of the luminiferous ether had a very strong hold on the physics of the day. One couldn't really think of explaining matters concerning electricity and light without this luminiferous ether, which was the medium through which light traveled. Light is supposed to consist of vibrations, electric vibrations, resident in this luminiferous ether. Actually Michaelson was terribly disappointed by his result. He had hoped to measure the speed or demonstrate the earth's motion through luminiferous ether. The apparatus was very, very sensitive, and the instruments that he used in this were very original, very sensitive, very important. It was an enormous discovery. In 1907 he was the first American physicist to get a Nobel Prize and, of course, the first Jew to get a Nobel Prize. It was a very unlikely journey from Strelno to Virginia City to Annapolis. From these two things I've mentioned, Michaelson and the remarks of Roland, you can see that American physics was no great shakes. And furthermore there was no American Jew of importance in physics in the nineteenth century or even the early part of the twentieth century.

Now we have to look a bit at the American condition. There was a series of immigrations of Jews to America—there was the original one of the Portuguese, then later a large immigration from Germany, which made a great success of it, and then came this massive immigration from Eastern Europe, Russia, Poland, etc. Now these people who came were not scientists, nor were they people of a scientific culture. And they came to a country which had no important tradition of scientific culture, as you can see from the part of the speech I read by Henry Roland. They came fresh from the towns and villages of Eastern Europe or from the small towns of Germany. Well-to-do people were not immigrants. There was no reason to go. So these were mostly poor people, who came and adapted themselves to the situation here more or less. Some did very well, when you think of those like the Lehmans and that whole group, who started as peddlers much as Michaelson's father had done. As for scientists there were really none, and there was no tradition in the Jewish culture to go in that direction. Well I entered the scene myself, and I lived with it as it came along, as I said, in 1898, and by 1926 I had decided I would study physics. I sent off my dissertation and was one of the few Jews in the whole United States that had studied physics. But the same is true more or less of the other sciences. There were fewer in chemistry in a way, because chemistry was very, very difficult in the sense of finding a job. To this very day it is a difficult field. At that time it was almost impossible to get into the universities. But there were people who tried, and that's the important thing. So by 1926, the time I'm talking about, I knew of almost every Jewish person in the United States who might be studying or had done physics as well as some students. Of course the American Physical Society, although it had grown prodigiously, was very small. But the level, the cultural level of physics and the position of the physicist, apart from a few exceptions which I can mention, like Millikan and Compton and the few bright lights in the United States, was quite low. It was so low that when I visited Copenhagen and Göttingen, Germany, after I got my degree, I found that while they subscribed to our journal, they waited till the end of the year to get the twelve monthly issues at once, to save postage. Thus we have not just a Jewish experience vis-à-vis science but a whole American experience.

But the generation of Jews who had come over in the late nineteenth century produced offspring who then entered the American scene without the complications of the *shtetl* or anything else. The air was free, education was free, they could follow their own inclinations. They could break away from the confines of the Jewish tradition of hundreds of years before, from the rabbis and the customs, and they could look at the Western world, Western culture, which then was open to everybody rather than just to the few rebels and revolutionaries of the previous century.

It took a little time for this to take effect, but when I was a young man entering college, quite a few were interested in fields other than law and medicine, which were the traditional fields. All over the United States, in the universities and everywhere, there were young people becoming interested in science. The cultivation of science changed very much from the nineteenth century. In the nineteenth century the patricians, the aristocrats, were interested in science. From the time of Thomas Jefferson on, there certainly was an interest in science. But it was more the kind of interest that reflected the interests of the upper classes, the broad questions, the philosophical issues. And actually, when Tyndall came from England to give lectures on science in the United States, he could fill Carnegie Hall, and they came in their carriages and so on. Tyndall gave lecture demonstrations. He made so much money, which he did not want to take with him, that he endowed Tyndall fellowships at various universities. So the interest was there, but it was a different kind of interest. As soon as the science subjects became more professional and you really had to work at it, using mathematics and so on, most people dropped out and went into other things: art appreciation, archaeology, etc. So the real hard work was taken on by the boys from the farms, the middle classes, and so on. Except of course for the Jews. They weren't there yet. But in the next century the very small percentage that had any interest in science felt really driven to it. I don't know just what stimulated that interest. In my own case it must have been the first verses of Genesis, which are very noble verses, about the beginning of the world and how it was created. A young boy who didn't have much sense of *tachlis* (practical values) became interested in this, and I think that is true of others who entered the field of science. Of course jobs were very hard to find. As I've told people, in my case I got my doctor's degree in 1927 and there was no question of a job. I didn't worry about a job because there just were no jobs. And it was possible for me, on a small fellowship from Columbia—which I might mention was $1500—to go abroad. I paid my own passage, and carried on my studies. And that was a new world, because there for the first time you could see science as it was being made by the creators of science—very often quite young men, younger than I was, Werner Heisenberg, who recently died, Erwin Schrödinger, and so on. What happened was a very interesting experience, especially for those who are educators. There is an enormous difference between gathering and having knowledge and having a feeling for the subject. I discovered in Germany, which was the place to go then, because that's where it was happening, that I knew more than German students of my period, but it was not a question of knowledge. I've described it as a new libretto, but not the music, not the tune. And this has to do with getting into a tradition. I've observed that most people who have made their mark in science actually studied with other people, of a similar type. The books were available, but there is something to tradition, even in science, which looks so cold. It is very hard to describe, but I suppose this is so in all fields, that there is an old tradition, a human tradition, which carries on. What was happening in the United States was that we had an enormous number of colleges and universities, and some of them were considered quite ridiculous. Ohio had something like three hundred colleges described by the phrase "cow college." They were looked down on everywhere in Europe and in the large eastern universities as well. But we had something we didn't realize. We had a time bomb going, because those places had students, and many of them were very bright, and all they needed was a certain kind of leadership. It was because of what my generation picked up in Europe and could give to American students that ten years after the period I am talking about, 1927, when the *Physical Review* stood in such low esteem, only ten years later, it had become the leading journal in the world. We were able to give all those students a proper education, put them on the right track. Of course the period for each student is only about four years. You need only multiply to arrive at the very large number we developed. Thus when the war came, that is, the Second World War, we had people who could do the job. But this was a very sudden transformation which occurred.

In the years before the war, the situation was very different from anything younger people here and others can think of now. There was no government support until after the war, and my laboratory at Columbia never got a nickel from the government for the research which we were doing. You might ask where the money came from. Well it didn't. There was no money. I had an associate, Professor Zacharias from MIT, who taught at Hunter College in New York, a regular full-time schedule—at that time sixteen contact hours plus committee work. But in addition he put in fifty hours a week in our laboratory, for which he got no pay. It was a privilege, in that sense. Of course the equipment was not as good as it could have been if we had received better financial support. What I am describing, then, is a nascent period which was not very visible from Washington or otherwise in the general community, where the United States had built up an enormous cadre of young people who were very capable, very interested. They came from a few schools. I'm talking of my generation. I had one at Columbia. Oppenheimer had a brilliant school for theoretical physics, especially in California. And so on a number of places. There was something that I would consider in some respects a Jewish impact, in the sense there is a certain tendency, perhaps coming from the Jewish culture, which thinks of these problems from a broader point of view, that's rather normative. It is just as difficult, and sometimes more difficult, to do an experiment or solve a problem of no special importance except to show skill, as it is to do an experiment that is of profound importance. And you can see that Michaelson was one of those. He experimented on light, the velocity of light; he found instruments to do it, the method was not very important. But the result was very important. It is the result that could change your outlook, rather than the result which would show that he had done it, how clever one has been to do it.

Now I find it very difficult to trace the Jewish impact through science on the United States and, vice versa, the scientific impact on the Jews. Actually that's a very important thing. The fact that Einstein was Jewish, or some of the other culture heroes of that sort, is a matter which gives enormous confidence to young people even if they aren't so very gifted. However mistakenly, they feel that there is something in them and that there is something perhaps to emulate. It may not be appropriate to their ability, it may be tragic at times, as I've seen it, but there is this impression and this feeling and I think it exists. If some of the other minorities in this country had similar heroes to point to, I think it would make an enormous difference. Somehow or other, as I said in the discussion before, the Jews tend to overestimate their ability and their cleverness. It may result in failure, but it certainly results in pride and makes life rather interesting.

There is another point which is I think very interesting, a Jewish quest for novelty. I think the novelties in the theatre were brought to this country largely by Jewish groups in New York, newer writing, newer stage settings, that sort of thing. I think that happens almost across the board: when you have new things coming up, new ideas, you will have the Jews becoming interested in that.

Maybe it is the same sort of esoteric desire that makes them interested in the diamond business. Things that are out of the humdrum or current fashion are the sort of things we go for. Well, fortunately as the Jewish immigrants of the first and second generations were coming up, there was a tremendous basic advance in science. A whole new science had arisen, a whole new point of view. One is the theory of relativity of Einstein, and then there was quantum theory in quantum mechanics, which came at that time. These were brand-new outlooks which came up during the period I'm talking about, 1926. Now this was very new. At the universities and elsewhere, the established people were too busy to learn this new magic, It was the young people of my generation that got down to it, and suddenly the students were attracted to us. This is where the Jewish influx into the sciences started. Always with the new ideas, picking up the new ideas, whether they were originally Jewish or not doesn't matter, but they were new, iconoclastic ideas. This is more or less a Jewish characteristic even in politics, so that a new period opened and we began to have Jews in the universities. I was the first Jew appointed in the physics department at Columbia University. They didn't have even one in chemistry till the end of the war. But this new material came along, and then one other thing. At the American universities in an earlier day, the departments were more like clubs, so it wasn't a question so much of anti-Semitism whether they would appoint a Jew but whether he would fit into the club. The answer in most cases was obviously no. He didn't have that rather gracious, suave manner which was the accepted collegial way these people talked about issues. There were others who were invited to the president's house (Nicholas Murray Butler) and things of that sort, and I never was—but, on the other hand, it didn't interfere with my promotions. Actually I never met the president until the Nobel Prize was awarded to me, but I was the first Jew to hold the rank of University Professor.

As the science advanced, the substance became much more important than the form. And all at once things changed. Then came the war, and that is when things changed very drastically. Because the war and the application of science to weapons required the newer people, our group was called on to solve very great problems which they hadn't dreamed of before. I personally was connected with both Los Alamos and the radiation laboratory in Cambridge, which developed radar. We dealt very much with the military. After the war we were still there, still knew those people. The power of science had been recognized, and then you found very powerful governmental committees, federal governmental committees, at which you would have groups of scientists, and none of them was without a very strong Jewish representation in this field. The government began supplying money and so on. So that as the thing developed from 1946 onward, you had this great supply of money, this entrance of the Jews everywhere, the barriers to a large extent that had existed before had disappeared.

What effect did it have on the Jews of America? I've thought about that and I don't really know. Of course it opened doors. That is to say, a Jewish young man could follow his interest into various branches of science and feel assured that he would have an equal, an almost equal, chance in the general job market, appointments, access to laboratories, access to equipment, and everything else. Now that's a very, very important thing. And it's happened and we've seen it. Now as for the specifically Jewish thing, to what degree has this affected them as Jews in the sense of being a part of the Jewish tradition, trying to follow this tradition, follow these customs, be learned in those fields, etc.? I would say that I can count on the fingers of one hand those I know who are affected in this way. Science, being universal, doesn't lend itself to a particular tradition, certainly not to an ancient tradition. So I would say in this sense that it is a part of a universal tradition, an opening of this tremendous world of science to the Jewish community. How it would be absorbed in the Jewish tradition, what part would be more or less specifically Jewish, I don't know. I don't discern anything. I'm a member of the Board of Governors of the Weizmann Institute in Israel, and I don't see that the scientists there relate uniquely to the Jewish tradition. They follow some of the customs, they celebrate Pesach, in their way, but more as a nationalistic affair than as something Jewish in the Jewish religious tradition in order to find learning in that direction going back to rabbis. It may be a good thing, in fact I'm sure it is. Because nothing that goes on for hundreds and hundreds of years is not in need of reexamination, of change, deeper understanding from deeper knowledge. It is a very difficult thing to hang on to, just as anyone that wants to live in the ancient temples of Mexico would find it difficult. And I think the same problem has occurred. These battles have occurred in the history of the confrontation of religion, any religion, with science. I only have to bring you back to the experience of Galileo. He was a true son of the Church and published ideas which were heretical from the point of view of the Church with the general idea that he was strengthening the Church. The Church at that time didn't see it that way and he was condemned, and the Church has tried these last four hundred years to live it down, and to come to terms with it. I think that this will continue to be the situation of science and religion. I don't believe they are opposed. The battle between them is more of a civil war because they both try to do the same thing. Religion, traditional religion, has to be a practical subject. Mankind is fearful, uncertain. It sees the world, nature, more or less as an enemy. He needs help. And he turns to religion, one kind or another, for help, to tell him his place in the world. That's what I mean when I say it's practical. Religion has to give an answer when questions come up. Science is the other way. It also wants to give an answer to people about their place in the universe. All these terrible things happen around man, humanity—lightning, thunder, earthquake, disease, typhoons, the skies, they don't look friendly. Religion tries to make it meaningful, and not so unfriendly, by dealing with it in profound and universal terms. Science, by patient investigation, by experiments, and so on, bit by bit makes the world reasonable and habitable, and so on. But necessarily slowly and necessarily in conflict, more or less, with the immediate answers which religion has to give. Just as Mr. Carter has to have an answer to a question, you have got to have an answer. So very often, because of the need for immediate answers, it turns out that those things in which religion was very strong, were wrong. But since so much of morality, so much of custom, depended on that, it couldn't stand by itself, it needed the secular arm to support it. It needed the military, it needed the police, it needed the government, more or less, to support it. You couldn't expect more than that, because when things become so established you have to call in the secular arm to support it. We saw this in the history of religion in the Catholic church. In America too, in the Colonies, where they had to support the traditional theme lest morality and stability disappear. So that is where science comes along.

Now, what of the effect on Jewish tradition, Jewish values, Jewish customs, Jewish religion down through the ages, what will come of that? What effect will science have on it? How they will be married in some form, I can't say. I think they will be. Because you begin to see more and more a yearning on the part of many young people for the kind of security which tradition gave them. And some are very recent converts. How this will be welded into a kind of unity, as Thomas Aquinas was able to do, in his time, for the Catholic church, we don't know. But I put this forward as a task for Judaica scholars and thinkers.

Questions and Answers

Q. Do you think that the talmudic tradition had anything to do with the Jewish interest in science?

A. Well I suppose that the Jewish tradition was a molder of Jewish character, whether you had studied it or whether you hadn't. I would say to that degree, I cannot trace a direct line. Although many of my colleagues in Israel are very learned in the Talmud—perhaps they wouldn't have been in Israel if they weren't—but they are not necessarily scientists of great renown. But I don't know the Talmud myself. It's all second- and third-hand. It may be that kind of reasoning which is essentially the case system and very practical. It may be called distinctively Jewish, although I wouldn't really go out on a limb and say that it had something to do with it. It does carry an intellectual tradition. It carries a tradition of argument. There is one other point. At one time, in an interview, we were talking about bringing up children, and I mentioned that I came home from school and my mother would ask me, "Did you ask any good questions today?" which I think is a Jewish thing, and the Jewish thing, in a sense, was not a question that was antagonistic, it was a question really helping to bring out and clarify the meaning, and I think that would be in the talmudic tradition as far as I know it.

Q. How would you compare the current generation, say under thirty-five, under thirty years of age, to the group that worked in World War II?

A. Well, they're not under thirty. They are nearer fifty because whether under or over thirty they are all marvelous. They are wonderful people, enormously skillful, enormously knowledgeable, resourceful, really marvelous. The present generation too. They are so learned. There is one thing that I miss though, but that's only because of my age, I guess. My friends and I were more interested in the philosophical, broader implications of what we were doing. These people are immensely more skillful and knowledgeable but more sharply focused. Maybe you have to be that nowadays. The number has increased tremendously. The competition is very intense, so that you can give a reason for it, but I do miss the kind of basic skepticism which informed my colleagues when I was young.

Q. What do you think of Israel's developments in the field of atomic energy and possible possession of the bomb?

A. Well, I wouldn't fault the atomic scientists. You ask a very serious question. I once discussed the same question with Ben-Gurion. I told him that once Israel acquired atomic weapons, it would mean the end of Israel. Once you elevate the weapons system to that degree, it wouldn't take more than two or three or maybe only one to polish off Israel—a small territory, concentrated population, think of Tel Aviv alone, Haifa. I would say Israel ought to do everything possible to avoid the introduction of atomic weapons. And I think, if you rely on it, there may be a psychological thing and deterrence, but I do not believe in deterrence. I've not found it necessary to turn to religion to think of ways of countering that. If I think of it in terms of a religious war—I can't answer the question.

Q. What is your personal view of religion?

A. I have abandoned neither religion nor Judaism. If I am asked my religion, I say Orthodox Hebrew, by which I mean the church I don't attend. I have a kind of very strong identification with this, and I think the whole idea of God as builder of the universe, not giver of the law, is a very significant one for me. I would never try to weaken anybody's religious faith. I think it would be a terrible thing. I did that once or twice when I was young, and I regret it. I myself, coming from a Hasidic background, was deeply moved by the rites and attitudes in Mea Shearim, very deeply moved by them. It's very much a part of me. But that's a different matter than trying to face the problem of the world. I think it gives me another understanding on matters which people who haven't had my experience would find utterly strange. And I think I find that true of many Jews when they see Hasidim in Mea Shearim. I've never visited the Lubavitcher in Brooklyn, but I can see that people would scorn it. I always find it very moving. I would be very understanding and I wouldn't scoff at it. I'd take it as a fact, it exists, and I believe people feel that way, not wanting to change their beliefs, and if it helps them, they are lucky in a way. But it is not the road of reasoning to which I subscribe.

MARSHALL SKLARE

Jewish Acculturation And American Jewish Identity

I. Introduction: From Self-Segregation to Acculturation to Assimilation

From its inception, American sociology has been interested in racial, ethnic, and religious groups. This interest originally stemmed from two sources: (1) the fact that a substantial proportion of the American population have been identifiable as members of minority groups, and (2) the belief that the relationship between the dominant group and the minorities may pose problems for American society.

What has been the approach of social scientists to the presence of minority groups in American society? If we study the work of early American sociologists on the subject of ethnicity, we notice that the regnant school of thought is that ethnic groups (generally referred to as "immigrant groups") would go through a three-stage process. They would start at the stage of self-segregation, progress to the stage known as acculturation, and end with assimilation. Assimilation would mean that they no longer constituted a significant entity in the society, though to be sure individuals might retain some ancestral memories as well as continue to use family names which would indicate that their country of origin was not dominated by Anglo-Saxon culture.

In sociological writing the word *ghetto* has frequently been used to describe the first stage—the stage known as self-segregation. This usage is unfortunate because the term *ghetto* should only be employed to describe situations of imposed segregation. For the majority of American ethnic groups, segregation has been elective rather than imposed, though to be sure groups have not always had perfect freedom to decide where they would live and what occupations they would follow.

The sociologists of yesterday assumed that after some years of self-segregation, and certainly by the time the second generation would come to maturity, ethnic groups would progress to the stage of acculturation. Acculturation would involve taking on many of the culture patterns of the majority, although continuing with some culture patterns inherited from self-segregated immigrant parents.

The final part of the process was assimilation, namely, the merging into the general society of members of a minority group. Sociologists of an earlier era did point out that the cycle of self-segregation to acculturation to assimilation would not proceed automatically: it could be interfered with by the presence of prejudice and discrimination. As they saw it, prejudice and discrimination would not only make it difficult for individuals to assimilate, but would create psychological pressures as well—individuals would hesitate to assimilate since by so doing they could be accused of cowardice, of deserting their fellow ethnics who had suffered rejection by American society.

It was also felt that the movement from self-segregation to acculturation to assimilation needed to be a gradual process. If all individuals moved precipitously from one stage to another, resistance to the final step of assimilation would emerge on the part of the dominant group. A differential rate of assimilation within the minority community was thus desirable; it would have the advantage of not exceeding the absorptive capacity for assimilation on the part of the dominant group. It was assumed that those who were well-educated would assimilate before those who were ill-educated, and that those who were members of the middle and upper classes would assimilate before those who were members of the working class.

To be sure there were those who had reservations about the validity of this cycle. Marcus Hansen, for example, a historian at

Harvard, advanced another conception which was later to be given wide currency by Will Herberg. Hansen contended that the assimilation of the third generation was not inevitable. He suggested that the grandson of the immigrant, feeling himself to be fully an American, might wish to remember and even to perpetuate what his second-generation father had wanted to forget. Nevertheless the dominant theory was that the trend to assimilation was irreversible. The great society would swallow up all ethnic subcommunities, particularly those which were white and had originated in Southern, Central, or Eastern Europe.

II. Assimilation as an Incorrect Prediction

It is apparent to us today that the early conception of an orderly cycle from self-segregation to acculturation to assimilation was an incorrect prediction. One of the reasons for the incorrect prediction appears to be that ideology played a considerable role in its formulation. Sociologists who were members of the dominant group tended to be committed to Wasp culture. They viewed the cycle as a natural phenomenon, given what they conceived to be the nature of the relationship between minorities and dominant groups. Overall they regarded assimilation as desirable—desirable both for the dominant group as well as for the minority group.

Sociologists who were members of minority groups did not, as a rule, advance a different view. Generally they were marginal members of their particular ethnic group. In most cases they were eager to be assimilated. Hence they had no objection to what one sociologist has termed "Anglo-conformity." In sum, neither scholars who came from the dominant group nor those who originated from various minority groups looked very hard for evidence which would cast doubt on the cycle of self-segregation to acculturation to assimilation.

Today it is clear that American Jewry, as well as a variety of other white ethnic groups, has not gone through the orderly cycle of self-segregation, acculturation, and assimilation which earlier generations of sociologists had predicted. Some American Jews, for example, can even be characterized as occupying the position of self-segregation. Furthermore, the self-segregation group is presently composed of members of the second and third generation as well as members of the first generation.

There are other aspects of the theory which reality has not validated. The acculturated group includes not only members of the second generation but of the third and fourth generations as well. Furthermore, some members of the first generation are acculturated rather than self-segregated.

In respect to assimilation, it is evident that while some Jews have assimilated, assimilation has not proceeded as predicted. Jewish identity is far from disappearing. If anything, the Jewish community as an organized entity has gained in visibility in recent decades rather than diminished in visibility. In fact this lecture series constitutes evidence of the fact that the cycle is far from completed. The lecture series is based on the assumption that the Jews are a living entity in American society rather than a historical curiosity. The existence of this series suggests that earlier social scientists made an imperfect prediction of what would occur in the future. We should remember that this prediction had its source in a belief in the melting-pot ideology. And it was reinforced by a less-than-perfect understanding of the dynamics of ethnic-group life.

III. The Pervasiveness of Acculturation

If I were asked where on the cycle most American Jews are presently located, the answer would have to be that they are on the level known as acculturation. Acculturation of course spans a wide spectrum. There are considerable differences among Jews in respect to where they are located on the acculturation scale. Furthermore many are more highly acculturated than they know.

My belief is that if we were to examine a variety of indicators of acculturation, it could be demonstrated that considering the culture that Jews brought with them, they have taken giant steps in incorporating various aspects of American culture. In some cases they have sought quite deliberately to blend American culture with values and patterns of Jewishness which they wish to retain. While we are not able in one essay to analyze who is at what level of acculturation, we can address ourselves to the more modest task of delineating how it is that Jews acculturated with such great speed and drive. What are the factors which transformed a group which spoke a different language from the dominant group, which had a style of dress different from the dominant group, and whose very religion was in opposition to the religion espoused by the dominant group?

1. The first matter that is involved in understanding the speed of Jewish acculturation in the United States is the fact that the United States has no medieval past. There is no history here of the Jew existing as a pariah people. There were, to be sure, some legal restrictions against Jews in some of the constitutions of the states which composed the original Union. However these were removed during the early part of the nineteenth century and were not of great importance even when they were on the statute books. We should also remember that there was, and still is, considerable interest in the conversion of Jews to Christianity. John Adams and John Quincy Adams, for example, were highly interested in such conversion, though to the best of my recollection this interest was not alluded to in the *Adams Chronicles* as presented on TV.

Even if there has been interest in converting the Jew, this would not involve conversion to a religion which has dominated the American continent for hundreds of years. American Christianity, whether Protestant or Catholic, was itself new to these shores. It had no status here as an ancient or medieval religion. Furthermore it is not always intimately connected with the great monuments of the American past or with the great events of American history. As we have seen, the Jew can celebrate the Bicentennial without compromising his Jewish identity.

In acculturating, then, the American Jew does not have to do violence to his Jewish past. He does not have to leave a ghetto. He does not have to be a traitor to his ancestors. In sum, the acculturation of Jews could proceed without feelings of overwhelming guilt and conflict. The acculturation of the Jews could proceed without their feeling that they must deny and bury their heritage. I do not mean to minimize the family conflicts which were engendered by acculturation—there were to be sure some serious rifts between the first and second generation. Nevertheless we must stress that the acculturation of the Jews could proceed without their feeling that such acculturation was a price exacted if the Jews were to have the same rights as others.

2. A second factor involved in the thrust and speed with which Jews acculturated is the fact that the history of the Jews is a history of acculturation. That is, Jews have lived in a variety of countries and hence in a variety of cultures. They are experienced in adjusting to a dominant culture. Their experience became evident when, in modern times, the ingathering of Jews took place in Palestine. It is even more evident today in the State of Israel, despite all of the efforts which have been made to absorb and integrate all of the segments of Israel's Jewish population.

It has frequently been said that the history of the Jews is a history of acculturation. If Jews have been influenced by cultures which were unfriendly to them, it is to be expected that the influence of American culture would be especially strong, for as we have noted, American culture had no medieval past. Even though there has been considerable prejudice and discrimination against Jews in the United States, on the whole such manifestations have not resulted in a feeling of embitterment on the part of Jews.

Contrast Jewish experience with that of others. Many immigrant groups which came to the United States had no familiarity with living as a minority and adapting to a dominant culture. The Jews, on the other hand, had a wealth of experience in that form of accommodation which we know as acculturation. They also had a great deal of experience both with segregation and self-segregation*

3. In explaining the speed of Jewish acculturation, we must assign a role to the fact that the Jews lacked a homeland. All of the immigrant groups who came to America came from a homeland. To be sure, in some cases that homeland was under the domina-

* Salo Baron's theory that Jewish survival is more likely in a multi-cultural society than in one dominated by a single culture is an important point, but I will not deal with it systematically here. It involves a full-scale examination of how pluralistic American culture has been.

tion of a foreign power—the English in the case of the Irish, and the Russians in the case of the Poles. Nevertheless the Irish and the Poles felt that their country was *their* homeland. In fact, although they lived on American soil, some of the Irish and Poles sought to use the United States as a base to defeat the foreign nations which ruled their homelands.

The Puerto Ricans are a classic contemporary case of the easy availability of a homeland, with the consequent slowing of acculturation. This is ironic since Puerto Rico is a part of the American Commonwealth, though to be sure there are separatists who would like to end Puerto Rico's ties with the United States. Furthermore, Puerto Rico itself has undergone considerable acculturation to the American way of life.

If the constant movement of Puerto Ricans to and from their homeland is at one end of the spectrum, the Jews are located at the opposite end of the spectrum. The Jews are a group which had very little interest in returning to the countries from which they came. Accordingly, their emigration rate has been minimal. The German Jews who came here in the nineteenth century, and who gloried in German culture, generally did not return to Germany. Furthermore very few of the German refugees who came in the 1930s availed themselves of the opportunity to return to post-World War II Germany.

The Jews from Eastern Europe who came in the 1880–1914 period showed the same lack of enthusiasm for emigration. A few of the ultra-Orthodox did return, and there was a small circle of Jewish radicals who repaired to Russian soil when Tsarism was destroyed, as well as a decade earlier when social reform was in the Russian air. However, the vast majority of Jewish socialists, communists, and anarchists were not motivated to return to Russian soil; they had the good sense to continue to preach their radicalism from the safety of New York, Philadelphia, and Chicago, and later from Los Angeles and Miami. Finally, the East Europeans who came to the United States during and after World War II had little interest in returning to their former homes. They would have to return to communities which were, in effect, cemeteries, and in many cases they would have to live in countries dominated by communist regimes. Understandably they did not wish to be reminded of the Holocaust every day of their lives.

4. If a homeland to which the Jews felt strong bonds was absent, there was another significant factor which was influential in speeding Jewish acculturation. This is the factor of upward social mobility, by which I mean the rise in class position. The Jews are well known to students of American society as a group which moves up much more rapidly than others. Indeed in two generations Jews have reached the lofty class level occupied by denominations located at the top of the Wasp group. Depending on the area of the country, these denominations are most commonly the Presbyterians, the Episcopalians, and the Congregationalists. It should be remembered the Jewish advance is all the more remarkable since it occurred in the face of prejudice and discrimination.

The reason why such rapid upward mobility took place so quickly is a large and difficult question. What we are interested in is that the rise of many Jews to the middle and the upper class has had the effect of speeding acculturation. The rise brought with it new relationships with Gentiles, it depleted neighborhoods and areas of the city where a distinctive Jewish life-style had established itself, and it gave the Jews new aspirations. Some would say that it also gave them new pathologies.

5. The next factor that must be examined is the question of values. There has been, and there still is, a great deal of loose talk to the effect that many Jewish values are the same as American values. Such talk is sometimes a thinly disguised device to improve intergroup relations and to demonstrate that Jews have been model citizens. Nevertheless it is correct to say that certain American values and certain Jewish values (if properly modified) can overlap. That is, if certain Jewish values are modified they are capable of a smooth articulation with American values. In cases where such overlap was possible and where the benefits were substantial, Jews were motivated to modify their value structure. When they did so their acculturation was speeded enormously.

The example which is most frequently adduced is the value of education. California, with its multitiered system of higher education, represents the ultimate in the American belief in the value of education, the rightness of education, and the availability of education to all who wish to use it as an avenue of upward social mobility.

Jews too believe that education is a social good. However, in traditional Jewish culture the education which is prized is education in the realm of the sacred. Secular education is viewed as distinctly inferior to sacred education and should only be pursued after the individual has achieved mastery in the area of the sacred. Furthermore, in traditional Jewish culture education is prized only for males. There is very little emphasis, if any, on providing equal educational opportunities for women.

We must remember that some of the Jews who came to the United States had already encountered secularism before they arrived here. Those who did not were soon touched by it. Thus the ground was prepared for shifts in attitude which would create value homophyly. Jews speedily relinquished the idea of the primacy of sacred education, and, at a later period, also accepted the idea that females as well as males should be educated. Thus Jews began to take advantage of the educational opportunities which were afforded them. They did so much more extensively and more intensively than any other ethnic group coming from the European continent. Secular education led to a great deal of acculturation—a degree of acculturation more extensive than most Jews realized.

6. Another factor which has worked to speed the acculturation of the American Jew is that the element of European Jewish society which we may designate as the *proste* came here in very large numbers. Indeed the *proste* came to dominate the Jewish community. Some have contended that America is the revenge of the *proste yidn* upon the *scheine yidn.*

There is little question that immigration to America was a selective process. Although it did not reach down to the very lowest levels of Jewish society, America was inordinately attractive to those at the lower levels of Jewish society, whether in Western or Eastern Europe. Up to 1914 in Eastern Europe, emigration to America or to other Western lands (or, as an alternative, to the large cities in Eastern Europe) was especially attractive to individuals in modest economic circumstances and in relatively modest status positions. It is apparent that many of the immigrants who came to the United States lacked the strong ideological commitments of those who stayed behind. This was especially true in the area of religious commitments.

All of these characteristics of the pre-World War I immigrants became apparent after the Russian Revolution. The Russian Revolution involved a radical restructuring of society and meant that those who had been firmly rooted in the Jewish upper class, and in the upper reaches of the Jewish middle class, were now declassed. The old status hierarchy was shaken to its very foundation. After the Russian Revolution there arrived on American shores elements of the elite of the Russian Jewish community, including those strongly committed to various ideological causes, which included Orthodoxy, Zionism, Hebraism, and Yiddishism. The victory of the Bolsheviks also resulted in the migration of radicals who faced imprisonment or worse if they remained in the Soviet Union.

The domination of the *proste* (the crude and common Jews) was noticed as early as the eighteenth century. Haym Salomon, who in recent decades has achieved a place in American Jewish history which he did not occupy in his own lifetime, wrote to his relatives in 1783 advising them to stay in Europe. "Your *yichus* (ancestral reputation) is worth very little here" was the way he put it. Even those who came here with the most impeccable *yichus* had to achieve social position by virtue of achievement rather than ascription. Jacob Schiff is perhaps the best example. Upon his arrival he did not automatically occupy the role which his singular *yichus* entitled him to. Rather it was his financial genius, his great generosity, his communal devotion, and his imposing manner which made him the leading figure in the American Jewish community.

By definition *proste yidn* had few inhibitions. They were eager for acculturation. Lacking the conservatism which comes from an aristocratic background, they were prepared to move rapidly on all fronts: economic, educational, and cultural. They did not arrive here wedded to a style of life to which they were deeply committed. They were open to the new, and they were eager to achieve the recognition which they could not attain in Europe.

7. The final factor in our analysis of rapid acculturation is the

persecution which the Jews have endured, together with their exclusion from society. Because of this history the Jews could not bring themselves to rebuff the invitation to participate in American culture. However, when Jews came to perceive that full participation in American culture would involve melting into the melting pot, they sought to retain their Jewish identity and to call a halt to further acculturation.

The fact, then, that the Jews had so long been outside of society meant that they were inordinately attracted to American culture. Thus for Jews America was more than a place to make money. It was a kind of promised land, a kind of holy land. The term *goldene medinah* did not only have the meaning that the streets were paved with gold and that America was a land of great economic opportunity. The phrase *goldene medinah* had the additional meaning that America is a place which gives the Jew an equal chance (or at least some chance), a place which does not subordinate him, and a place which is open to his talents. Jews who used the phrase *goldene medinah* were quite aware of American prejudice and discrimination. Nevertheless they viewed America as a veritable paradise in comparison to the countries from which they had come.

IV. The Problematics of Assimilation

Now that we have analyzed the factors responsible for the speed and impact of acculturation on the American Jew, we need to turn to the question of why acculturation was not followed by assimilation. We should, of course, bear in mind that individual Jews did assimilate. In the eighteenth and nineteenth centuries, such assimilation was common in the South, in the Middle West, and, later, in the Far West. In our own day assimilation has also occurred in places of high Jewish concentration, including the Middle Atlantic and New England states. If assimilation did occur in many individual cases, why did it not become a mass phenomenon? Why has the loss of Jewish identity been more the exception than the rule?

1. Perhaps the most frequently adduced reason for the lack of

mass assimilation is the hostility of non-Jews. There is little question that Gentiles, whether Wasps or ethnics, were not particularly eager to assimilate the Jew, and that some of this lack of eagerness can be traced to the factor of prejudice. The attitudes of middle- and upper-class Wasps is especially important in this connection. (Jews who were candidates for assimilation were not interested in assimilating into minority groups whose acculturation was less than their own and whose social status was limited). The ambiguities of the Wasps were quite evident. On the one hand they encouraged assimilation by rewarding those who wished to subordinate their Jewish identity. On the other hand, when they realized what mass assimilation would mean, they were not so sure that it should be encouraged.

We must reckon, then, with the ambiguous stance of the Wasp and the possibility that the attitude of Gentiles was a factor in discouraging assimilation. At the same time, however, we must recognize that any effort to account for Jewish survival purely on the basis of Gentile attitudes is necessarily incomplete and one-sided.

2. It is apparent that demographic factors have been an important influence in making the American Jewish community viable. Although Jews are less than three percent of the total population of the United States, the American Jewish community is the largest community in the millenial history of the Jewish people.

An important point about the size of the community is that it is concentrated in a relatively few urban centers. To be sure, Jews now frequently reside in the suburbs rather than the central city, but even in suburbia there tends to be areas of Jewish concentration. The point that needs making is that the American Jewish population is sufficiently large and concentrated to maintain a variety of Jewish institutions, to offer a variety of services, and to be a sufficiently large group to be visible. Indeed, given the size of the Jewish community American Jewry has had high visibility. Finally, although intermarriage is a very serious problem, the size of the Jewish community is such that intermarriage is not a foregone conclusion; the marriage market is large enough to assure endogamy for all those who want it.

3. A factor which is seldom mentioned in any analysis of American Jewish survivalism is that anti-Semitism in the United States has not been strong enough to motivate assimilation. There are a variety of responses to anti-Semitism in the modern era. These responses are as varied as the feeling that it is dishonorable to assimilate as long as there is anti-Semitism and the reaction that the parent owes it to his child to assimilate so that the child will have the chance for a less stressful and embattled life.

As we have noticed in our analysis of acculturation, anti-Semitism in the United States was quite different from what it was in Europe. Furthermore, the Jewish reaction to anti-Semitism in the United States was different than on the European continent. The American Jewish attitude has generally been that anti-Semitism was more temporary than permanent, that anti-Semitism is, in fact, un-American. It violates American values, it contradicts the American creed, and in the final analysis is subversive.

Given all of these beliefs about anti-Semitism, it is not surprising that Jews felt no strong desire to capitulate to anti-Semitism by assimilating. Rather, their reaction has been to fight anti-Semitism, a reaction which has given rise to Jewish intergroup-relations agencies both on the national as well as the local level. Furthermore, the reaction of fighting against anti-Semitism has motivated programs even in Jewish organizations which are not specifically established for the purpose of combating anti-Semitism. American Jews have felt that they have both the right and the duty to fight anti-Semitism. At the same time they have felt that anti-Semitism would not necessarily doom them to remain at the bottom of the class level of the society. One could be both Jewish and successful. One could find economic opportunities in fields that had not been preempted by Gentiles. One could obtain an education despite the quotas which were in existence at some of the elite private universities.

4. Another factor which needs to be analyzed is that of the existence of pluralism. As we have pointed out, the idea of the melting pot has a long history. On the other hand, there were always pluralists who felt that the melting pot was unsatisfactory and even illegitimate. Social workers such as Jane Addams came

to understand the danger and the illegitimacy of demanding that immigrants strip themselves of their heritage. And if some of the strongest advocates of the melting pot came from the Jewish group itself, as in the case of Mary Antin, the most persuasive argument for pluralism was, appropriately, developed by a Jew—the late Horace Kallen.

The new pluralism, or the "new ethnicity" as it is generally known, is not a direct descendant of Kallen's pioneer efforts to develop a justification for pluralism. In any case, the new pluralism is an important factor in assisting the continuance of Jewish survivalism. There are some students of American society, Jews included, who are worried about what the new pluralism may bring. They fear that it could ultimately be used to justify a restriction of Jewish educational opportunity and professional advancement, and more generally, promote a fragmentation of our society. Be that as it may, the current acceptance of pluralism (as well as the earlier existence of a pluralistic philosophy) must be considered an important aid in making assimilation only one option and in suggesting that the option of survivalism within the framework of acculturation is an acceptable and viable alternative for American Jewry.

5. The next factor which I would like to develop may strike you as rather quixotic. It is that one of the reasons why Jews have not assimilated is that they score very low on any scale of religiosity. On the whole, American Jews have been strongly secularistic in their mode of life.

Indeed, until the growth of cults in the 1970s, there were very few American Jews who displayed the behavior that we saw in Europe: the need to believe, the need to find a religious philosophy without which the individual feels he cannot continue to live. Franz Rosenzweig is a notable case in point and he is the quintessential example of the wondering Jew who ends up choosing Judaism.

The relatively few American Jews who did have a deep need to believe tended to be repelled rather than attracted by Christianity. If Judaism was impossible for them Christianity was doubly impossible. Furthermore, most recently Christianity has been tainted for Jews by something which did not exist during Rosenzweig's time, namely the fact that the Holocaust took place in Christian countries and that Nazism was able to flourish in what was ostensibly a country whose population was Christian, both Protestant and Catholic.

All of us know that at the present time there exists an organization with the name Jews for Jesus. We also know about young Jews who have become followers of Reverend Moon. We know that there are young Jews who have been converted to the Hare Krishna movement and to other Eastern religious cults. Thus some young Jews have been caught up in recent developments on the American religious scene. However, by and large Jewish secularity has persisted and has functioned as a protective mechanism, insulating the adult Jew from attempts to convert him either to Christianity or to religions which historically have had no encounter with Judaism.

6. In explaining the lack of mass assimilation we must consider the nature of Jewish culture. If we do so it soon becomes obvious that despite the impact of secularism there is a fair amount of agreement among Jews that Jewish culture is both suprasocial as well as social. Thus Jewish culture is not comparable to other ethnic cultures, though, to be sure, some of these cultures—such as that of Greek Americans—are strongly intertwined with religion.

The suprasocial nature of Jewish culture means that it can retain a hold upon individuals for more than sentimental reasons. Furthermore, it can appeal to individuals who have had no contact with the homeland culture. Elderly East European Jews of the first generation may be sentimental about their Jewishness as they think back to the life of the *shtetl* or to that of larger communities in Eastern Europe. But for those who lack such bonds, the factor of the suprasocial nature of Jewish culture means that Jewish culture can still function to contain assimilation. As I have emphasized, secularity is strong among Jews. As a result, the suprasocial character of Jewish culture may have limited impact on some Jews. A case could be made for the fact that given Jewish secularity, the suprasocial nature of Jewish culture might result in alienation rather than in attraction. However, given the thrust of

American culture—a culture where religion operates as a significant factor in the social system—I would contend that the suprasocial nature of Jewish culture attracts more Jews than it repels.

Although very little is said about it publicly, it is apparent that not only is there the feeling that Jewish culture is suprasocial but many Jews, including those who are quite secular in orientation, believe that Judaism is superior to Christianity. The point, which has been made publicly in literally thousands of sermons and speeches before Jewish audiences, is that Christianity is an offshoot of Judaism. Listeners do not take this statement as a simple historical judgment. Rather they take it to mean that Christianity "needed" Judaism—that Christianity could not establish itself without extensive borrowing from a superior religion—Judaism. And the view of Christianity held by many Jews is that Christianity did not gain the upper hand because it was superior to Judaism. Rather it "won" because it was inferior—because it was imposed by officials of the state, because it appealed to a large mass of gullible individuals who were receptive to the miracles which it promulgated, and more especially to the belief in the divinity of a Jew named Jesus. Christians can therefore be viewed as intellectually naive, religiously unsophisticated, and as adhering to a religion geared to the masses. All of this is seen in contrast to Judaism, which stresses demanding ritualism and high standards of learning. And in the view of some Jews, Judaism's glory is that it has prophets who were mere humans but who saw through sham and hypocrisy and had the courage to denounce the evils which existed in their society.

7. In addition to the belief that Jewish culture is suprasocial there is a related phenomenon: the feeling that to be a Jew is to be a member of an elite people. It would take us far afield if we were to try to trace the process by which the Jewish group developed a belief in its own eliteness. Eliteness is rarely discussed publicly because of the fear that it will be resented by Gentiles and boomerang against Jews. But it is constantly present and constantly reinforced. Thus the awarding of the Nobel Prizes in 1976 served to underline in Jewish minds that the eliteness of the Jews

still persists. As a consequence, if you assimilate you enter into a group that is not superior to the Jewish group. On the contrary, the belief is that the Gentiles are inferior. Is it the Jews or the Gentiles who produced the three titans of the modern age: Freud, Einstein, and Marx?

Jewish eliteness has a variety of implications. It means that as high as one may climb in the class or status structure of the nation, there are enough Jews of similar accomplishment with whom to form a clique. However high one's brow level, there are enough Jews to interact with. Finally, being Jewish is taken to mean that one automatically becomes a member of an elite by virtue of being born Jewish.

These points about Jewish eliteness become quite apparent if we take the example of the Poles and the current rash of Polish jokes which has infested the nation. The Polish joke is based upon the fact that the Pole is inferior, is at the bottom of the heap, and belongs to a group which is the very antithesis of an elite group. From this perspective, the Pole who has attained elite status is conflicted about his identity. What does he have in common with his fellow Poles? Even if he accepts his identity as a Pole, he suffers under the burden of being an exception. He has achieved elite status despite the inferiority of his group. Jews experience something quite different—namely the feeling that one may have achieved eliteness precisely because of one's Jewishness.

8. In our discussion of how the Jews acculturated so quickly, I made the point that acculturation is speeded because of the lack of ties with the land from which one came. However there is now a new homeland—the State of Israel. Despite all of the problems which it has encountered, and all of the demands it has placed upon American Jewry, there is great pride in its existence. It has been a vital factor in retarding assimilation. Very few Jews reacted to the establishment of the State in the way which Arthur Koestler did. For him the establishment of a Jewish state meant that he could honorably assimilate. There was now a Jewish homeland; those who wish to retain their Jewishness could repair to the homeland, leaving Jews in the Diaspora free to assimilate. The Jews of America have not taken their cue from Koestler. Indeed

the emergence of the State of Israel has been a factor in heightening Jewish identity rather than in diminishing it.

An additional point must be made about Israel, namely that Jews of diverse backgrounds can relate to it. Jews of very diverse patterns of Jewish identity can find something in Israel to which they can relate. From the standpoint of Jewish identity, Israel can function as a kind of Rorschach. Since it itself contains so many diverse patterns of Jewish identification, there is always something in Israel to validate the most diverse types of Jewish identity.

9. In our analysis of acculturation I discussed the concept of America as a *goldene medinah* and highlighted the fact that this concept was a spur to acculturation. If one carries the concept of the *goldene medinah* far enough, however, one not only acculturates but positions oneself close to that of the assimilationist.

From this perspective it is fortunate that attitudes to America have undergone modification during the last decade or two. In its most radical form, there has emerged the feeling that America is imperfect, corrupt, polluted, declining, and a threat to world peace. These feelings had a strong impact on young Jews during the late 1960s and the early 1970s. Their elders did not develop a similar allergy to America. As has been evident during the Bicentennial, they are still capable of considering the establishment of the country an event worthy of celebration. But the dethronement of America has affected wide circles in the Jewish community in the sense that it has placed a heavy shadow over the theory behind the melting-pot ideology.

The dethronement of America has a sad aspect to it. Nevertheless it has assisted the building of Jewish identity and the awakening on the part of some of a greater Jewish consciousness. No longer must everything Jewish be measured against how it conforms to American culture. Take the position of Classical Reform Judaism in the United States. Classical Reform fitted Judaism to America because what was American was superior. For example, for all practical purposes the left wing of Classical Reform proceeded to change the Jewish Sabbath to Sunday since Sunday was the Sabbath of all civilized men. Given the end of America as the *goldene medinah*—the ideal culture to which all decent men should aspire—no longer can a case be made for shifting the Jewish Sabbath to Sunday. In fact the number of Reform congregations which hold their main service on Sunday are now so few in number that they are sociological oddities.

10. The last point which I should like to make about the resistance to mass assimilation is that American Jewry has gone so far as to test the climate for assimilation. The test found that America was unreceptive. Such unreceptiveness is not simple anti-Semitism or even the patterns of group exclusivity which we analyzed earlier. Rather it has been a resistance traceable to the feeling on the part of the Gentile that he wishes to remain the kind of Gentile that he is.

The testing of the Gentile took two forms. One was led by Eastern European Jews and the other by German Jews. In the case of German Jews the test was the establishment of the Ethical Culture movement. For the East European Jews it was the promotion of a variety of leftist movements. The interesting thing about both tests is that they did not involve assimilation in the classical sense. They made the demand upon the Gentile that he meet the Jew halfway. In the case of Ethical Culture the demand was that the Gentile give up his loyalty to Christianity. In the case of Jewish leftism the demand was that the Gentile give up his belief in capitalism.

It soon became obvious that Gentiles were not prepared to move in either of these two directions. It became apparent that Jews could only assimilate if they were prepared to meet Gentiles on Gentile turf. Interestingly enough, Jews in the United States have considered this a form of capitulation and they have had no strong desire to capitulate. Finally, some Jews committed to Ethical Culture and to radicalism have retained links—however attenuated—with the Jewish community.

V. Summary

The conventional wisdom has been that American ethnic groups would move through three stages: (1) self-segregation, (2) acculturation, and (3) assimilation. Most American Jews have reached the second stage and have done so with great speed. Many are more acculturated than they know. The factors that have transformed a group which spoke a different language from the dominant group, which had a style of dress different from the dominant group, and whose very religion was in oppostion to the religion espoused by the dominant group, into a subcommunity which is so "American" as the Jews include the following:

1. America had no medieval past.
2. The Jews had a history and familiarity with acculturation.
3. The Jews lacked a homeland.
4. The Jews were able to climb the class ladder very quickly.
5. The factor of value homophyly operated to speed acculturation.
6. America was dominated by *proste yidn* rather than *scheine yidn.*
7. America and American culture was overwhelmingly attractive, given the history of the Jew as an object of persecution and exclusion.

While many Jews have acculturated, the majority have not moved to the final position on the cycle: assimilation. What has kept American Jews from moving beyond the stage of acculturation to that of mass assimilation? The following factors are the most significant:

1. The attitude of Gentiles to Jews.
2. The size of the American Jewish community has been sufficiently large and concentrated to make Jewish life possible.
3. The comparative weakness of anti-Semitism and the ability of the Jew to penetrate those areas of the culture that he was interested in without having to pay the price of conversion to Christianity or the denial of Jewish identity.
4. The rise of a new pluralism which seeks to supersede the older philosophy of the melting pot.
5. The secularism of the Jew has operated as a protection against conversion at the time that American society—with all of its secularity—has retained a religious base. This religious base has served to retard assimilation.

6. The retention, despite secularization, of the belief that Jewish culture is suprasocial as well as social.
7. The fact that there is a widespread belief that to be a Jew is to be a member of an elite people.
8. The emergence of the State of Israel and the impact which it has had upon Jewish identity.
9. The end of America as the *goldene medinah,* a process which may be painful to view but which provides the possibility of the strengthening of Jewish identity.
10. The rebuffing by Gentiles of Jewish-led movements which were assimilationist in effect if not in intent and which would have spelled the end of Jewish identity.

***

Prognostication is a dangerous art. We need not burden ourselves with the making of predictions about the American Jewish future. What is evident in the contemporary Jewish community is that while there is considerable intermarriage and numerous instances of assimilation, considerable efforts are being made to stand fast and halt the cycle at the second stage—namely, acculturation. There is also the contemporary phenomenon of efforts to strengthen Jewish identity. Frequently these efforts take the form of a process which we may call "reculturation"—the return to Jewish forms and culture (or, more technically, what are considered to be Jewish forms and culture). In some cases reculturation also includes the creation of new Jewish forms and culture. Some of these new forms are controversial and, in the minds of critics, even dangerous. Such controversy is inevitable, and under specifiable conditions it can even have a salutary effect.

Centuries ago an anonymous Jew placed a graffito on the Arch of Titus, which was erected in Rome to celebrate Titus' capture of Jerusalem in the year 70. The graffito consists of three Hebrew words: *Am Yisrael Hai* (the Jewish people still live). Today, Jews not only live in the very city which Titus destroyed, but they have established a new Jewish Commonwealth. And in addition to the

State of Israel there is the impressive example of Jewish survival in the United States. It is evident that Jews continue to exist as a recognizable and—despite their comparatively small numbers—highly significant segment of American society.

RONALD S. BERMAN

The American Experience: Some Notes From the Third Generation

It is a hallowed tradition that Jews in this country have contributed to its greatness from the beginning. We ought naturally to take account of their role in the Revolution and in the course of the following century. But it was really after the great emigration from Eastern Europe that Jewish culture engaged American culture. At first there were only differences; and there were many like Henry Adams who could see only those differences. The pilgrimage from the East brought to a new country unmanageable numbers of poor people. Their religion and language were strange if tolerable; their dress, taste, and manners seemed to the onlooker to be deplorable. This mattered a good deal before it was learned that vulgarity is itself a matter of pretensions to style. The Jews of the East had not passed through either Reformation or Renaissance: and were indeed only just coming to terms with the Enlightenment. Except for backwaters like Sicily or the Ukraine, they were the last people in Europe to discover the secular state. Yet these immigrants managed to engage American culture—to compel its attention, change its mind, endow it with a different set of values. We are within a larger occasion approaching a centennial of this emigration, and perhaps we ought to reflect on the gains and losses of a century of Jewish American life.

There were distinctions among Jewish immigrants, but these were not confined to nationality. The Russians of my own family were suspicious of Rumanians but, in a spirit of high-mindedness, willing to share the New World with them. In moments of feeling it was natural to call attention to nations, tribes, or other antecedents, but Jews of the great migration were divided—and connected—in other ways. As Irving Howe has reminded us, they formed benevolent associations, *Landsmanshaftn,* clubs, camps, congregations, unions, political parties, leagues for the reform first of their own conditions and then of the world. They studied in the same night schools, worked in the same places, lived in the same neighborhood, built their lives, in short, around similarity. Most important of all was their venture into public life and policy. First local then national, it became as characteristic of the Jewish electorate to vote heavily as it was of the Irish electorate to vote often. This was citizenship of a kind previously denied. The civic organization of European Jews is often described as isolated, and the ghetto has sometimes been used as a metaphor of character and mind. But Jews in Eastern Europe could not attend universities freely and had very little future in either professions or government. They formed a connective tissue of social organization not because they were clannish and probably not because they were a minority. They understood even before the turn of the century that public life was the first form of individual rights. Before you could be a person you had first to be a citizen. In this belief they were no different from Periclean Greeks or Renaissance Florentines.

One thinks of life in the old regime as a kind of persistent assault and battery, but what mattered more were restrictions on will and choice. The Jews of the *shtetl* were shut out of normal commerical life, and the Jews of the cities had fewer rights than other proletarians. There was virtually no freedom of movement and certainly no franchise—it was as if one were to live in the Soviet Union today. This makes understandable a cultural obsession with organization. It is one legacy of the emigration that had better endure if individual rights are also to endure.

The problem of the first generation was survival in a hostile environment. The material success of American life came hard and not to everyone. There is no need to dwell on sweatshops, strikes, and infamous standards of work and pay. Modern Jewish life remembers that, and parents obsessively compare the freedom of the professions to old forms of servitude. Each generation of Jews learns the wisdom of economic independence; but it is hard for parents to transmit; in cultural life too we are always one war behind.

Our scholarship has established the great social (and psychological) theme of the first three generations. But both scholars and readers have imperceptibly aged, and we must now talk about not only the fourth but the fifth generation of Jews since 1880. One of the surprises that has greeted them is the assumption that while they constitute a separate ethnic group they are no longer a minority. Insofar as government is concerned, that distinction rests upon other kinds of identity. The assumptions around this may be that religion is no longer a serious determinant in this country; that Jews are part of the majority; or that a minority is a temporary condition. This would have been surprising to our grandfathers.

The great migration began among people who knew from force of circumstances that they formed a definable minority in the nations of the East. All the force of legal definition and social habit had made that so. There was nothing in the New World to make them change their minds. The nature of industrialism made sure that Jewish immigrants, like Irish and Italian immigrants—and very much like the present illegal work force of Western Europe and the United States—conformed to a pattern. Mass immigrations of the twentieth century, unless they are propelled by war, begin with the drumming-up of opportunity. A working force primarily of young men and women is identified; a profit is made from their embarkation or passage over the border; jobs that no one else wants are reserved for them. The loneliness of these mass movements of the twentieth century is characteristic: Puerto Ricans work grimly to support or bring over their families to the mainland; Algerians and Yugoslavs lead lives of urban desolation in order to support communities in their own homeland. It was not much different for the Jews of New York, although I think it was harder.

The Jews of the migration were a great many people, with a common language and religion, but that did not make a community. After economic survival the problem was the formation of a community out of the materials—and these were very miscellaneous—that had been brought along. There were some very serious questions: Would social authority be exerted by religious or secular leaders? To what extent would the ghetto impose its isolation once again? Was the socialist tradition transferable? Was Jewish culture itself? The last was of particular interest, for anyone could see that democracy in the United States expressed itself in terms of social change. This was good for political freedom but rather dangerous for tradition; the difficulty was not only to make a community but to have it endure in a country more or less indifferent to the past.

Most immigrant groups subordinate their languages; which become dialects and private or hidden forms of communication. They are occasionally taken up as causes and given temporary respect. But Yiddish was from the beginning assumed to be a rival of English, and it remained what it necessarily had to be, a public language. The new life was expressed through Yiddish diaries, novels, drama, newspapers—and especially through the rapidly accumulating traditions of the first two generations. It was also the language of social and political debate. Through what then seemed to be its endless resources, the motives of our life were laid bare.

Its themes are familiar to us all, but even as we read Shakespeare not to find out how *Hamlet* ends but rather to experience its language and ideas, we read these still sturdy and vital records for the pleasure of their company. Jewish cultural life could not ignore the great theme of real life, which was poverty. It found itself, sooner than it wished, addressing the conflict between the traditions of Jewish life and those of an open, changeable democracy. A tremendous amount of Jewish writing is about the loss of authority in parents, in religion, and of course in the traditions of life as well. Many a Yiddish stage play is a melodrama about generations; which is essentially a story of the conflict between what is old and known and what is new and necessary.

Having acknowledged the power and beauty of Yiddish culture after the migration, one has regretfully to ask where it is now. In the same place as Mayan civilization and other interesting but extinct species. Life after the migration was, so to speak, temporarily immortalized by works first in Yiddish and later in English. But these never ascended through history and biography to literature. Although a modern epic, this life never found its poet, and instead of informing the present it remains the preserve of scholars, teachers, students, librarians, and the National Endowment for the Humanities. Another lesson to remember, then, is the fragility of great enterprises. In 1920 there was a pulsating Yiddish world, half-secular and half-Orthodox. Because of our success, however, we are not nearly so ethnic as we used to be.

Life in the generations after the migration—even that event itself—was pretty well ignored by the writers of the West. They were preoccupied with other things: the war, consequent changes in American life, the problems of a majority. Because of that our experience remains essentially private; not taught at most schools or universities, pretty well lost to the popular imagination. The Jew did become a part of world literature, but in an equivocal way. During the migration and the time of the first two generations, Pound and Eliot, Fitzgerald and Hemingway wrote about Jewish presence or intrusion in their world. In *The Great Gatsby* we find out who fixed the Black Sox in 1919; in *The Sun Also Rises* the Jew is the only character outside shared codes of feeling and morality. In Eliot and Pound he is a dissolvent of European culture, worse even than Fagin in *Oliver Twist;* Jewish fiction and letters were subliterary; and as seen from the outside, Jewish experience never found a writer like Scott or Faulkner who could deal with race, religion, or the past. Great works of fiction have a kind of symphonic persuasion; they enforce their familiarity because of their power to order and display common thought and feeling. The particularity of Jewish experience has not yet been put in that form—although in history, painting, and the debate of Jewish intellectuals all the materials are still there. So the present generation does not have a common art form or language that makes its collective experience remembered.

The third generation found the literature—and culture—of Yiddishkeit much less relevant than it had been to their parents. They were very much on their own, conscious of the loss of original belief with little to replace it. It may be heretical, but I think this generation was never at ease in America, although it has been supposed to have been assimilated. The children of the thirties had families who remembered hard times and who were certainly experiencing them once more. The depression—which I think is one of the two or three definitive experiences for modern Jews—transformed their evolution. It didn't bring families together as televised mythology tends fondly to believe, although at times it did bring out remarkable individual acts of kindness and human goodness. I can still recall my grandmother, the patron saint of every bum in New York, who before the day was well started set me (at the age of five or six) to making sandwiches with her for the men down on their luck who would be sure to come by that day. But in the large the depression encouraged multiple employment in families; finished the job of disintegrating parental authority; delegitimized those skills and trades that had attached the generations; kept Jews out of work and on strike—and kept them out of the established world and its closed institutions.

Daily life from the thirties to the fifties took place within a kind of Diaspora of its own. By now the Lower East Side had been left behind, for Jews had begun their movement which, beginning with Williamsburg, Borough Park, and Flatbush, was to ascend eventually through Hempstead and Mineola to Great Neck and even Southampton. Human history, Emerson suggested, is the lengthened shadow of a man; but I suppose that evolution can also be seen in the lengthening tracks he leaves behind him. Before the war Jews were pretty well centralized in urban neighborhoods, still lived in blocks of tenements, or apartments which were beginning to replace them. And daily routine contrasted severely with the usual dreams about America; it meant taking the subway to a store or factory, putting in a long and physical day of labor, saving as much as possible in the way of personal expenses, trying desperately to maintain the associations of family and *shul* (a Jewish institution which antedates the Jewish Center) against the centrifugal force of American life.

The daily life of the first generation was based on survival. The third generation was somewhat more ambitious. It wanted to compete in American life, and it wanted to dominate that life. Energies once displayed in union halls and in other great debates were more quietly, but with the same intensity, mustered in classrooms and libraries. Jews discovered that wherever there was open examination and a system based on merit, they could go as far as talent allowed. They also found that there were limits. The irritants of restrictions in residence and exclusion from hotels could be borne; but quotas in education and debarment from professional or business practice could not. So that there were opposed impulses in Jewish life: to become part of middle-class America; and to separate oneself, and criticize its assumptions. Jews in the academic world (for example), which was highly stylized, might become psychologically divided, hoping to transcend differences but convinced that acceptance would never really be possible while differences existed. Many of them, it seems to me, worked on the wrong end of the equation; seeking to change the differences rather than affect the acceptance.

Because of their own situation Jews were more than a little concerned with social justice. When they reached the New World, they had applied European socialism to the factories and sweatshops of which it was so lucid and natural a criticism. The world view of socialism had a special consolation: it went beyond religion, race, class, and nationality. It was essentially a faith in working-class brotherhood. But it was built upon certain assumptions that appeared to obsess American Jews, appearing whenever there was a social movement that attracted them. Jews were vulnerable to ideas which promised that social change would occur after changes in human nature itself. All the movements of the left—socialism, communism, radicalism, liberalism—promised more than social justice. They promised perfection. And the minor movements of this century, from psychoanalysis to Ethical Culture, which were of special interest to Jews made the same extraordinary assertions. They proved to resolve the differences between Christian and Jew, Ego and Id, history and human nature.

It is both moral and idealistic to entertain such hopes. But they are, of course, a hidden variant of religion itself. As the old religion wanes another takes its place: but secular religion can be as messianic as any other; and dependent on its own mysterious revelation. Jews of the past two generations have wanted to believe that man and society are perfectible, and they have accepted some assumptions that go beyond either evidence or reason. There has been a rage for equality, which is a useful standard but otherwise a fiction. There has been revulsion from authority, although Jewish tradition is built upon the relationship of knowledge to ignorance, which is otherwise known as authority. There has been the phenomenon of Jewish pacifism and an accompanying disdain for the immorality of the state—although Israel exists by force of arms and national will. Its defeat would certainly be a victory of principles, however, for those who might enjoy them. There has been the kind of adoration of social change which resists the knowledge that it has to end somewhere; that the material world does not offer an infinity of alternatives. Most people remember Archimedes saying that he could move the planet with a lever long enough; few remember that he said he needed also a place to stand on. So do we.

There have been two kinds of universalism in which Jews of my generation have indulged. One is Judaism as a secular religion; and this accounts for an extraordinary emphasis on style and feeling, with the corresponding absence of dogma and definition. For some, Jewishness becomes either a state of mind or a preliminary to (perhaps a religious equivalent of) World Federalism. To some extent universalized Jewishness is liberalism—and to an unsuspected degree simply the doctrine of feeling good. The last decade was a time of the Children's Crusade, and things, even for adults, have seemed since then as if they could be understood as part of a world-religion without the complications of ritual, doctrine, dogma, or (especially) tradition. The earth is good, people are good, health foods are good; other religions, especially in the Orient, are more good than our own; the whole experience of life being too basic to be complicated by ideas necessarily parochial.

The political variants of this idea reflect on both domestic and foreign policy. The point of lectures from a thousand Hillel houses has been the likeness of Jews and the rest of the world; and, wherever it was possible, to assert some principle of human goodness to Third World development, or to ascribe to some other political system and religion a set of virtues that have escaped our own, Jews were often ready to convert their own particular into the world's universal. Before the United Nations was despised it was adored, and this was because it was seen as overcoming on a national level those distinctions and conditions that Jews often found personally unacceptable. And of course, the distinctly critical stance of liberalism, and of Jewish liberalism in particular, made it natural to view our religious and secular structures from the viewpoint of a perfect and nonexistent universal.

The second kind of universalism is familiar to any reader of academic or of Jewish novels. It is the faith we all have in being taught, trained, loved, bought, educated, organized, and persuaded out of the agonies of personality and into a higher and better form. This is a country, one might think, composed exclusively of communes, centers, and retreats, and every other possible kind of brotherhood against mortality. To each diet and exercise, with each membership and every enrollment, some small degree of certainty is ventured for. And we tend to sacralize these things, to feel, especially when young, that there is faith in such good works. The first kind of universalism explodes our faith, spreads it over a universe too large for any context. But the second kind focuses too much upon too little, and finds a religious comfort in the security of the right cause. It is like Protestantism reduced to vegetarianism.

Perhaps our problem is not so much how the world sees us as how we see ourselves. Consciousness, after all, is already a high state of mind, and not at all something that needs to be raised.

There are some lessons to be drawn from this brief history of our own centennial. The first generation taught us that the unhappiest conditions of strangeness and poverty can be surmounted. The second created a culture of enormous power, usefulness, and beauty. The third abandoned that culture, looking for another and more general human community to validate its existence; it endowed the United Nations with moral powers and psychiatry with magical ones, experiencing and leaving behind virtually every religious substitute known to man. Perhaps the fourth generation will find the real thing.